OF LAN SEA AND SKY

escapades of a
modern day adventurer
and entrepreneur

MALCOLM SNOOK

Order this book online at www.trafford.com/07-2592
or email orders@trafford.com

Most Trafford titles are also available at major online book retailers.

Note for Librarians: A cataloguing record for this book is available from Library and Archives Canada at www.collectionscanada.ca/amicus/index-e.html

ISBN: 978-1-4251-5759-3

We at Trafford believe that it is the responsibility of us all, as both individuals and corporations, to make choices that are environmentally and socially sound. You, in turn, are supporting this responsible conduct each time you purchase a Trafford book, or make use of our publishing services. To find out how you are helping, please visit www.trafford.com/responsiblepublishing.html

Our mission is to efficiently provide the world's finest, most comprehensive book publishing service, enabling every author to experience success. To find out how to publish your book, your way, and have it available worldwide, visit us online at www.trafford.com/10510

www.trafford.com

North America & international
toll-free: 1 888 232 4444 (USA & Canada)
phone: 250 383 6864 ♦ fax: 250 383 6804 ♦ email: info@trafford.com

The United Kingdom & Europe
phone: +44 (0)1865 722 113 ♦ local rate: 0845 230 9601
facsimile: +44 (0)1865 722 868 ♦ email: info.uk@trafford.com

10 9 8 7 6 5 4 3

For my wonderful daughter Francesca.
If I can inspire you to love life, your fellow man and the wonders of nature, I will not have entirely failed you.

Contents

Introduction

It's not unusual to see a biography appear of a pop star or footballer. If someone is in the public eye, if they have fans, the book will of course sell. The fact is though, that all around the world there are people very few of us have ever heard of, whose lives are at least as interesting. I hope my life is interesting to anyone who has parted with hard cash to buy this book! I didn't set out to lead an interesting life, as such, but thankfully all sorts of other people have inspired me to try all sorts of activities. What I have always wanted to do is to take the gift of life and live it to the full. Then there's a snowball effect. As a result of living the kind of life I have, I've come into contact with more and more exciting, adventurous, talented people, in many spheres of life; from sailors, military people, explorers, to great swing dancers and musicians. Some, like John Ridgway you may have heard of. Other fabulous characters who I've met and been inspired by you won't have heard of at all. I want to record something about them, as well as telling my own story along the way. They include an old gentleman by the name of McLeod who built a hotel in Scotland, an east end character who started a sailing club for youngsters in east London, a young villain who went on to be a great skydiver and entrepreneur, a deserter from the Foreign Legion, an aviator who restored a World War Two Spitfire that had been stored in crates for years, a man now ninety one who still teaches swing dance, and who was many years ago a dancer at the Cotton Club, the Roxy Theatre and the Savoy Ballroom Harlem.

All these great people, and more, appear in these pages, some briefly, others in greater detail. In all cases their achievements are greater than mine. I hope you enjoy meeting them as much as I have. There are other stories here too. Of growing up, of making careers decisions, making mistakes with relationships; even the everyday part of anyone's life provides lessons others can learn from. It's people that make the world go round, we can learn so much from one another. I wish now I'd spoken more and in greater depth to my parents and grandparents. If you are lucky enough to have yours do it now. I know quite a bit about their lives thank goodness. How one grandfather was a conscientious objector in World War One, who nonetheless went to the trenches as a medic. I know how the other grandfather, in a coma was put with the dead bodies near the end of World War One. A telegram announcing his death was sent to Grandma, but thankfully someone realised he wasn't quite dead, possibly when they came to bury him. He made a full recovery. Things would be different today, for three months later he was back in the trenches. I know about my father's life in the RAF during World War Two and something of my great grandfather's life as a newspaper typesetter and father of the union chapel. I know about my mother's musical achievements and how she rebelled against her own parents, there's a lot of her in me. People don't have to be famous to be fascinating and indeed, most fascinating people are not, I suspect, famous.

One of a handful of sketches still surviving, made by my father's father, in 1918, towards the end of World War One after coming back from the dead.

CHAPTER 1

Growing Pains

DROMINA IS THE name of a beach in Ireland. I've never been there. It is also, temporarily, the name of the yacht, well motor-sailor to be precise, on which I sit typing this, a short history of my life, to be followed by a book about, what may be my last big adventure.

Arguably my first adventure, as such, was when my parents took my sister and me, at quite a young age, on the grand tour of Europe. We went to France, Belgium, Luxembourg, Lichtenstein, Germany and Switzerland that I can remember. The longest stop being at Davos in Switzerland. Dad already knew his way around the area, having previously taken a party of kids from the school where he taught.

I loved Davos, I think we all did. There was a new cable car being constructed at the time, on a mountain called, well to be honest I can't remember now. It might have been the Jacobshorn, but I think that's had a lift on it for much longer. Looking at the maps on the internet, I think it must have been the lift to the Bergrestaurant on the Gotschnagrat. Wherever it was, in the mountains around Davos, when one cable car ascended another descended, at least that was the system there at that time. However, during construction, they had one cable car on one side and an open platform for taking building supplies to the top on the other. So as we went up, en famille, the open platform came down. At the top there was a sort of wooden chalet arrangement, primarily for the workmen, but open to visitors. The chalet housed something of a café and had a balcony with a single wooden rail around it and a deep drop beneath. The large restaurant and facilities which must be there today, were still in the early stages of construction.

At the top, despite it being summer, it was snowing. The four of us went into the chalet, and, while Mum and Dad had a tea or a coffee, my sister Margaret, and I discovered the snow covered balcony. Perfect for making a slide. Not only that but at the end of the slide you could grab the rail and swing out, over the drop, if you dared. We did.

Presently, having turned the balcony into a death-trap, we were called inside. There was a problem. Construction was going on at ground level too and a bulldozer, levelling a new car park had bulldozed through the power supply. There was an emergency generator, but it wasn't very powerful. It should be possible to winch us down slowly using this source of power, but it would take a very long time. In addition, the cable car was currently at the bottom, the open platform at the top.

To Margaret and me this sounded very exciting. Disappointingly, from our point of view, the open platform in fact had a tiny sort of kiosk in one corner. A one man hut if you will, which under normal circumstances was for the one man who would operate the controls within. The controls would be redundant with the emergency power, so the four of us would have to squeeze into this one person space. We did, somehow, and the workmen, who were mostly Italian stood on the platform itself to go down. I distinctly remember that the cable was covered in ice and as the cable flexed, or ran over wheels on the pylon supports, great lumps of ice would fall on the workmen underneath. They didn't seem that bothered. I was impressed by their toughness. I believe we made the local newspaper that week, but that's something my father told me some while later. Sadly, I can't recall having seen it.

At what age it first occurred to me that I didn't want to live like everyone else I cannot be sure now. I do remember walking home from my senior school every day and swearing three things, over and over, no commuting, no lawnmower and no mortgage. All vows I would break, although hopefully never again. Likewise, I can no longer remember the precise age, at which I started sailing at the Lea Avon Sailing Club, then based on Highams Park Lake in East London. I could check with friends and possibly work it out, but it probably doesn't matter, suffice to say about the age ten to twelve. For several years the sailing club was my main activity outside school, until my parents persuaded me to give it up and concentrate on studying for my GCE 'O Level' exams.

Ken Ford, Commodore of the Lea Avon Sailing Club, mover of mountains and designer of probably the most beautiful training dinghy the world has ever seen.

The sailing club was run by a wonderful man, named Ken Ford. Not a rich fellow, but passionate about the club and about sailing. There were two fleets of boats at the club and a solitary Merlin Rocket. The larger fleet comprised, probably thirty or more, of a class of dinghy called a Fly. Constructed primarily of marine ply, this one design, single sail racing dinghy was a thing of beauty. Ken was her designer. Sleek, fast and elegant, with wide, varnished side decks, I've not to this day seen a more attractive small dinghy for kids to learn in, nor one with the performance. I find it hard to believe the little boxes I see kids learning in nowadays, what fun are they? If the kids fail to fall in love with sailing it could be that these boring little rectangular things with tiny sails are to blame. I can't help wondering how Flys' failed to catch on in a huge way.

I debated this point recently with a sailing friend who said kids would sail in an old car tyre, with a broomstick and a handkerchief. We came to the conclusion they would, but that it wouldn't necessarily hold their interest long term. You'd have to be quite an optimist to think a little box would either. As usual I expect it comes down to money. The larger kids, or more experienced members of the Lea Avon Sailing Club got to race in one of about ten British Moths, another very attractive racing dinghy, but somewhat larger. And then of course there was the occasional chance to go out in the Merlin Rocket, clinker built, wonderfully varnished, and a whole different look with a tall bow and a jib as well as a mainsail.

My sister and I around eight and ten years old respectively with one of the sailing club's superb British Moths.

Being based in East London this was no rich kids playground. The idea of the club was that you built your boat first and sailed it second. Of course things are never this simple and boats did become available when a kid left the club. In these cases it was usual for the inheritor of a dinghy to be expected to re-paint, re-varnish and refurbish the boat, before taking 'ownership' and going racing. Naturally, in reality, the boats remained the property of the club. However, the concept that you 'owned' your boat, maintained it, took responsibility for it and always raced it meant the boats really were cared for, and there was rarely any shirking at packing up time, since everyone wanted to ensure that 'their' boat was safely packed away, undamaged!

The club operated all day Saturday and Sunday and Wednesday evenings. Wednesday evenings were for boat building and maintenance, and tuition, although all these activities went on at weekends too, alongside racing. All in all it was a hive of activity, even before the big project. The big project was to build a two storey clubhouse. Not pay to have one built mark you, but for a bunch of kids, plus Ken , with some help from an architect, who was one of the parents, to build a pretty large and imposing structure. It would have boat storage and workshop below with social amenities up top. The big project didn't have a big budget. If indeed it had a budget at all! What it did have was Ken Ford, who begged, borrowed, harangued and hassled and obtained help and material from anyone who could provide it, until somehow he got all the supplies and permissions in place.

The major part of this striking edifice was constructed from old railway sleepers, and seeing it rise into the sky, as it seemed to us kids, from out of the deep wet muddy holes we dug with traditional hand implements was a source of immense pride. A bottle containing a scroll with the names of all the kids who were in at the beginning lies buried in the foundations. Winter and summer, come rain, come snow, the work went on, until finally it became a working clubhouse, the result of sheer hard work and passion. I visit it sometimes, even now, although I can't go in. The club no longer exists and I believe the local authority has control of the building. I don't know what it's used for. Back in the sixties it was ground breaking if you'll excuse the pun, in so many ways. It used recycling, the building blended with the landscape and both building and club gave something to the community and young people in particular. Some of these ideas are embraced rather more today, in theory, and yet I don't think it could happen again, not with our over regulated, nanny state, society; kids on a building site – good heavens no.

The Lea Avon Sailing Club's flagship a totally stunning, clinker built Merlin Rocket.

I more or less only see Ken at funerals and weddings these days and even that wouldn't have come about, if my cousin Mick, who I introduced to the club, hadn't married Ken's daughter. What an inspiration that man was though, and I'm sure that thought would be echoed by very many of my age who grew up around that beautiful appendage to Epping Forest that is Highams Park Lake.

I did have one other conflicting interest at the time, and that was motorsport. At about the age of thirteen I was allowed to go to a Formula three race at Crystal Palace. Dave Walker won the main race for Gold Leaf Team Lotus, his teammate Bev Bond crashed right under my nose, very literally as his steaming car came to rest on the banking right at my feet. I was hooked. This was exciting. Professional racing driver, that was what I was going to be, simple, obvious.

A Fly in action against the beautiful backdrop of Highams Park Lake as it was in the 1960s.

I probably had a bit of a reputation as a loner and a swat at school, although my exam results don't support the latter idea much. Fact was I just had different interests from pretty much everyone else around me. My mother had won a scholarship to the Guild Hall School of Music at some time in her youth and was a talented violinist. My father and sister were musical too and I wanted to join in. My mother arranged for me to have private violin lessons with an elderly gentleman named Reg Adler in Chingford. He was such a wonderful, gentle human being, who gave so much to so many youngsters, and adults for that matter, that I find it impossible to paint a complete and satisfactory portrait of him in words. He was a gentleman in the truest sense of the word, but for all his kindly demeanour and the twinkle in his eye, he had steel, discipline, determination to see a project through and a strong work ethic. Totally devoted to music and to teaching he was a genuine unsung hero of everyday life in the suburbs.

The kind of dinghy kids get to learn in today. You decide.

For me, post eleven, playing the violin in an east London school was not the easy route to popularity. In fact it was no route to any kind of popularity. It reminds me of that song A Boy Named Sue, you have to grow up tough, mentally if not physically as well. Reg Adler was the music master at McEntee Technical College which was a large part of the reason my parents and I were so keen I should go there. I think I was the only boy in the school orchestra, I was certainly the only boy who played the violin. Everyone else was into football, which, whilst I enjoyed playing it and even went to a couple of West Ham matches, never really lit my fire. I was overjoyed we won the World Cup in 1966, was a big fan of Geoff Hurst and Bobby

Moore and I might have felt differently about the game if I had a chance of making the school team. However, the sports master and I weren't on the same wavelength, possibly not the same planet.

It could never happen today, that's one beam and a bunch of kids building their own clubhouse, with the leadership of Ken Ford and a single architect.

And up she goes.

A typical day on the building site, small work-groups of youngsters getting on with it.

The finished clubhouse, with storage, workshop, social amenities and race control. A remarkable achievement and a monument to the dedication, drive and vision of one man, Ken Ford. Worthy of a knighthood at least.

One of the other teachers got a rugby team going for a while and I played wing forward for two games, but getting flattened wasn't really my idea of a good time. In the upper sixth we were given the opportunity to take the whole of Friday afternoon off, this being our sports period, provided we could show we were using the time for a sporting activity and not just bunking off. I got out of there and took horse riding lessons on Chingford Plains. Also in my last year or two at school I got myself on a British Schools Exploring Society expedition to arctic Sweden. I saw an appeal for money, for this expedition, on television. The appeal was made by Magnus Magnusson. I wrote to him, explaining that I couldn't offer any money but would love to go! A little cheek works wonders. God bless his memory, he supplied the details. I formally applied. My headmaster gave me a favourable reference, my pocket money and all I could make, plus a sub from Mum that never got paid back, were all thrown in, and suddenly I was on my way to the arctic for the seven or eight weeks of the school summer holiday.

I well remember the excitement of receiving a list of compulsory equipment to be bought and going shopping for it 'up in town'. When I got back to school after the expedition, no one was in the least bit interested in what I'd been doing, but the experience changed me, or perhaps reinforced in me an idea of who and what I was. It's always struck me as ironic that despite my poor relationship with the sports teacher I was probably the only kid in my year who made a full time living from sport for a six year period, soon after leaving school. It wasn't sailing, horse riding, exploring, or motor racing however.

The British Schools Exploring Society Expedition was broken up into groups. Most were making topographical maps. There were some military cadets too, and my own group was making a geological survey. We took a ferry from Harwich to Gothenburg and then a train all the way north, via Uppsala, right up to Kiruna, where we took a break, and then on further north. The train terminated at Narvik, but arrangements had been made for it to stop and let us off in the wilderness of pre Chernobyl Lapland, on the Swedish side of the border. I was given to understand that the expedition would make maps on behalf of the Swedish Government and that in return we could take mineral samples home for British Universities.

My group, of which I was the youngest, was led by a Doctor John Gunner. He selected an area in a hanging valley about twenty miles from base camp, which he felt revealed much about the area's geological past and we set to with plane tables and started mapping. This went on for about six weeks. We lived at 'Geology Camp' in Vango Force Nine tents, three to a tent. There were patches of snow, but mostly the rocks were exposed. The weather was a bit changeable towards the end, hot one day, raging blizzard the next. On the whole though it wasn't too uncomfortable. I made good friends with a guy called Stuart, who gave me my first, and to date only experience of potholing when we got back home.

Each day several of the geology party would go out armed with geological hammers and collect interesting mineral samples, garnet mica schists, augen gneiss and basically all manner of damn heavy rocks! These were stockpiled in the main valley in which our hanging valley hung. Towards the end of six weeks, when the map was nearly finished Dr Gunner asked for some volunteers to take the mineral samples to base camp. I fancied a change of scenery, so I volunteered. About four of us went. We knew we would have heavy loads and we expected there to be sleeping tents and supplies at base camp. On this basis we took our enormous, framed rucksacks for the rocks and sleeping bags only. No tents and no form of groundsheet.

We climbed down into the main valley and loaded up with the sample rocks. It later transpired my load of rocks weighed over eighty five pounds and being the youngest and physically smallest, I had the lightest load! We had to go a short way down this valley, then up one side and down the other to meet a trail called the Kunsladen, or something similar. It translated to the Kingsway and ran down another valley. About eighteen to twenty miles down this valley and we would climb out of it and down the other side of another ridge to base camp. By the time we were on the Kingsway it started to snow, but it seemed just as arduous to go back as to go on. We went on, and along the way collected some boletus mushrooms to supplement our dehydrated rations.

Here I must make a confession. The rations were, I'm sure, scientifically worked out, so everyone had enough, protein, carbohydrate, sugar etc. Being me, I'd traded my Tate and Lyle Golden Syrup and possibly some other foodstuff with some Lapps, in order to get myself a reindeer skin to take home. As a result my sugar level would possibly have been a little low. When we got to base camp, horror of horrors, there was no one there and there were no sleeping tents, only store tents, single skinned, with no groundsheet. Our Black's Icelandic sleeping bags were good, but they weren't meant to be laid straight on the bare tundra.

By morning I was suffering from exposure and hypoglycaemia, (low blood sugar). I was having some interesting hallucinations. Luckily, the expedition doctor, who'd been out visiting another group returned by chance for some supplies, and after the application of some warmth and hot sweet tea I was right as rain within twenty four hours.

Back at Geology Camp we finished the map and still had a week left. It was decided we'd walk across the Swedish, Norwegian border and on to Narvik and back. For the fun of it. It was fun too. The scenery was spectacular, as was the light. There were reindeer and lemmings, lakes and rivers, snow and sun, mountains and valleys. It was incredibly beautiful. On occasion we witnessed the Northern Lights or Aurora Borealis as well. After two or three days we looked down on Narvik Fjord from the hills above and tried to spot the sunken warships from the battle of Narvik. I remember too seeing some bits of German aeroplane from the war scattered on a hillside. After one long hot day, of walking with tent and clothes, food and primus on our backs, several of us stripped off and jumped into a glacial melt water lake. Thank heaven we were in good shape. The shock was indescribable.

At the end of it all, it was pack up, back on the train and then the ferry home. Dr Gunner gave each of us a private debrief on how he saw our performance. I don't know how critical he was of others of course but I remember being a bit disappointed with my de-brief. I know it helped me though in later life, and even though I've now forgotten his exact words they contributed to a determination to prove myself, that helped me many times in the future. Such as when unpopular decisions had to be made as chief instructor of a parachute club and when setting up my own business and at other difficult times. Well meant constructive criticism can be a blessing, even if, being only human, most of us find it hard to take at the time.

A year before my arctic expedition I had been to The John Ridgway School of Adventure for my summer holiday. The school is located at Ardmore near Rhiconich, just south of Durness and close by Cape Wrath, in north western Scotland. I've visited the place several times since, although not recently, and consider it one of the most beautiful places I've ever seen. John Ridgway was another inspirational character, as was his lovely wife Marie Christine. They ran the school each summer, and every winter would go off on some small adventure or other, such as tracing the source of the Amazon, or some other trifle. This was after his record breaking transatlantic row with Chay Blyth naturally.

The course was hard work, very hard work, but well thought out and though I shouldn't be the one to say it – character building. Amongst other things we climbed the mountain Foinaven and did a survival exercise, which involved being dropped in the sea near a remote island and being left to put the skills we'd been taught into practice. They made sure we were good and hungry too, by having us prepare a meal and then taking it from us before they dropped us in the sea! There was also climbing, abseiling, canoeing, orienteering and of course sailing. The only relaxing part of the course was a trip with John on his yacht, during which he took time to talk to each of us in some depth.

I disagreed with him on one fundamental, but I can't recall too many conversations from so long ago, so clearly this one was special. Again I've been very lucky to meet another inspiring personality. I remember John Ridgway telling me I could achieve anything in life if I wanted it badly enough. I disagreed with him then and I do so now. Not as an excuse for any ambitions I've failed to meet, nor without a good deal of respect, for both him and his views. At the time I was still dreaming of being Formula One World Champion, but I believe you need a degree of talent and more controversially a degree of luck. Wasn't Stirling Moss good enough to be World Champion? Did the likes of Jean Alesi, winner of only one Grand Prix not try hard enough? There are many examples of drivers with great talent and ambition who just failed to achieve the ultimate prize, or whose talent was wasted in the wrong car at the wrong time. Nonetheless, there is wisdom and experience in the John Ridgway viewpoint; if you are going to chase a difficult goal or ambition, you do have to want it badly, stretch yourself and believe you can do it.

I wanted to race cars badly, and later I got to! I was not your archetypal rebel at school obviously, but when there was a racing car show on at the Walthamstow greyhound track, or on a ferry on the Thames, as happened a couple of times, I played truant to go. Then and only then. I know truancy is a big problem in many schools in this day and age, but for me, at that time, it was a big step to take. It was at events such as these shows, and through pestering the likes of Roger Williamson, David Purley, and James Hunt, in their Formula Three days, for autographs, that I came to realise, that being a racing driver isn't a job you just apply for! I could just about afford to take myself to Brands Hatch or Crystal Palace on public transport, as a spectator, from east London, but I wasn't going to have enough money to pay to go racing, even when I left school and got a job. This was something of a shock, and a bit of a blow to my ambitions! Once I realised that I would need some money behind me before I could commence my climb to the podium, I was back to the 'what shall I do when I leave school?' question.

Not unnaturally, during my last few years at school I also discovered another distraction. Girls. My first date was with a fellow pupil from my mixed sex school. She was slightly podgy, but I didn't ask her out on the basis that less attractive girls are more likely to say yes, a system employed by some around me. In fact Debbie was charming, popular and very attractive with bobbed blonde hair. You could have knocked me over with a feather when she said yes and I was, of course, a bundle of nerves. I defy anyone to forget the first time they ever went out with a member of the opposite sex, although, if this was also Debbie's first date, which I doubt, then I'm sure she wants to forget it! Still, publish and be damned eh. I took her to the Regal Cinema in Highams Park. Sadly, like so many cinemas, it later became a bingo hall. The film was a Marty Feldman comedy. There were some other local kids in the audience, with whom I'd previously had some fights and whilst I might never have had a second date with Debbie anyway, the heckling certainly ensured it.

Next up was my first real girlfriend. Strangely it was playing the violin that opened the door this time, rather than being a hindrance. Post sailing club I started attending a Saturday morning music school for 'talented' kids. How I got in is a mystery to me. However, I ended up on the first desk of the second violins next to the leader, the totally gorgeous Glynis. Now Glynis was a tall slim blonde and a complete babe in anyone's book. We dated for some months and I was utterly devastated when she dumped me. If you're old enough to remember a band called 'The Sweet' well that was the era and you can probably remember the high boots, flares and all the other wacky things from the seventies – the decade taste forgot! In fact Glynis was a big fan of 'The Sweet', despite being a classical violinist herself, and she managed to obtain one of the lead singer's silver lame covered, leather catsuits. I don't know how she got it and I don't want to.

My biggest adventure with Glynis was when we parked my dad's big old Zephyr Six, just off the road on the edge of Chingford Plains for some heavy petting. When Glynis and I parted ways I was still technically a virgin, and so was she, but I learned my first real lessons about women's bodies from her, and she really was lovely. However, on this occasion, when it became late and time to take her home, we climbed into the front bench seat, wiped the condensation from the windows and I started the car. I engaged first gear with the old style column change, let the clutch out and everything was working perfectly. Except, that we weren't moving. The car had sunk axle deep in the mud, the back wheels were doing their thing, but to no avail.

I had Glynis push, covering her new, knee high, red leather, pride and joy boots in mud. No go. Next I took Dad's carpets out of the car and tried employing them under the back wheels. No go. I flagged down a passing car, a big old Rover. Eight kids got out of it, four guys and four girls. One or more of the guys played rugby for the George Monoux Grammar School – our arch rivals. Never mind, they agreed to push even though one of the fellas was somewhat embarrassed when his girlfriend asked why we had pulled off the road! Despite nine pushers, carpets under the wheels and me driving, in a nice, clean, mud free environment, the car was still firmly stuck.

We waved down a second car. A Cortina with an Irish guy and his wife stopped. They had a tow rope. With the tow rope attached diagonally up to the road, with the Irish guy pushing, in addition to the Monoux Grammar School guys, their girlfriends and Glynis, and with the Irish chap's wife towing with the Cortina, there was a loud sucking noise and the Zephyr struggled out of the mire. By now we were very, very late. Thank yous' were hastily made and we headed home. Glynis's new boots were in such a state we had to hide them in the bushes, for retrieval later and cleaning when parents were out of the way.

My big worry was the state of dad's car and would I ever get to use it again. I put the keys back on the sideboard and waited for all hell to break loose the next day. Dad didn't say a word, nor the next day, or the next. He's just toying with me, I thought. Of course I didn't dare ask to use the car again. A week later, the weekend again, dad suggested I walk down to the library with him. As we left the house he commented how dirty the car looked. Here it comes I thought, but no, he'd only just noticed and since I hadn't used the car all week, no blame was laid at my door. Amazing. I didn't confess until I was in my thirties!

The summer after my arctic expedition I went back to Rhiconich, with a mate called Andy, to do some hill walking and climbing. I had a tiny two man mountain tent by Ultimate Equipment. It was state of the art at the time and very light with the inner and outer tents sewn together along the ridge and a built in ground sheet. There were two vertical poles, one taller than the other and it was just possible for two people to lie down in one direction, the feet end having the lower pole. At the higher end there was a bit of a bell shape so you could bring a few belongings in from the rain, but that's all.

We camped about a hundred yards from the Rhiconich Hotel, by the stream for fresh water. When the weather was good we went climbing, when it was bad we tramped into the hotel, muddy boots and all and watched Wimbledon on the TV. The hotel was run then by a Mr McLeod, and he was a character. I was told much later by the subsequent owners of the hotel that the old gentleman had built it himself.

There were two bars, one, the public bar was frequented by the local fishermen, a tough lot. The other was the lounge bar, slightly quieter, slightly more comfortable and with a choice of one hundred scotch whiskies. Andy and I set about sampling them all. Of course your palate is shot after the first, but I decided I liked Aberlour, and I've had a bottle ever since. Not many people visit the hotel in winter I suspect, but in summer, McLeod used to get two or three girls from Aberdeen to come and help out as waitresses and so on. There were three when we were there, slightly tricky as there were only two of us. The girls were of a similar age to Andy and myself and very attractive. After work they spent quite a lot of time with us, unofficially, and since Mr McLeod locked up, we had to push them back through the window late at night, which involved a little bit of climbing, but we had all the gear for that. One of them became a fairly serious girlfriend for a while, we corresponded and she came down to London for a visit. I visited her parents' farm in Rothienorman near Aberdeen too. In fact I was fooling around with her friend first and Mary came down to the tent to tell me what she thought of me, which wasn't entirely complimentary. Nonetheless something clicked between us. My mother would have been delighted if I'd married her, and she was a fabulous girl, but I was not up for settling down so early. Unfortunately the tiny tent had to withstand a little damage with four of us fooling around at a time in there. Andy was no puritan either!

One day while Andy and I were at Rhiconich our primus stove sprang a leak, so we couldn't heat any food, or even make a hot drink. I asked old McLeod if he had a soldering iron I could borrow. "I dunna lend ma tools ta anyone laddie" he replied, then promptly offered to solder the primus for me, which he did. Bear in mind that Andy and I had been abusing his hotel, tramping mud, running off with his staff, watching his TV, getting drunk. I thought he was a fabulous old guy. That evening, to say thank you I offered to buy him a drink. "No one buys me a drink in ma hotel laddie" he said and threw me out. Hilarious, of course I was back in the next day.

Some years later I took Sian, my then girlfriend to the Rhiconich Hotel and we actually stayed there as paying guests. Mrs McLeod was no longer around but Mr McLeod was.

I asked him if he recalled the incident from years before and was disappointed to find he did not. About a year later I returned to the Rhiconich Hotel again, this time with Angela, of all of them she was the love of my life. I said hi to Mr McLeod and asked him if he remembered me this time. "Aye I do laddie and that's not the same lassie ya brought last year". My love affair with Angela didn't go the distance, but that wasn't the reason. I spent quite a bit of time talking with Mr McLeod on those two visits and at the end of the second one he said to me "dunna come back next year laddie, it'll no be the same". I didn't go back again for years, then finally the inquisitive side of my nature compelled me to return. I found the hotel in the keeping of a couple from Sheffield. Although I'd not met them at the time, they frequented the hotel, as climbers, in the same period Andy and I went there. We added up the years and it turned out that old McLeod died within a year of that last previous visit. They loved him and the place as much as I did, and do. I hope they still have it.

CHAPTER 2

Careers Decisions

I'VE LOST TOUCH with him now, but my mate Andy was an important friend in my youth and an interesting character. Our parents met in the maternity hospital when I was being born, at the same time as Andy's older sister Rosemary came into the world. Andy's about a year younger than me. I hope he won't mind me saying but he could be a bit clumsy, on the other side of the coin, however, he's a genius. Straight A's, at A level and in quantity, a great degree and a great career in the oil business. He always seemed to land on his feet, except when he made his one and only parachute jump and landed down wind, on a disused, gravely, tarmac runway, ouch, but that was Andy. When I say he always landed on his feet I mean career wise, where one oil company sponsored his university years and another then bought out his contract for megabucks when he qualified. Then he went skiing one year. Probably to a posh resort in Switzerland. There he got into a two person gondola and an attractive English girl got in opposite, they chatted and then skied down together. Andrew had just met the Honourable Charlotte Ashton of Hyde, whose father Lord Ashton was also Chairman of Barclays Bank. They married and Andy's career has taken them around the world. Last I heard they were living in New Zealand, and I hope they're still living happily ever after. It always tickled me though, that Charlotte, who I never got to know on account of their travels, must surely now be the Honourable Charlotte Bartlett. Has a sort of ring to it don't you think.

I'd always been attracted to boats and my father, who was a science master at another school, and also their careers advisor, was keen that I should join the Merchant or Royal Navy. An ambition that appealed to me too, given that the budget to go motor racing would take a while to come by. I loved my parents deeply. I followed my dad's advice and regrettably took subjects suited more to this possible career path than to any aptitude on my part. I don't want to be critical of my parents, they did far more for me than I've been able to do for my own daughter and were as near perfect parents as is humanly possible.

However, I gave up subjects I was reasonably good at, to study those I hated and tended to fail at. It's a strategy which, these days, puts me in mind of World War One generals pouring reinforcements into lost causes and failing to exploit the places where breakthroughs were made. History was one of those subjects I gave up and which today I soak up like a sponge and love. At the time, struggling with subjects I found terribly difficult and didn't enjoy caused me a huge amount of stress, I exorcised my feelings with long walks around the streets, or in the forest of an evening, but brooding on it didn't help, nor did the stress my parents put upon the importance of my exam results to my future. What would I end up doing if I failed. Ironically the career path I was struggling to get to was closed off to me anyway for medical reasons! If, I'd studied subjects I was good at and enjoyed I'm sure I could have achieved three A levels and gone to university. Yet again, though, my life would have been very different, probably more conventional. I can't help wondering if it's all mapped out for us from day one and we just walk the line.

Be that as it may, if anyone reads this, who's of an age where they're deciding what to study and what to do in life, I suggest you study the things you enjoy. If you're good at something you can generally make some kind of living from it. And if you like a thing you tend to be good at it. Finally, you should end up in a career that interests you. Luckily I discovered something I was good at, and it gave me some of the happiest years of my life, but not just yet.

The day I took my last 'A'Level exam was a day of relief, if not one of satisfaction. One of my few school friends and I decided we should go out and celebrate. Neither of us had a lot of money, I made some by caddying for a golfer at the club on

Chingford Plains. He was a strange character, he spent much of every round, telling me in graphic detail what he'd be doing to his wife when he got home. Either he thought I was already an experienced man of the world, or he enjoyed embarrassing his young caddy. Whatever the truth of the matter he also gambled quite large sums on the outcome of his games and when he won I could reckon on a good tip.

Phil and I had never been to a real nightclub, only local youth club discos and the like. We'd heard about a new nightclub in Victoria, so we took the underground up to town, with all we could afford, only to find the nightclub shut that night. Nothing daunted we found a black London taxi. London's cabbies know everything that goes on in town. "We've just finished our 'A'Level exams and we want to find a nightclub to celebrate" we told him. He took us to Kensington High Street and pulled up almost opposite a nightclub. It was called 'Thursdays' I think. He pointed it out and said "well there's a nightclub over there, or you could try Lulus, up the street, second turning on the left." We thanked him, paid and crossed over to take a look.

It was expensive. We decided to check out the other place first and then decide. We took the second turning on the left and walked a long way up it, no sign of a nightclub. Perhaps we'd misheard, perhaps it was the first turning on the left, we tried that too, but there was no sign of a nightclub, perhaps he meant past the second left, but on the High Street. We started to walk back in that direction. A young couple were coming the other way, arms around one another. "Excuse me" I said, "do you know where Lulus is?" The girl answered, "Yes" she said "It's up that side street on the left", pointing to the street we'd explored first off. We decided we must have missed it, since she confirmed the taxi drivers directions perfectly. As we set off I heard a slap and turned, "how the hell do you know Lulus" I heard the young man shouting at his girlfriend. We walked up the side street. We saw no nightclub, we did see some very beautiful girls and some very happy looking men entering and leaving a certain house. I'm sure we both had the desire to find out more, but not the courage, the experience, or most crucially, the funds. We ended up at the actual nightclub drinking very expensive drinks and returning broke on the last train home.

Before my mediocre A level results were received I applied for a Board of Trade eyesight test, with a view to becoming a navigating cadet in the Merchant Navy. I saw myself in a white uniform on the deck of a cruise ship, surrounded by glamorous ladies. Well, it wasn't a bad dream! Generally, you go along, look at some colour recognition books, do a couple of lantern tests, which simulate ships lights at various distances and you're given a result, you've passed, you've failed. Simple. Not so for me. I was told I was borderline, so borderline in fact that they couldn't decide whether I'd passed or failed. I was told by the gentleman in charge that he'd confer with someone else, his boss I suppose, and they'd drop me a line in a day or so. Naturally when the letter came it was bad news, they'd decided to play safe and fail me.

I figured, that if it had been such a close run thing, then, if I could persuade them to test me again I might get lucky and scrape through. I wrote back and enquired about the possible grounds for appeal. They replied that I could appeal if I thought the test was unfair in some way, or if I'd been cured of the condition. Well the second option was a bit of a laugh, as there is no cure for colour-blindness, whilst the first would require a slur on the chap who ran the test. I opted to call their bluff and appeal on the grounds I was no longer colour blind! Now all I had to do was come up with a cure for colour blindness. I thought about various 'alternative' therapies and spoke to a Chinese acupuncturist. Now acupuncture does not claim to cure colour blindness, however, I used to have migraines as a youngster and acupuncture does claim to relieve migraine. When you have a migraine you can see all sorts of things, colours, lights and so on, and the acupuncturist thought there could be a link between my migraines and my colour vision problems. Well it was worth a try, possibly I could wave good-bye to my migraines and I'd get a letter from the acupuncturist to The Board of Trade suggesting it was worth testing me again, fantastic!

I had four sessions of acupuncture and people who say it's painless must have some sort of sensory deficiency. He even stuck needles in the corners of my eyes just about. As well as my temples, thumbs and other places. The ones in my thumbs went in at the base and it seemed like they were going all the way up to the knuckle, ouch. Then there were the migraines I got in the evenings after the sessions, it was horrible. I don't get migraines anymore though, and I got my letter to The Board of Trade. I appealed. They responded and said they'd test me again.

Now I don't remember where the first test took place, but I do remember being surprised that the second test was at a different address altogether, in the region of High Holborn, central London. When I got there, it wasn't just a case of a few books and lanterns and there were about six 'experts', not just one guy on his own. At the end of the tests they announced, unequivocally that I was colour blind. Now the funny thing is that years later I took that same test, several times, for my racing driver's licence and every time I passed with 100%. I think that acupuncturist started some process that sorted the problem over time, but of course I couldn't wait to appeal, nor did I know, what, if anything, was happening. How different, again, my life would have been if I'd ended up in the merchant navy. Or the marines.

My next career idea was to apply for a commission in the Royal Marines. I was invited along to HMS something or other, a shore based establishment. I went through a couple of days of building bridges across non existent streams and undertaking all manor of tests. Then, eventually, I got to the final interview with three senior officers. Now, obviously, they do some background checks before you can get a commission in the armed forces and one of the questions they asked me was "Have you ever failed a medical for the merchant navy?" Well to me it wasn't a medical, a medical is where they stick things up your bum and all that malarky, I'd only ever failed an eyesight test, so I said "no". Now they don't tell you why you failed, but I think they thought I was a liar and I think it's a question of interpretation. Anyway, no marines.

Now, having taken the wrong subjects at 'A' Level I wasn't going to get into university, so I needed a job at worst, career at best. My father pointed me in the direction of the Inchcape Group of companies and I became a management trainee, instantly breaking one of my vows and becoming a commuter. I caught the train each morning from Highams Park, like hundreds of others and trundled up to Liverpool Street. I'm not sure if by then it was still steam, or diesel or electric, I can remember the steam trains from that station for sure. From Liverpool Street I walked to City Road and a desk in Inchcape Export Ltd. From there I purchased items requisitioned by the Shell Petroleum Company, which were then shipped to oil rigs around the world, everything from heavy plant to workman's gloves.

It was quite interesting and there was this fabulous girl Terri from Harlow. As a management trainee you get moved around a bit and I had a spell in the in house travel agency, but the best bit was a 'character building' outward bound type course, management trainees got sent on. I think you possibly had to volunteer, or apply, but in my case I got a cruise on the tall ship 'Sir Winston Churchill' from London to Alderney in the Channel Islands. That was right up my street and a wonderful experience, shortly afterwards I left the company. Perhaps I should feel guilty about taking their training and then leaving. I know it's been a big debate in industry since. British companies have shied away I think, whilst I have the impression, the Germans for instance have not. Frankly if everyone gives good training, then, even though people tend to move around more these days, the common good is served and all benefit. It's tough when it's your money though and especially hard on small business.

Had I stayed at Inchcape, though, I'd have lost my soul as well as my mind, it wasn't the right place for someone like me. Recently I've started to read Patrick O'Brian's novels about the Royal Navy in Nelson's day. Having been on a tall ship and climbed the rigging, and been out on the yards certainly gives you a perspective, one which would be a severe test of the imagination in other case. Thank you the Sail Training Association and of course Inchcape. I also met a Naval architect from America recently and we discussed sail training. He said he was surprised that the world's greatest navy didn't have a sail training ship when so many others do. He was of course referring to the US Navy, I suggested to him that what he really meant was the world's biggest navy!

CHAPTER 3

Skydive

DURING THE FEW months I was at Inchcape I'd started a new hobby. On my wages I couldn't afford to go motor racing, but I could afford to go skydiving. I read about the RSA Parachute Club in my father's Readers Digest. I hitchhiked down to Thruxton near Andover and took a weekend course. Students trained for around eight hours on Saturday and jumped, weather permitting, on Sunday. Of course as happens so often in the UK the weather on Sunday did not permit. The result was that I telephoned regularly to check the weather, and took a day off work, mid week, to go and claim my jump.

I'd only ever been in an aeroplane once up until then. That was the first commercial jet airliner, a DeHavilland Comet, in this case operated by Dan Air. That was when I was sixteen and went on a school skiing trip. The parachute club at the time of my first jump was renting a Cessna 172, a tiny aircraft, even as light aircraft go. There was room for a pilot, who had the only seat, and then kneeling on the floor, two parachutists and a jumpmaster. I was number one, so I knelt at the front next to the pilot, with my left hand across my front mounted reserve parachute, to protect the handle, and my right hand on the dashboard of the aeroplane. Behind me was Paul Young, dapper, tough, ex Guards and French Foreign Legion, the no nonsense jumpmaster. Behind the pilot and next to Paul was number two, safely tucked up, well away from the open door.

We bounced down the grass runway and up into the air, circling slowly up to two thousand five hundred feet. At about two thousand two hundred feet Paul threw out a wind drift indicator to tell him where the correct opening point was, and then directed the pilot to the right place next time around. All of this was totally new to me, little did I know that a few months later I'd be Paul's colleague, and not too long after that a jumpmaster myself. For now I was on an adrenalin charged high, taking in the noise, the blast that came in the door, the sights and the smells. Well, we won't go into the smells, but it wasn't me.

My sister and my mother's father visit me at the parachute club, where the Cessna 180 is part way through being re-painted in Midas livery. This grandfather's love of life and his anti war stance made a big impression on me and in part at least his attitudes have inspired the way I live, and my desire to create an organisation to campaign for peace.

When the order "on the step" came I climbed out purposefully into the position practiced on the ground, the slipstream makes it necessary to be purposeful. Then, when Paul shouted "go", I went. Simple, and seconds later I was blissfully guiding my parachute down on to the drop zone for a nice safe landing. I field packed; a way of bundling it back together for transportation only, and returned to Tony Rolfe who was kitting people up for their jumps. Being mid week, he wasn't too busy. "How was it?" he enquired, "great" or words to that effect I replied, "want to go again?" he said. After the training weekend's disappointment and the wait, the idea that I could do two was a surprise. "Er yes, can I?" I was kitted up and off again before I knew it, and still being charged up with adrenalin from the first jump it all went terribly well. I was now on a new path although I didn't know it yet.

It was two weeks or more before I found myself back at the parachute club, with weather suitable for students to jump. This time I wasn't charged up with adrenalin in quite the same dosage I think. It wasn't all quite so new, which left a little spare brain capacity to ponder things. Anyway, I felt fine as we climbed into the sky. Paul, the only man in the world who can wear a crash helmet all day and remove it without a hair out of place was jumpmaster again. However, in place of Jamie the pilot for my first two jumps there was Werner. Now Werner was a lovely guy and a good pilot, but it's funny how any little change can add to your nerves when you're feeling nervy.

Then there was a radio call from Boscombe Down. Near Thruxton there are several military airfields, the biggest being Boscombe Down which in those days handled some pretty big traffic. They instructed us to hold off for a while, while something came through. We flew around in circles with the aircraft banked right, ie with the open door downwards, and I was again next to the open door. Now there's no danger of falling out at the wrong time due to centrifugal force, or is it centripetal force, I failed my 'A' Level physics of course. No that's not the point, it's just a bit disconcerting to a novice parachutist, who's being given too much time to think about it. There's too much of a good view down and you start to think, why have you put yourself back in this situation, you got away with it twice, isn't that enough for you, and so on. I got more and more nervous and I wasn't enjoying myself, to be honest scared comes to mind.

However, when Paul ordered me "on the step" it felt like a relief to be getting on with it. Much like waiting to step on stage on opening night, my nerves went away immediately, I was occupied. I did a pretty good jump and of course afterwards I wondered why I'd got so worked up. That was the toughest one though, first freefall was difficult, and later on still I had a couple of malfunctions on early square parachutes, but mentally that was my toughest jump, number three, never forget that one.

A student jumper descends under one of the club's Double L round canaopies.

On one of those early trips to the parachute club I got a lift back to London from a couple of nurses. When we got back to the nurses home, well there was a party going on and it seemed rude not to. So I stayed and then walked, I don't know how many miles across London, in the early hours to get home. I was eighteen or just nineteen and still living at home. I remember I was amazed to find my parents still up, sitting in the living room waiting for me to return. It's hard to credit now, in an age of mobile phones and internet on the go, but in 1975 our household didn't even have a phone, my parents were waiting to hear my key in the door, but dreading a knock from the police. Oops.

When I took up skydiving as a profession I overheard a conversation between my parents which wasn't a happy one. Dad was not impressed with me giving up my career path at Inchcape to go live in a hut built of wood and paper on an airfield, where I would earn eleven pounds a week for risking my life. I remember he blamed Mum for encouraging me to go to the John Ridgway School and on my arctic expedition. The description of the hut is no exaggeration, it had been a temporary building in 1939 and this was 1975. It had a concrete base and a wooden frame. On the inside of the wooden frame was some kind of early plasterboard, or maybe that had been substituted later, the outer skin was just tarred paper.

Thruxton airfield as seen from the aircraft. The triangular grass section at the top, just left of centre is the student drop zone.

After, dare I say it, just five jumps Bob Acraman the parachute club owner invited me to join the staff. He'd heard about my little faux pas with the marines, knew I wasn't suited to an office job and I like to think he saw some potential too. At the time I was also talking to John Ridgway about a position at the Adventure School, but the Adventure School was a summer job only and the parachute club was year round. The parachute club won. I think there were some club members who were a bit put out that someone with so little experience was getting a job at their club and getting free tuition and free jumps and so on. On the whole though I was made very welcome. Of course living at the club and working a six day week my progress was rapid.

To become a British Parachute Association instructor at that time one had to take a potential instructor's 'PI' course, then a full instructor's course and to be a club chief instructor 'CCI', one had to take an advanced instructor's course. There were number of jump stipulations and, 'time in the sport' requirements too. Bob Acraman acquired a dispensation for me from the time in the sport requirement, for my PI course, on the basis that I was working full time at a week round club, whereas most candidates were weekend only jumpers.

Well, I say Bob got me a dispensation, it wasn't actually quite like that. At that time, in the mid seventies, there were two major full time civilian parachute centres and quite a few weekend only clubs. The two full time clubs were Thruxton where I worked and the Peterborough Parachute Centre run by John Meacock. All the clubs were affiliated to the British Parachute Association and operated under their auspices. Now, Bob, was I think, respected by most of the other operators. He was a hell of a skydiver, with thousands of jumps, who had run the Rhine Army Parachute Association. Everyone knew him, or knew of him. I'll tell you some stories about him shortly. However, Bob wasn't good at doing things by the book. With his experience he figured he knew best how to do things and he tended to go his own way. Possibly some of the others did too, I don't know, but Bob told the BPA what he thought of their rules once too often, and accordingly, relationships were frayed with the association and some of its leading lights. In many ways I believe he appointed Paul Young as CCI and later myself because he knew we'd run a tight ship and keep on good terms with the BPA.

Back to the story. I thought I was booked on a potential instructors course at Peterborough, all properly registered and arranged. In fact I turned up with a letter of introduction from Bob, and without the necessary two years in the sport. Thankfully, skydiving seems to attract quality people and although I was unexpected and outside the norm so to speak, the powers that be recognised that this was Bob Acraman at work again and that it wasn't my fault I was in this predicament. They also bought the argument about me working full time at a full time centre, which didn't apply to most candidates, obviously. I had all the other requirements and I was allowed on the course, but it was a heart in mouth introduction to Charlie Shea-Simmonds the National Coach and Safety Officer, and to John Meacock, the two most powerful men in the BPA, and the sport, at the time.

Parachute design has changed much since 1976. In those days a freefall parachute had a spring loaded pilot chute (mini parachute) which was released, usually, when a ripcord was pulled removing four pins which held the pack closed. The pack had four cones, with small holes through them, attached to the inside flaps. The outer flaps had holes with grommets, these were placed over the cones and the ripcord pins were then inserted through the small hole at the top of each cone, to hold the arrangement closed, with the spring loaded pilot chute nestling underneath. Pull the ripcord and the flaps with the grommets should slide off the cones and the pilot chute leap out into the slipstream. In fact there were a number of potential problems. One was that the spring in the pilot chute, if placed right under a cone, could put upward pressure on the cone and hinder the other flaps from sliding off. Another problem for a student, trying to maintain a stable attitude and fall face to earth, could be that the pilot chute would not jump far enough and would be trapped in a vortex, or volume of dead air, behind his/her back and therefore not lift the main parachute off. Many parachutists decided that two pilot chutes were a good idea, one was almost certain to jump out and catch.

I had subscribed to this view myself and it could have cost me my life. The only jump I ever really messed up was my first freefall. It's a bit of a pressure and I was used to Paul Young despatching me. As I said earlier, small changes can make you nervous. For my first freefall, Bob the parachuting legend, and my boss and employer, decided to put me out himself. Just to add to the pressure. In order to fall stable a skydiver pushes his or her hips (centre of gravity) forward to pull themselves face to earth. We were taught to look for the handle by moving the head only and not de-arching, or pulling the hips back, sort of leaning forward for a better look. This change of posture could roll you on to your back and put the parachute underneath you. Not the healthiest place for it to be.

I committed this cardinal sin on my first freefall and accordingly rolled on to my back as I pulled the handle. The pilot chutes found a way out, but one came out between my legs and the other came out to the side of my right leg. Being attached to one bridle cord and with my leg between them, they weren't going anywhere. The correct action would have been to deploy my front mounted reserve parachute, but I did the instinctive thing and kicked, to get the pilot chutes off. It worked, for me. Bob should probably have put me back on the static line (known in parachute slang as the dope rope and I felt a dope too), and made me practice 'dummy ripcord pulls' again. But being the maverick character he is, he took the judgement that I'd be ok, bit like falling off a horse, and put me straight into another freefall rig and took me straight back up. Bob was right, I was determined not to show myself up again. I never thought about the consequences of getting it wrong again, I just didn't want to let myself or Bob down and freefall number two was virtually perfect. I never looked back.

Sadly, somewhat later, whilst I was on my potential instructors course there, Peterborough Parachute Club had a fatality. Their first I believe. This is still a very rare thing in skydiving and as tough as he was, mentally and physically I would say, I imagine John Meacock, the owner and Chief Instructor, was shaken. The fatality was a novice freefall student who did exactly as I did on my first freefall. He had two pilot chutes, he rolled on his back, the pilot chutes caught one each side of a leg and instead of deploying the reserve he tried to kick them off. In his case, they didn't come off. I knew none of this, I'd been in a classroom lecture. Later in the day I bumped into John Meacock outside. I still had not heard the news. He asked me in a casual sort of way how many pilot chutes I used. "Two" I replied, "why?" he queried. And to my eternal shame I gave him the stock answer, "because I can't get three in". He walked away. I can't describe how I felt later when I heard the news. Short in stature John was a big man, he gave me a second chance and helped both me and the RSA Parachute Club out in a very big way at a future date.

CHAPTER 4

The Legend Of Bob Acraman

THERE WAS A time, when I thought I might try to write a biography of Bob Acraman. Stories about him are legion in the army, or were, it's a long time ago now. Getting hold of Bob these days is difficult. He's somewhere in Nigeria, wheeling and dealing. Here are a few of the shorter stories, some are second hand, others I have first hand experience of.

Bob himself told me that he'd been a petty criminal in the east end of London as a youngster. A judge had given him the option, jail or the army. He'd joined an infantry regiment, but jokingly, or not, said he didn't like to walk everywhere and so applied to become a para, in order that he could fly everywhere. In those days it wasn't so easy to get into the parachute regiment or brigade. Soldiers had first to pass pre-para selection, later Bob would be in charge of pre-para selection, for a while, and he made it tough. He stole a piano from the officers mess and sank it in a shallow lake in Wales. Would be paras were given the map reference and told to report back to Sgt. Acraman and tell him what was there. If they came back and said "it's a lake Sarge" they were off the course, failed because they had not actually been to the exact map reference. Only those who found the piano stayed on. One group was marched, by Bob, to the top of the Brecon Beacons in the snow and ordered to strip. Bob stripped too and then told them the story of Little Bo Peep and other nursery rhymes, before telling them to dress and marching them back down. They must have thought he was mad, which of course he is, totally barking, in a wonderful kind of way.

There's a story about one recruit being given a tractor tyre, the big one off the back and being told to report with it to a sergeant at Edinburgh Castle by a certain time. The poor sod was then told to report back to Sergeant Acraman at Aldershot, with his tyre, in an equally short space of time.

Another group had to cut down a tree each, strip the branches and keep their tree with them throughout the course, in bed, in the loo, marching down the road, everywhere. Bob must have been in his element thinking up ways to test people.

I'm told Bob was made sergeant and demoted several times and was finally cashiered from the army for streaking through the officers mess during a formal do. This is second hand but it fits with everything else. In many ways it must have been the army's loss. However, Bob worked the system. Bilko-like he confessed to me he'd run a delivery business on the side, using army Landrovers for a long while.

There was a time in the seventies when Her Majesty's Government made quite major cutbacks in the armed forces, and there was a programme of careers advice to help ex military personnel into civilian life. Bob ran a successful business. The RSA (Robert Sydney Acraman) Parachute Club trained 7,000 students in a year at its height, and it was profitable, despite me earning a whole £22 a week by then! The MOD, or someone, thought it would be a good idea to hold Mr. dishonourable discharge Acraman up as an example of what entrepreneurial flair could do in civvy street. All our student parachutes at that time were stamped RAPA, which of course stands for Rhine Army Parachute Association, where Bob had been Chief Instructor. I'm sure you follow what I'm saying here. When this was queried, the answer was that it stood for the Robert Acraman Parachute Association.

One day a researcher for the TV programme 'This Is Your life' got in touch with the club. The famous, record breaking aviator, Sheila Scott was to be featured. In her early years as a pilot she had flown parachutists at Thruxton. I should explain that the RSA Parachute Club was not the first club at the airfield. The first ever UK parachute club had been established at Thruxton after the war, called the British Parachute Club. They jumped from old bi-planes called Jacaroos. Bob had jumped at this club but he'd never, ever, met Sheila. The opportunity to go on television was too good to miss though. On he went and greeted her like a long lost buddy. She didn't know him from Adam. Although he's not famous, Bob would make a terrific subject for the programme himself.

Club owner, army and parachuting legend Bob Acraman in action. His reserve parachute is slung to the side to make it possible to see the tiny accuracy disc he's aiming to land on with one foot.

Bob needed a new challenge and he had a good business record with the parachute club. He decided to start a sort of adventure school. Not like the John Ridgway one, but a bit like army basic training. He approached the bank and they were only too happy to advance Bob plenty. He bought what had been an isolation hospital, just a few miles up the road from Thruxton. In it we installed an assault course, a trainasium and various other bits of kit such as a trampoline and other pieces of sporting ephemera. The trainasium is a confidence building obstacle course through the trees, which gets higher and higher and has gaps to jump across, tipping planks, rope bridges etc. It culminated in a choice of a fan jump or a death slide to get back down. A fan jump is a piece of parachute training equipment, you jump off in a harness, with a rope which operates a big fan to control your descent. The 'death slide' is just a long rope slide, with a T shaped handle on a pulley.

Customers would go around the course clipped on to a safety line, the staff all had to do it without!!! We had a sales rep by then who was fond of telling people he was SAS, he even got married in his SAS uniform. In fact he was TA (Territorial Army) SAS and he had to be rescued from the trainasium when he froze halfway around! Paul Young became chief instructor of the new venture. I became chief instructor of the parachute club. This put a few noses out of joint again I think, a bit like my original appointment. The reason being that I had very briefly left the parachute club to try and earn some money as a salesman myself. I'd been planning to marry my first fiancee Cindy Higgins at the time and needed to make something realistic in the way of salary. When Bob asked me to come back as CCI, on a salary which would be about competitive for the time maybe £7,000 per annum, I was overjoyed, It was like coming home.

The adventure school had the potential to be a very good thing indeed. Bob approached some inner city councils and offered to take problem and deprived kids for a holiday that would give them some self discipline, and self confidence at the same time. Just as Ken Ford's sailing club had been ahead of its time so was Bob's Adventure School. One council took him up on it and we had some ordinary paying customers too, but the recession bit and the new business was struggling from day one. It was being supported by profits from the more established parachute club.

In an effort to make some extra money Bob accepted a suggestion from some sort of battle re-enactment society. Many people have heard of the 'Sealed Knot' who re-enact English Civil War battles, but in fact there are lots of these groups, and military vehicle conservation groups and so on. One of these organisations got in touch and asked Bob if he'd be prepared to make the Adventure School into a World War Two Prisoner Of War, POW, camp from which they would try to escape. You can imagine how that idea would appeal to someone like Bob, just as much as he needed to make some money from the place. Of course the press got hold of the Butlitz story as it became known. Bob strutted around as camp commandant, with an ex girlfriend of mine, now an ex wife of his, all dressed up as his mistress. The publicity did us no favours whatever and the damage done by the would be escapers tunnelling away, cutting electrical wires etc. etc. not to mention the cost of putting up watchtowers and so on, well I'm sure it can't have made a profit. It was a hugely amusing weekend though!

I realise now, as I approach fifty, that Bob must be the best part of twenty years older than me. However, he always seems to have looked the same to me. I can't help wondering if he ever looked young. The way he looked gave him a sort of gravitas, you felt he was a man with experience. He had a pretty good sense of humour on the whole. The only time I saw it fail was on his fortieth birthday. I think it was Jacqui's idea. Jacqui was the parachute club's full time rigger, who made sure all the kit was properly repaired when it needed it and was otherwise in good order. She had a business making jumpsuits too and they were damn fine. I had two during my career. Anyway Jacqui's idea or not, we got Bob some Phyllosan. You may remember the advertising slogan 'Phyllosan fortifies the over forties'. Well, sense of humour failure, I really thought we'd all be out of jobs!

Bob was a hard man. When the Adventure School's financial problems really started to drag the business down, compounded by the general recession which hit parachute club profits too, a finance company sent some heavies round to 'reclaim' Bob's Range Rover. They broke into it in the middle of the night, but Bob heard them and went out with a loaded shotgun. Two of them were in the vehicle. Bob ordered them out, but unbeknown to him a third heavy was hiding in the bushes. This guy jumped Bob from behind and the gun went off, luckily no one was hit and a fight ensued. The double barrelled shotgun was smashed over Bob's head at one point, with sufficient force to bend the two barrels, John Schofield (more of him later) who shared the house with Bob called the police. The heavies turned out to be members of the British Judo Team I was told recently There was also a well known story in parachute club circles about a row in a pub where some idiot insisted on poking Bob with his finger. Bob bit it clean off!

Bob himself tells some stories about his time in Aden, where apparently amongst other misdemeanours, he laid some explosive at the bottom of the officer's latrine trench. Just enough to give some of them a shock later!

He's undoubtedly done some questionable things, but the opportunities Bob gave me and others were fantastic. I've had some great times since, but my youthful experiences at the parachute club opened my eyes to many things, taught me to stand on my own two feet, trust my own judgement, make tough decisions and more.

Exactly what Bob does in Nigeria these days I couldn't rightly say, although I'm pretty certain arms dealing has or does come into it. I'm sure he's had a go at farming and selling palm wine of all things and I think these days he has a bar. I've heard he's been involved with the UK government or possibly acts as a conduit between them and the Nigerians on certain matters, and I've heard other stories, one involving the SAS which of course I can't verify, let alone publish. Of course that's how legends grow, and that's what Bob Acraman is, in parachuting circles, a legend. Suffice to say he's still living a hell of a life, and amongst all his other talents he's quite a gifted guitarist. And he must be approaching seventy now.

CHAPTER 5

Interesting Doors Begin To Open

AFTER MY POTENTIAL Instructors Course at Peterborough I took my full Instructors course at the Army Parachute Association at Netheravon and later I took my Advanced Instructors course there too. In those days they used De Havilland Rapides at Netheravon, a wonderful old canvas and wood bi plane, with upside down Gipsy Major engines. Another aeroplane with character was the De Havilland Dove. This was also an early piston engined airliner, which used the same motors as the Rapide, but was an alloy bodied, low wing monoplane. Bob bought one from a chap called Nick Grace who ran a small air freight business and frequented Thruxton.

I got the impression that Bob and Nick were quite good friends. For us, the Dove was a marvellous thing. We could get about eight jumpers in it and we could all sit forward of the door. Four things are important here. After years of struggling with small Cessnas where we had to kneel, we could now sit, on the floor since seats are too heavy when you want to get as many people in as possible, plus their equipment, but this was still luxury. Two, the door was at the back, so we could all sit forward of it, out of the icy blast you understand, skydiving in the UK is no picnic in winter! Three, it climbed a lot quicker so the time to get cold dropped dramatically, and four, we could put a relatively large group in the air all at once, now we could practice larger relative work formations. Another minor advantage was that we could all listen to Pink Floyd on the climb to altitude, to put us in the right mood!

Nick Grace, who sold Bob the Dove, had purchased a Spitfire, largely in bits, in crates, from the Strathallan Aircraft museum. After the war it had been sold to the Spanish and converted to a two seat trainer, before ending up at the museum. Nick rebuilt and restored it, which was the subject of a TV documentary. Every single rivet had to be replaced. It is one of a very few original 'Spits' still flying. Years later I happened to watch a Jimmy Saville 'Jim'll Fix It' programme where a terminally ill youngster was given a flight in the 'Spit' by Nick. I was shell-shocked at the end of the programme when they dedicated it to Nick, saying that between filming and broadcast Nick had been killed in a car accident. It was this event that led me to track Bob down in Nigeria as I felt he'd want to know.

After our first jump from the De Havilland Dove, on the day we acquired it.

Our main aircraft prior to the Dove, which was also owned by the parachute club, was an old Cessna 180. This is what's known as a tail dragger. In other words it has two wheels at the front and one small one under the tail. It's more difficult to take off and land than many light aircraft which have a tricycle undercarriage. That is to say, they have three similar sized wheels, one under the nose and one on each side, but still fairly near the front. An aircraft with a tricycle undercarriage taxis with its tail horizontal. With a tail dragger aircraft, like most World War Two fighters you have to get the tail flying first, then get up to speed to rotate the aircraft (pull back) and take off. The rotation of the prop on the other hand means the aircraft wants to swing as well.

Finding suitable pilots for this beast was one of my tasks as chief instructor. In the early days of my career at Thruxton it caused me another problem though. Bob had contracts with British Aerospace and RFD GQ Defence Equipment. For the former we demonstrated the parachuting capability of a British transport aircraft, the Hawker Siddeley 748 and for the latter we undertook test jumps on new designs or adaptations of parachutes. When you earn £11 a week and you jump out of aeroplanes all day, being offered £20 a jump to try something new sounds wonderful, ah the foolishness of youth eh.

One of the first jobs for British Aerospace involved a trip to Africa. I didn't get to go. Paul Young who had been Bob's Chief Instructor for some time was senior to me and someone had to keep things running back at Thruxton. The result was that I was left in charge of the club for a couple of weeks. Bear in mind that I was twenty two at most, probably twenty one when this occurred. Quite a responsibility. There are a lot of regulations both British Parachute Association and Civil Aviation Authority, then there's the small matter of being responsible for peoples lives, throw in a large cash turnover and customer satisfaction and Bob left me in charge of all this.

Sometimes, these days, when I meet people in their early twenties, who seem to take life so very lightly I wonder just how I could have had so much left in my hands at the same age. I'm not trying to blow my own trumpet, it's just an observation about how the world, or Britain at least, has changed so much, kids seem to grow up quicker to start with and then sort of stop. The very night Bob and Paul left, some idiot drove a truck into the back of our Cessna 180 which was parked and securely tied down at the flying club. The only damage was to the rudder, but this is not a common aircraft with spares readily available. Now, it's one thing telling customers they can't jump because the weather's unsuitable, telling them they can't jump because you have no aircraft, when you've taken their money and trained them is a bit more tricky.

Don't ask me how I knew, but I had a feeling John Meacock at Peterborough had a 180 rudder. I called him, he did, and being a very decent chap he let us have it. Hippy-like I had acquired an old Morris Minor, ex GPO van, which, being a bit tatty I'd painted orange with a paintbrush. I drove up to Peterborough through the night in this strange jalopy, and then straight back with the rudder, having already arranged for an engineer to be standing by. Even so we'd be a few days without the Cessna, it needed to be checked for other damage, airworthiness is not something to be taken lightly. Therefore, I arranged to hire something else, a twin engined 206. Luxury by comparison. Anyway, training and parachuting continued uninterrupted throughout Bob and Paul's absence, we turned a healthy profit and by the time they came back the 180 was flying again.

Our work for British Aerospace and for RFD GQ Defence equipment make interesting stories in their own right. The Hawker Siddeley 748 is a relatively short take off and landing turbo prop cargo plane. Its main rival at the time was a Fokker which was a high wing monoplane. The 748 is a low wing monoplane. The 748 is the better flier I'm told, but, the high wing of the Fokker has other advantages particularly on rough jungle runways and so on. All design is a compromise, you pays your money and takes your choice. Of course customers want it all though. There was quite a sales battle going on. Now, I'm told, and it seems logical given the design, that the 748 was never envisaged as a military parachuting aircraft. However, when governments who were 'would-be' customers asked if it could be used for military parachuting, the answer had to be yes, otherwise more points to Fokker.

The cargo door was on the port (left) side, between the wing and the tailplane. The tailplane, like the wing was also low mounted. Stand in the open door and look aft (backwards) and you're looking down on the tailplane. I hope I'm painting a picture here. Now imagine the aircraft is flying, a 100 knot gale of slipstream and propeller blast is whooshing down the side of the aeroplane. When you jump, that blast is going to blow you backwards. Going over the tailplane is not an option, you've got to get down under it!

It can be done, making the 748 a viable military parachuting aircraft, but certain conditions have to be in place AND it's disconcerting for the jumper who thinks about things. The conditions are, one, the jumper has to leave the aircraft in a military parachuting position. That is the type of position used on mass jumps where a fixed line (static line) opens the parachute as you leave the aircraft. For these mass drops such as the one at Arnhem the idea is to get as many soldiers out of the aircraft as quickly as possible and group them in a small area, (the drop zone) so they can form up into a cohesive force quickly. The risk in pushing soldiers out very tightly packed is entanglement so a military jump position is legs together with arms over the reserve. Not being spread like a freefall parachutist the military parachutist cuts down through the air feet first. This then is the first condition for jumping from the 748 even if you're doing freefall, first clear the tail! The second is down to the pilot. He has to fly the aircraft as slowly as possible, with the landing flaps down. This reduces the slipstream and creates a certain amount of downdraft. Some pilots feel a little nervous flying an aircraft close to the stall. We were told that a nervous pilot in Brazil had caused one jumper, who possibly compounded the problem by leaving the aircraft in a freefall position, to lose his head, on the tailplane, literally. As you can imagine this cheered us all no end.

The upshot was that all parachute demonstrations were done by RSA Parachute Club personnel (who could be relied upon to adopt the correct position) and the pilot would always be a British Aerospace pilot, who could be relied upon to fly slowly! Sometimes vehicles had to be parachuted out of the door too! There was some effort to sell British parachutes as part of the package, hence the link with RFD GQ Defence Equipment.

Personally I made two trips. The first was to Denmark where we were trying to sell the 748 for coast guarding duties. Quite a few of us went and it was a nice easy demonstration on to a large airfield. We stayed in a fabulous hotel, I had something resembling a suite, with a spiral staircase leading to a double bed in mid air virtually. We were guests of the British Defence Attache at a reception, and also had a wonderful meal at the Yacht Club in Copenhagen. At the age of twenty two all this was a very new and exciting experience.

Several of us, on the staff, had inoculations for all sorts of weird and wonderful places, so that we could go pretty well anywhere at the drop of a hat. However, it's not possible to have visas in place for everywhere all the time, so they had to be arranged as necessary. Out of the blue one day we had a call from British Aerospace. The sales team were in Madagascar. They had no idea before going there that the Madagascans were interested in a parachute capability. Not only did the Madagascans want a parachute aircraft to replace their wonderful, but ageing, fleet of DC3s, but they also wanted their own people to jump the 748, not merely a demonstration you understand.

Now knocking a few of your customer's heads off is no way to win friends, but the answer still had to be yes. So British Aerospace wanted an RSA person out there to make sure the Madagascan parachutists knew what was required of them. In other words to instruct and act as jumpmaster, or dispatcher as well as to jump themselves. There were other considerations too. I believe deforestation is a problem in Madagascar now, but when I was there the drop zone was on top of a mountain, so as to be above the tree line, since we were in the midst of mature rain forest. Best for all concerned if the jumpers hit the target, which was my responsibility too.

A mixed lift of staff and customers in the Dove. It may look cramped but it was luxury compared with the small Cessnas that had served until then. In the foreground are Kevin and Paul left side, myself and Jacqui on the right.

Paul Young was my senior, at that time, at the club and would probably have been first choice. However Paul had been in the French Foreign Legion. He'd made sergeant, which is generally the highest rank a foreigner can achieve, the officers being French. After his first three or five years he'd signed on again, being commandant, so to speak, of a nice south pacific island and having a great life. As a sergeant on his second term he would have been considered a low risk for desertion. However, when he'd been posted back to Corsica he'd decided he'd had enough and deserted (also see Author's Afterword). Now, the only way to fly to Madagascar was via Paris. Not an option for Paul. So at the age of twenty two I was given this fantastic job.

I was told to hire a car and get myself to Heathrow where tickets would be waiting for me at a certain desk. I had to fly Air France to Charles de Gaulle and take a bus to Orly, or the other way around, then, after a few hours wait there was an Air Madagascar flight to Antananarive, the capital of Madagascar. I queried my lack of a visa. I was told that the Madagascan authorities wanted me out there, so there would be no problem. British Aerospace would arrange the visa for me while I was travelling, could they have my passport number please, and coincidentally, I would be met at the airport by a chap called John Schofield (not the same one who shared a house with Bob) he would have my visa ready and waiting.

Clearly my contact at the other end was white so he should stand out. Easy then. My sister was living and studying in Paris at the time, so she met me for a chat at Orly and about thirty something hours after the initial phonecall I was touching down in Madagascar. I looked and felt my best after this epic, having had a crying baby right behind me for the eighteen hours or so of the second flight.

Antananarive airport surprised me, as it looked quite smart and modern. As always happens when a long haul flight lands, everyone is in a hurry to get off and get on with their journey, or whatever their plans are. Not having a visa, my priority was to spot a white face in a sea of black. I couldn't see one. Nobody had arranged a visa for me and nobody from British Aerospace was there to welcome me to Madagascar.

Someone else had come to meet me however. Lieutenant Raymond Andrianavano, although only a Lieutenant at the time, was highly thought of in the Madagascan Parachute Regiment, because he spoke several languages, including some English for sure, and Russian and French I believe. He and several of his soldier buddies, having heard that a parachute instructor was coming out from England took it upon themselves to come and welcome me. Thank goodness. Not seeing my contact and being unsure what I'd do at passport control with no visa, I allowed all the other hurrying passengers to push past me until I was at the back of the queue trying to work out how I'd explain that I was legitimate, even wanted there to 'border guards' who were unlikely to speak English. I remember clearly another passenger dropping his bottle of duty free scotch which exploded on the airport floor, I nearly jumped out of my skin.

Seconds later, this soldier, Raymond Andrianavano, appears out of nowhere and says to me "parachutist militaire?" "Er yes, oui". Then before I could explain anything to him he dragged me right to the front of the queue. He grabbed my passport and slapped it down in front of the guard doing the checking. I could see three of Raymond's buddies on the other side watching. They, like Raymond, and the guards doing passport control all wore pistols on their belts. Not something you're used to seeing in England, maybe these days with heightened security, but certainly not then. The guard, policeman, whatever you'd call him opened my passport, no visa. He said something I didn't understand. Raymond's response was "militaire", in other words he's with us and he's coming in. I didn't like the look or feeling of this, the hairs stood up on the back of my neck..

The other lines stopped moving, the other guards took an interest, Raymond's friends took an interest. A heated argument developed and not understanding a word of it I couldn't tell which way it was going. I felt tight like a coiled spring, as if I had a heightened sense of awareness, when really I was bemused by events and in effect a passenger, I had no influence over the outcome. Next, the guard took Raymond and me downstairs, clearly to consult his boss. I could swear I saw cells down there out of the corner of my eye. The senior officer was playing cards with a couple of colleagues. We disturbed them, everyone, except me, spoke at once. After what seemed an eternity, but can only have been a few minutes, a red stamp was placed in my passport and I was ushered out. This time to the right side of the barrier, so to speak, where we were greeted by Raymond's buddies and I was reunited with my luggage and parachute. So that was all right then. I still imagined that British Aerospace would not have let me down like that, and had a final scout round for the elusive Mr Schofield. No, not there. Raymond and his mates had a black military Citroen Traction Avant waiting outside. Fabulous old car. They asked where I wanted to go. Well I'm booked in at the Hilton I told them and that's where we went.

I'd been abroad before, but nowhere like this. We drove through a shanty town of corrugated iron shacks, to the relative splendour of the Hilton, with a nice garden, uniformed waiters and so on. I'd had a considerable shot of adrenalin at the airport, but, by the time I got to the Hilton, my fatigue after all that travelling, no sleep, crying babies and the last couple of hours adventure was overwhelming. Raymond and his friends had been quizzing me about my skydiving career, my equipment and all sorts of things to do with the sport and the 748. They wanted to carry on the conversation in the bar, but I explained how long I'd been without sleep, arranged to meet them later and went to my room. The things I needed most were a bath and a sleep. I was amazed when I ran the bath and the water was a dirty brown colour, it looked like it had come straight out of the river. I'd never been to a place like this before! At least the water was hot and then there was the bed, never did fresh sheets feel so good.

When I did finally meet Mr Schofield, it was in the bar at the Hilton, sometime later. No one had told him to meet me he told me, "but you're here now so nothing to worry about eh". I supposed not.

I spent a couple of days at the barracks meeting the guys who would jump and going through with them what was required of them. I had to use Raymond as an interpreter but there were no difficulties. I took a taxi to the barracks as a rule, and I got quite a bit of time to do as I pleased and look around Antananarive, go to the market and so on. I don't know if it still goes on but when I checked into the Hilton a beautiful young girl seemed to take an interest in me. She was gorgeous, but goodness only knows how young. Whenever I went out she came with me. When I got a taxi she simply got in and told me what the fare should be. When I went to the market she bartered for me. When I was in the barracks, she waited outside for me, all day if needs be.

I became friendly with a sales engineer from British Aerospace and we spent our spare time sightseeing together. Another girl had attached herself to him. It seemed to be a regular feature, there were always girls hanging around and I guess they took it in turns, as new guests checked in then that guest was theirs for the duration, in their eyes anyway. How many guests took full advantage I have no idea. I can only say that I never took mine to my room and I'm pretty sure my colleague didn't take his upstairs either, but they weren't disheartened. Anytime of the day or night, if one of us went out, our girl would be there.

I only got to do the one jump in Madagascar sadly. I would have loved to jump one of their DC3s, but there were not flights in and out of the country every day and their next scheduled jump was not until after I was scheduled to leave. Otherwise they'd certainly have taken me. The one jump was obviously from the 748. Most of the jumpers would be on a static line doing the standard military mass drop kind of exit. Raymond wanted to do freefall with me. It was a bit like letting the cat out of the bag regarding the tail plane, but I had to explain to him that he'd have to do a military style exit and then adopt a freefall position. I didn't even want to risk a dive exit which would probably have been fine, but the consequences, if not, don't bear thinking about. Stick with tried and tested.

I got the mass drop on top of the mountain with none of them in the trees and then Raymond and I went to altitude and did our freefall thing. I had an early square parachute and I remember people appearing as if by magic out of the trees to watch. Everything went perfectly. The only way back to the barracks was in big old Bedford four wheel drive army trucks through the forest. This took a couple of hours, but they were passed happily chatting, with Raymond interpreting. Then back at the barracks the guys insisted I stay for a meal and of course they got me well drunk. I felt I was building good relationships and doing a good job for British Aerospace!

In the foreground is a World War Two Harvard trainer, but behind is the Hawker Siddeley 748 military transport we helped to demonstrate and sell around the world. Behind that is a De Havilland Dove chase aircraft used to take pictures, not the same Dove we later purchased however.

A day or so later, at breakfast, one of the British Aerospace chaps had his passport on the table at breakfast. Normally they were in the hotel safe. Special arrangements had been made for him to go home quickly as his wife or another close relative was seriously ill. I had a look through his passport to see where he'd been. One page had a very impressive looking visa. Sort of embossed in I think it was, and possibly even had some gold as well as the red ink. I can't remember exactly, but it was quite striking. Instinctively I said "ooh, where's that?" "Don't be silly" he said "that's Madagascar, that's where we are now". Well that's not what they put in my passport I thought. I went to the hotel safe.

I had a grubby little red stamp in mine and even I understood the implication of 'vingt quatre heures'. The airport, border guard had given me a twenty four hour pass to get my visa sorted and of course, in the rush of euphoria at getting into the country visa-less and in the course of looking for my contact and being hustled outside by Raymond I hadn't realised. By now I'd been in the country a week to ten days and I figured getting out again just might be a little interesting, depending on their attitude.

I telephoned my new friend Raymond at the barracks and asked if he appreciated that I only had a twenty four hour pass, which was well overdue? He came over to the Hilton and took me to see a number of high ranking officials or politicians, to try and get a visa retrospectively. I know we saw three or four different officials, I don't know their titles and of course I didn't understand a word of any of the conversations just to add to my discomfiture. I remember very well French colonial buildings, very grand with leather panelled doors, now in a state of disrepair, and avenues with tall grass growing up between the paving stones. But what really was going on in my head was that here I was in the country illegally and what Raymond and I had done was to tell everyone who probably shouldn't know! I put this to Raymond and he agreed that there was a small risk of arrest! "Don't worry though, I'll take you to see my General, he'll sort things out for you".

I don't know how easy it is for the average Lieutenant in any army to walk in and see his General, but clearly Raymond was on good terms. The General asked me a few questions about the 748 and skydiving and my present predicament through Raymond. It was all very friendly if somewhat formal. At the end he said he'd take care of things and clearly the interview was at an end, so I just had to trust that he would take care of things, although what he'd do exactly I had no idea.

I was due to leave in about forty eight hours. Life went on as before, and in fact we had a fabulous sightseeing trip around the island on the 748, but I was still worried about the twenty four hour pass in my passport. The rest of the 748 sales team were going on to Tanzania, on the 748, after I was due to leave on my Air Madagascar scheduled flight to Paris. I ordered a taxi to take me to the airport. The sales engineer I'd become friendly with decided to come with me. He, and the two girls of course, got into the taxi with me. My young lady, seeing my bags realised I was leaving, burst into tears and indicated she wanted to come with me. Ho hum. What can you do, can't even converse properly. At the airport we sat in a lounge, after I'd checked my main luggage in. I was in no hurry to go through departures. Then three of the big four wheel drive trucks we'd used to get back through the forest from the drop zone appeared, and Raymond and all my guys got out. They were of course armed. No one was going to argue with that lot. I heaved a sigh of relief, felt elated even, and greeted my buddies. They escorted me out to the aeroplane, I was first on board and nobody looked at my passport or even spoke to me, what the aircrew made of it I have no idea. Soldiers were still scattered around the apron and on a balcony when the aircraft taxied off. There was what could almost be described as a party atmosphere, quite bizarre.

It was the biggest adventure of my life. At such a young age it was wild. I've not told too many people about it since for fear it sounds too far fetched, but there it is. It happened and living the life I was at the time it seemed fitting, somehow, that such a thing would happen to me.

CHAPTER 6

Test Jumper

THE OTHER COMPANY we did work for was RFD GQ Defence Equipment, one of only two British mass parachute manufacturers at that time. Before they could submit a parachute to the military, it had either to have a large number of dummy drops behind it, possibly running into thousands, or a much smaller number of live drops with an experienced parachutist who could report findings. The military don't like to risk their people too much in peace time, they cost a lot to train and if civilians will do the job at £20 a jump I guess they don't have to!

There were two main projects for GQ as we called them, that being the parachute part of the company. RFD make life rafts and survival equipment, so you can see why they got together. One project was jumping a new conical canopy. Nothing groundbreaking, but it was very good for what it was, as I recall. The other project, was with hindsight slightly comical, rather than conical.

There are two ways of measuring the diameter of a round parachute. The Americans' measured them spread out flat on the ground, so their I24 reserve was 24 feet in diameter when laid out. It's flying diameter when pulled into shape is rather less and it's actually a very small parachute. GQ thought it more meaningful to describe a parachute by its flying diameter, laid out on the ground it would be much larger. Therefore, their 22 foot steerable is actually a huge canopy, enormous, much, much bigger than the American I24. The MOD had purchased a great many for parachute regiment mass drops. This big canopy would take the weight of a soldier and his weapon, ammunition, pack, food etc.

The other sort of jumping the army indulged in was HALO, High Altitude, Low Opening. This is the sort of thing practiced by the Special Air Service, all of whose soldiers are also skydivers. It's a way of delivering small teams behind enemy lines, generally for sabotage, or information gathering, or both. There are plenty of books about the SAS so it's no secret that they have a lot of specialisations and in one team you'll find a medic and a radio operator, an explosives expert and so on. Although they duplicate many of the skills, in case of losses, they can't duplicate loads of equipment, not on a mission delivered by parachute. Equipment means weight. Therefore, if the radio operator lost his Bergen (rucksack) the mission would be out of communication, if the explosives expert were to lose his Bergen, blowing things up could be a problem.

An SAS jumper in the 70's looked like some sort of Action Man toy, with his two parachutes, his Bergen, his oxygen bottle and mask for high altitude, his personal weapon etc. It's a wonder they could walk.

Nowadays parachutes pack up much smaller and they're lighter, even quite big canopies. In those days an SAS man had something called a Tactical Assault Parachute TAP as his main parachute. This was what's known as a high performance round. Modern square parachutes are really flying devices, more akin to gliders, or hang gliders than traditional parachutes, which were effectively controlled descent devices. When a round parachute is in operation there's an area of high pressure near the apex, or middle top if you prefer. There's a vent hole there on a low performance round, to allow excess pressure to escape, otherwise it would have to get out under the hem of the parachute. Inevitably it would get out from one side then the other, setting up an oscillation or swinging action. The human being on the bottom would inevitably swing into the ground very hard, which isn't the idea.

The next development was to put some slits in the back of the parachute, pressure escaping there would give the canopy a little forward drive and by manipulating those holes with control lines you could make the parachute steer. Due to the fact that these holes were in a low pressure area, the parachute had a mere 5mph of drive and turned slowly, ideal for students, but not for great accuracy. The final development in round parachutes, before the squares came along, was the high performance round, of which the TAP is one example It's a big one, to carry the weight of a soldier and all his equipment.

In a high performance round, the apex is pulled down so the high pressure area is made bigger, like a doughnut sort of shape. The extended high pressure area has a series of slits cut into it, which direct air backwards, or forwards if you wish, control lines can reverse the direction. A high performance round has greater forward speed, because the drive comes from the high pressure area. It turns faster for the same reason and for another, with a high performance round you can make one side of the canopy drive forwards at the same time as making the other side drive backwards for a really sharp turn. It's also possible, on most, to stall the canopy, letting a lot of pressure out of that high pressure doughnut, so you sink like a stone, potentially useful if you're being blown off course or overshooting, just don't land it like that! High performance rounds probably made 12 to 15mph at best, some claimed more I believe. All this complication, inverted apexes, lots of slits and holes, control lines branching off in all directions, it made them more prone to go wrong frankly. Part of the canopy could go through a hole or slit and try to inflate on the wrong side for example, and then it would lock there.

At the time high performance rounds were more or less state of the art, square parachutes were very much in their infancy and not yet readily available on the market. Only category eight jumpers and above were allowed to use high performance rounds in the sport, they gave greater accuracy and were more fun too. When a high performance round parachute malfunctioned it could be quite violent, because of the extended high pressure area, it could swing you around like crazy, therefore you had to get rid of it, cut it away, for which there were a number of release systems available, and then you could deploy your last line of defence, the reserve parachute. Reserve parachutes were, in my day, straightforward, low performance rounds that could be relied upon (generally) to save your life.

The SAS soldier was subject to most of the same considerations as the sport jumper, so his reserve was a reliable, low performance round. The I24 in fact. Which you may recall is a very small canopy. So, if the HALO jumper experienced a malfunction on his high performance Tactical Assault Parachute, he would have to perform a cut away and deploy this itsy, bitsy, teeny winy half bikini. Which couldn't support his weight and that of his kit. So in order to save his life, the kit would have to go, and then maybe the mission would have to be aborted, certainly it would be compromised. Given that high performance rounds did malfunction from time to time, this was not a happy state of affairs. So a new reserve for the SAS was called for.

As I'm sure you know, when tax payers' money is spent there are all sorts of regulations, tendering and goodness knows what, which in my opinion makes things more expensive nine times out of ten, but there we are. In this instance someone, somewhere put two and two together, to make six. Well we've got loads of these 22 foot steerable canopies (huge remember). Why not make a few of them into reserves for the SAS. GQ knocked up a reserve container. The parachute in its normal role was deployed from a bag on a static line, so the bag went in too, but this time with an enormous pilot chute to lift the weight. So you had an enormous canopy, made of bulky fabric since it was never designed to be small or light. This was enclosed in an inner container, plus all its lines, then an outer container and pilot chute. The whole thing was bigger than any main parachute I've ever seen. It was designed to be worn on the front, because the TAP was on the back and that's not small. An SAS guy would also have to have worn a Bergen, oxygen and a weapon, they'd have loved it!!!! The container was so huge, GQ put a curved housing for the ripcord so the handle could be brought into view.

Since I was going to be first, (in fact the only person ever to jump it as it turned out) I experimented with the contraption on our packing table a few times, pulling the ripcord and pulling the canopy out by hand to make sure everything worked. It all operated as it should, so I prepared to jump it. Things called rocket jets, which were release devices were fitted, so I could get rid of it if necessary and I wore one of our nice reliable, low performance round student canopies on my back as a reserve. Not perfect, since this had the pin and cone closure I talked about earlier, but I was used to them and packed it myself, it was an acceptable, calculated risk. Some of my test jumps were filmed for the Royal Aircraft Establishment at Farnborough and I had to go along later and talk about them when the films were shown.

There were a number of difficulties. To deploy a front mounted reserve it's obviously nicest, not to mention safest, to be falling back to earth. Usually all too easy to do by accident. Not so easy when most of the weight you're carrying is just in front of your hips! I had operated the ripcord, several times on the packing table and, it would appear by some fluke, possibly the angle the ripcord pins happened to be inserted, or the angle of pull being different when not wearing it, but they'd come out ok. On my first jump with the behemoth, I pulled the ripcord, having rolled on my back ok, but it wouldn't come out. The pins simply wouldn't go through the curved housing at whatever angle they were sitting or I was pulling. Adrenalin is a wonderful thing, I pulled so hard the whole housing came away and the parachute opened. So it worked anyway. Although I could never ever see it being accepted in the role for which it was intended. GQ tried to kid me they'd designed the housing to come away if necessary, pull the other one chaps.

I had to do ten jumps on this contraption, earning twenty pounds a throw. It would enable me to buy a stereo music centre, as they were called in those days. My first, real, material possession since becoming a parachute instructor. However, the tests weren't over yet. Some, know it all Colonel, appeared, who was a skydiver. He insisted that the new reserve should be tested by someone wearing a tactical assault parachute on their back, just like his guys would be using. Sounds fine in principle but it makes no difference to testing the reserve whatever, none, zero, zilch. What it would mean is that I'd have a complicated, malfunction prone, high performance round as my only last defence against death. This idiot wouldn't take no for an answer, so I agreed to a compromise. If the first nine jumps went ok I'd do the last one with a TAP on my back. I was beginning to feel I could trust the 22 foot steerable to open and I'd only cut it away if the inner bag stayed shut and I had nothing, otherwise I figured it was so big, it would land me in one piece even with a partial malfunction, it had a net skirt, so a partial malfunction was very unlikely anyway, but the technical reasons for that don't need explaining here. The next thing our Colonel friend wanted, was to follow me out of the aeroplane and watch first hand.

I told him he could follow me out on two conditions. Bear in mind this is a civilian business, civilian centre, he had no authority whatsoever on our drop zone. I stipulated a time gap between me leaving the aircraft and him leaving, to create some separation. I also stipulated the length of his delay so that he would open above me, this would give separation on two planes, horizontal and vertical. The reason being that skydivers have been killed or suffered disfigurement, when a freefaller has collided with an open canopy, also in the days before square parachutes which can be flown in a stack, entanglement was considered one of the main dangers.

We took off for this final test jump I did my delay, deployed the 22 foot steerable and looked around the moment it opened, an instinctive thing borne of early training and habit. Whoosh, crack, bang there was the colonel just yards away on my level and facing, therefore travelling, towards me. We avoided one another, but I gave him a balling out on the ground that I hope will embarrass him forever and made it clear he was no longer welcome. He was never seen at Thruxton again.

CHAPTER 7

Display Jumper

Life at the parachute club wasn't all big contracts, test jumps and trips abroad. There was a demonstration team though, and that was a lot of fun. One of the instructors, a wonderful guy called Ken Townsend, who really dedicated his life to sport jumping, after following in his father's footsteps and joining the parachute regiment, had a contact with the firm Midas, who manufacture car exhausts, and he managed to get sponsorship from them. The Cessna 180 was painted gold, well bright yellow anyway, with the Midas logo in black down the side. Several of us had black and gold jumpsuits supplied and some square yellow canopies were purchased. There were a lot of demo jumps, but three stick in my mind particularly. One was a water jump into the river Trent.

Parachutists can be injured in all sorts of ways, most injuries are not caused by parachutes failing to open but by bad landings, or landings in the wrong place. Land on a road and you're an unexpected hazard that's quite likely to be run over, hit power lines and you may be electrocuted, water and you may be drowned and so it goes on. Water is considered to be one of the major hazards, not least because of all the equipment a parachutist wears, which can drag you down. Intentional jumps into water are very carefully planned, with safety boats, lifejackets and so on. It's a requirement to cut away as your feet hit the water, remember a cut away is not with a knife, but a quick release system. It can be very difficult to judge your height over water and some jumpers have succumbed to the temptation to cut away before their feet hit the water, only to find they were further up than they thought. It is a requirement for an advanced instructor's qualification to have made a successful water jump and mine went perfectly I'm glad to say.

The next memorable demo was for the opening of a nightclub called Neros at Southsea near Portsmouth. It's usual on a demo to wear a smoke canister on your foot, sometimes on both feet, in order to leave a trail in freefall, or under the canopy, or both. Sometimes a jumper will stick his foot out of the door of the aircraft and activate a smoke canister on the approach to exit. These various uses of trailing smoke, make it easier for an audience to see you, create an impression of speed and add to the show a bit. The smoke canisters get pretty hot and since parachutes are largely made of nylon, which melts, and since they cost a lot of money, one of the main objectives on landing, especially if there's a breeze which might blow your collapsed canopy about, is to keep the parachute well away from the hot canister.

For the Neros demo, the nightclub had arranged for a collection of beautiful promo girls to be positioned around the arena in white and gold romanesque dresses with castellated skirts, of a very short and flimsy nature. On landing I went down on one knee for a second and tried to bundle up my canopy and keep it away from the foot with the hot canister on it. A slightly eccentric, and I have to say slightly unwashed and odoriferous old lady, rushed out from the crowd. She grabbed my knee and started rubbing it, saying "it'll be alright dear" next thing she was feeling a bit higher up. My colleagues on the ground party were in fits of laughter and in no hurry to help me. Now I had to avoid burning her as well as my parachute and still persuade her to leave me alone. All I could think about was the injustice of being surrounded by all these beautiful, scantily clad girls and getting groped by a strange old woman.

The third most memorable demo was for some celebration, anniversary or something of the sort at GQ, the parachute manufacturer we did test jumps for. I doubt very much, having done it, if it was a legal demo. I did not organise it, and didn't see how tight the drop zone (landing area) was until I got there. Obviously Bob was in charge and to be fair to him it would have been hard to say no. Legally there are requirements about the size of the drop zone, distance to hazards and considerations like that. The GQ factory was in a valley, with power cables and a road nearby. There was even a water hazard nearby too, I think, possibly a canal, I can't remember now. I can remember the very small arena and the barbed wire fences and the barbed wire around the roof and so on.

Off on a demo jump, note the smoke canister attached to the wheel strut, to help on-lookers at ground level catch sight of the aircraft when its at altitude and just before the jumpers exit.

Drop zones can be illegal technically, but still not be too difficult, especially under a square parachute. This one was difficult, but we'd all be on squares wouldn't we. Well no, GQ didn't make a square parachute yet and at least one of us should do the demo on one of their canopies shouldn't we, otherwise it might look as if we thought they weren't any good. GQ did make a high performance round, their version of the American 'Paracommander' or the French 'Papillion' it was called a 'Pathfinder', very apt. We drew lots, so popular was the 'Pathfinder' option, even Bob, with thousands of jumps and by far the most experience didn't want to be the one with the round for this demo! I drew the short straw, literally. Of course it was windy, of course I got into the arena, but only after skimming the roof and lifting my feet to avoid the barbed wire and lifting them again to just miss the heads of the people in the front row. It was the scariest demo I've ever done.

My good friend Ken did one demo where there were two events near to one another, he jumped into the wrong arena, but they were quite happy to have a free display, what the real customer up the road thought I have no idea! On another occasion Bob Acraman was a guest at some event at the Army Air Corps at Middle Wallop. Sometimes we flew quite close to Middle Wallop, from the club, whilst climbing to altitude, especially if air traffic control at Boscombe Down wanted us out of the way. Someone commented on the aircraft, Bob looked up and said "Oh yes that's mine". He wasn't so chuffed when Ken threw a wind drift indicator out, right overhead and was even more horrified when someone climbed out, no one jumped though, it was just a wind up, life at the parachute club was like that, day in day out.

CHAPTER 8

Everyday Life As a Parachute Instructor

A NORMAL WEEK at the parachute club meant Monday closed, training on Tuesday, Thursday and Saturday. The Tuesday course was scheduled to jump on Wednesday, Thursday's on Friday and Saturday's on Sunday obviously, but jumping would take place on all the six days we were open, for any club member or visitor, weather permitting. Usually the classroom training only required one instructor and sometimes we'd swap at lunchtime, sometimes one instructor would do the whole thing. If it was a very large course then we might split them into two groups for the physical things like parachute landing falls, emergency procedures and equipment familiarisation. Always though there would be enough staff to run a programme of jumping out on the airfield, whilst training was going on back at the clubhouse.

In the summer we could work very long hours and the weather was our master. A run of bad weather could mean we'd have hundreds of first timers to jump when it got good, and on a good day we'd run from dawn to dusk, with two aircraft when we had them. Club members would pack their own parachutes, but students would leave them for the staff to pack, until they'd learned that skill too. In the middle of the summer we could parachute until gone 10pm, not be fully packed away until 11pm, then we'd want to eat and we could be up at 6am to get all the unpacked rigs re packed by 8:30am, to start jumping at 9am. The place had a real buzz to it at those times though, and we were young. It was a special place and a special time. The summer of 1976 seemed to last forever and it was wonderful.

The team that represented Britain at the World Championships, at that time, was called Symbiosis. They were regularly on our drop zone, living in Bedford and Ford vans with mattresses in the back. I can't help thinking about the movie Point Break when I think about them, they were the real thing and living the life, although not robbing banks I think! Charismatic guys though, and great jumpers, who lived for the sport. We also had regular visits from members of the Red Devils, the Parachute Regiment display team, affectionately known as The Freds and from the Royal Greenjackets Display Team.

Being young, and fit and adventurous, we had some wild parties at that place. One of the other instructors was my very dear friend John Field. He's ever so slightly older than me but our birthdays are just two days apart, so each year we had a joint birthday party. One of those years was also my twenty first. I knew that I'd be debagged, that is stripped and probably smeared with food and goodness knows what. Particularly, I expected some good natured abuse from a couple of the Freds, and/or Greenjackets. I replaced my belt with a padlock and chain, but someone, somehow had bolt cutters.

My upbringing at home had been very conventional, even conservative. Mum was a violin playing civil servant, dad was a school physics teacher and we all went to church. I wasn't a virgin when I went to live at the parachute club, I lost that a year or two before in a tent on the beach at Durness, on the north coast of Scotland, but I wasn't very experienced either. It was a revelation to me that people would come down to the parachute club for the weekend, sleep on the training room floor, with possibly forty other people in the room, and some of them would be having sex. Privacy was doing it under the football game table! When I joined the staff, I had my own room and sometimes there were female pupils who thought that, 'having' the instructor was all part of the fun. That too was a revelation. During my years as a parachute instructor I had three serious girlfriends and a number of flings, a couple of which I would have liked to be serious!

When I was first on the staff there were four girls from the village who used to hang out at the club, Rosie, Cindy, Angie and Sylvie. All of them were schoolgirls living in the village.

Most of their school friends lived in Andover, but the timetable of rural bus services mitigated against going into town of an evening. And anyway, the parachute club was an exciting place to hang out, lots of people, lots going on, and something they had, which I suppose their school friends back in town didn't. They spent as much time as they could with the Symbiosis guys, they were the British Champions and were regarded by lesser mortals and camp followers as 'sky gods.' Next in prestige came the instructors I would say, although when I started there I was just an apprentice instructor in effect. One of these girls from the village would become my first fiancée but when I first started working there she was too young to fool around with.

On Mondays I went into Andover to do my laundry at the laundrette. One week, the only other customer was a very attractive thirty two year old blonde. I was nineteen. She made some comment to me about laundry chores and I, very obviously and clumsily, said something about how living on my own had really brought it home to me, and before you knew it we were an item. She was divorced with a young son and lived in a ground floor flat in town. I still kept my room at the parachute club, but for a long time, I dated this wonderful woman, who taught me so much.

However, I couldn't see me spending my life with someone older and ultimately we split up. In addition, to be honest, I found I was falling in love with one of the four girls from the village. Cindy was coming up to her sixteenth birthday by now, and her main interest, the guys from Symbiosis, well, they were off to Australia for the World Championships. Not only that, but they'd decided to go there for six months, enjoy the weather, train and so on. For her, six months of boredom loomed large, waiting for them to return. I figured she'd go out with me, just to pass the time, as the next best thing. I also figured, that although this wasn't ideal I had six months in which to make her fall in love with me.

Our first date was on her sixteenth birthday and my plan

worked. One of my good friends at the club who was a bit of a father figure to Cindy, in fact Tony Rolfe who'd kitted me up for my first two jumps and who'd seen me flitting from girl to girl earlier, threatened to kill me! Until he saw how serious I was. Those two years with Cindy were amazing, my first true love I suppose, although I'd felt pretty strongly about Glynis in my school days, that never went very far, this would. Cindy already spent all her free time at the club and we were inseparable. Unfortunately her family weren't too keen on her settling down with me, or possibly they just didn't want her to settle down too young, whatever the reason they conspired to get rid of me.

Getting involved with Cindy also got me involved in the life of the village. I already knew a few people, notably the staff at the pubs and the post office. There was also a character called John Gill. He owned a very successful transport café based next to a roundabout on the outskirts of Andover. He sold part of the car park off and was pretty wealthy from that, but the transport café was very popular and exceptional value. So he was doing a booming trade there as well. The parachute club staff and regulars frequented the place a lot and despite the exceptional value we always pulled his leg about being tight. He took it in very good heart, the way it was meant and one day we arrived en masse to find him pegging out used tea bags on the washing line to dry. Hilarious.

John lived in the village and drove a Ferrari. One day a TV commercial was shot in the village with Sacha Distel. There was a flash car in the script and it failed to turn up, so John rented them his Ferrari for the day, doubtless for a small fortune. Well, they say money goes to money.

The village had an amateur dramatic group run by a lovely man named Derek Baker. Cindy wanted to join and an audition was called for. She wanted me to go along for moral support, and since we did everything together anyway, I went. On the night I was persuaded to audition too. I don't remember there being a noticeable shortage of guys or a surfeit of ladies but it caused a slight problem when I got a part, and Cindy didn't. Fortunately Cindy did get a part later and we were both involved in numerous productions.

Just as hours at the parachute club could be very long in summer, they could be quite short in winter, drawing dark early and less suitable weather. Jumping in winter can be stunningly beautiful, but it never goes on late. Therefore, I was involved in the village pantomime and usually one, sometimes two plays per year. I loved the experience. One of the early plays, a thriller in three acts, saw me cast as a policeman with just a few lines. Three days before the production, the lead actor was taken into hospital and Derek was talking about cancellation notices at the rehearsal that evening. I told him that if he wanted to take my little role, I could learn the lead in the three days remaining. I did too, an act per day and at the dress rehearsal I was word perfect.

There were to be three or four actual performances. On one of them I messed up a bit, overconfident, after learning all those lines so quickly. I skipped a page completely. Thankfully my colleagues just picked up from where I was and if the audience were confused they didn't show it. I think it was quite a confusing plot anyway! One of the members of the troupe wrote the pantomimes himself and they were a scream. We also did a bedroom farce one year where I played a randy plumber, very seventies, very British. No one was nude on stage, but there were a lot of scantily clad ladies and a lot of kissing. Quite daring for sleepy little village Thruxton I thought.

I cherish my photographs from all those productions, very happy memories. Our only production outside the village was in a drama festival at Salisbury Playhouse. I don't recall how many drama groups were involved, but we all had to do a one act play. Ours was a supernatural story, about a mother with two obnoxious children who ran her ragged. The neighbour had supernatural powers and she and the mother exchanged bodies so the neighbour could sort out the children. Cindy and I played the obnoxious teenagers, not challenging! The two ladies who played the adults were required to act their socks off, swapping persona half way through, and then back again at the end, they were, frankly, brilliant. We won a large silver plate that resided in one of the village pubs for a year. Derek was producer and director.

I've talked about special jumps at the parachute club, testing, demos and so on, but some of the everyday jumps, out of the hundreds, stick in the memory too. I remember one of my early relative work lessons with Paul Young. Most of my training was undertaken by Paul, he taught me to skydive and he taught me to teach.

Relative work is where two or more skydivers try to build a formation, link up and possibly change the formation. In competition you are judged on how many different patterns you can make in a set time. Taking extra time is punishable by death, so it's rarely done! Teams are generally in groups of four or eight. Before you can start jumping in a team you need to be able to fly, to the point where you can link up with one other person. Back then, I don't know if the terminology still applies, the first two in a formation were known as the pin and base. Therefore, the first skill you have to learn is to pin a base. Falling base is relatively easy if you'll pardon the pun, the base just has to fall stable and on heading, as a target for the pin. However close two people are when they leave an aircraft there's almost always a degree of separation on exit. The pin has to dive down to join the base and link up without going underneath. It is technically possible to move across and upwards relative to someone else but it's not so easy. The larger a formation becomes the slower it falls, so for the individual who goes below it can be game over.

I remember the first time I pinned Paul and the sense of achievement I felt, but I also remember a jump soon after that one, the image of which is imprinted on my mind, forever I hope. If you do enough skydives you will see some beautiful and unique things in the sky. Aside from those clear blue days without a single cloud, the sky is uniquely different every time you visit it. Even on a clear blue day the sight you see of the land varies with the seasons of the year. On this occasion there was a huge cumulonimbus in the sky, very tall and very white. It is not permissible to jump through clouds. There are several reasons. The most obvious is that you can't see what's in it. An aircraft for example, or if you are jumping in a group a skydiver who's already opened his canopy. In addition, you cannot be observed from the ground, nor can you see where you are going. Jumping through clouds is officially a no-no then.

Jumping through gaps in the cloud is quite permissible, given certain conditions, otherwise no jumping would ever get done! In Britain anyway. On this occasion Paul and I jumped beside this towering cloud, all white billows. Normally one doesn't really get an impression of speed in freefall, the ground looks much the same at 9,000 feet as it does at 10,000 feet. However, whizzing past this cloud with its particular texture created an impression of speed for me. Paul will have had an entirely different view, he was looking at me, with his feet facing the cloud, all I could see was him and this big white fluffy thing whizzing past. It was a stark black and white image, because everything Paul wore was black, excepting his white helmet, his jumpsuit, kit, boots, gloves, all black, that was his style.

Another of those jumps that has left a lasting photographic image on my mind was with a tracking student. Tracking is a way of making distance across the ground in freefall. It involves a position in which the arms are by the side, legs pushed out and close together and body slightly de-arched, so that you trap air and propel it out behind you, jet like. The body position is not unlike that a ski jumper uses. It's not an inherently stable position, it requires a degree of balance and skill. Done well, high speeds can be achieved across the ground, 80mph is generally reckoned achievable, of course you are falling still faster. Tracking is a very useful skill. When building a large free fall formation, the last person out can have a long way to travel to reach the formation. At the end it is necessary to split up and get away from each other in a few short seconds, so that you can open your canopy without risk of a collision. This is basically the major purpose in being able to track well. However, it's also a skill used by base jumpers to get away from cliff faces and in freefall, if someone mistakenly puts you out in the wrong place, you can possibly correct the error. A vital skill then. It's also a requirement within the BPA parachutist category system.

The parachute club staff had a tough life! Far right is Paul Young, the man who really taught me to skydive, next along is my best friend from those days, John Field. The hairy one with the moustache is me.

On this occasion it was the end of a summers' day and the student, John Lewis needed to prove he could track to move up a category. He would be disappointed if we couldn't do it, but a thin layer of cloud was moving across the drop zone towards the opening point. It's important in my opinion, not only to obey the rules, but to be seen to be strict so people know where they stand and won't try to badger you. The setting sun caused this thin layer of cloud to glow red, it was a stunning sight, the cloud being at about three thousand feet. From above we could see down through the cloud, so there was no danger of getting out in the wrong place, or of not seeing an aircraft or such like. My only worry was that observers on the ground might not be able to see us and we could be accused of bending the rules. On the basis that we weren't bending the rules, we would clearly jump.

I pointed out to John that the opening point was just beyond the ragged edge of the cloud anyway and told him that I would put us out at a point from which we should be able to track to the correct opening point. We left the aircraft over this magical, translucent red carpet and tracked parallel to one another for all we were worth. We clipped the edge of the cloud curtain and then it was time to open and glide down to earth, bathed in the glow of the setting sun, the last magical moments of a beautiful day. John got his qualification. I felt the joy of life as strongly then as I ever have, the sheer wonder of life, nature, comradeship, beauty, seeing someone else reach a milestone.

There used to be a ground breaking airline called Laker Airways or Laker Skytrain. Sir Freddie Laker was the pioneer of cheap air travel for all and three of his pilots used to jump with us. I don't think it reflected any lack of confidence in his aircraft! One of these was a great guy named Sid Hughes. I'm told that Sid was Sir Freddies most senior captain, I'm also told that earlier in his career he'd been involved with the development of the ejector seat for military aircraft. What I know for certain is that Sid was a lovely fellow who would often turn up mid week, when there were fewer crowds, in his lovely little Alfa Romeo.

On one occasion he turned up mid week, mid winter, wanting to practice some relative work with Paul and myself. It was one of those cold, clear days without a breath of wind, a day which was eminently jumpable but oh so cold. It was freezing at ground level and the temperature would drop dramatically with altitude. Strangely, the freefall bit isn't the problem, that's over in sixty seconds or less, but the climb to altitude in a slow moving Cessna with no door can be excruciating, even with heaven knows how many layers of thermals and jumpers under the jumpsuit. Faces and hands suffer particularly. Sid had forgotten his gloves. No matter, someone had left a beautiful pair of super warm gloves behind in the aircraft, strange, but they were there and we'd stuffed them into the pocket behind the pilot's seat until someone should claim them. We told Sid to use them. They were clearly expensive and he was reluctant. We told him he had to or he'd lose his fingers! Finally he agreed to wear them in the aircraft but said he'd stuff them back in the pocket when we got out as the last bit doesn't take long. I thought he was barmy, but it was up to him.

The last thing you want on a jump like that is an air traffic control delay, but that's what we got, so we went all the way to the maximum allowable limit without oxygen 12,000 feet, in fact as there was no one else around, we went a little bit higher. We were in the 180 and I was to go base, which put me closest to the open door, it also meant I got to do the spotting, I'll explain spotting in a minute. When we got to the exit point at ahem 12,000 feet, I had to climb out and hang on to the wing strut with one foot on the step, then Paul would get into a diving position as far out as he could get and Sid would also be in a diving position, half out the door. The idea being that you leave together, after a synchronised rocking, ready set go, to minimise the separation. As Sid was getting into position he was also trying to stuff the gloves back into the pilots seat pocket. Of course there's a gale whistling around inside the cockpit and whilst hanging on to the strut I watched a single glove fly past and hurtle back in the slipstream, away over the tailplane. So much for not using someone else's property then!

In those days I had a moustache. I swear I could have broken it off, our breath froze on our faces. Even with silk lined gloves, the pain when your numb fingers begin to come back to life is indescribable. I don't use the word agony lightly and it's hard to know what to do with yourself or where to put your hands. It was a great jump though.

I never met her, but Sid was married to a Laker Airways Air Hostess as they were known then, flight attendant if you prefer. Sir Freddie is well known for his pioneering work in aviation, but I think he had other qualities not so well publicised. Tragically Sid developed a cancer. I was told, by one of Sid's colleagues, and have every reason to believe it, that Sir Freddie sent him off to a ludicrously expensive private clinic in the USA to be treated with the latest, at the time, drugs. One of which they had high hopes for. I think it may have been called Interferon. Whatever the drug was it was expensive and I understand that lots of regular small dosages were called for. The point is it wasn't cheap, and Sir Freddie sent Sid to the clinic for as long as it took, he kept him on full pay, he sent Sid's wife to keep him company and kept her on full pay too. This is how it was told to me by one of Sir Freddie's other pilots, sadly Sid passed away, but I've felt a fondness for Sir Freddie, who I never met, ever since.

On the subject of the other Laker pilots who visited us, one, who shall remain nameless, was given the honour of being amongst the first to fly our new pride and joy, the De Havilland Dove. Even in the nineteen seventies this would be called a vintage airliner and it was very different from the modern McDonnell Douglas and Boeing jets flying the Atlantic. Unlike the other aircraft in use at the parachute club it had retractable undercarriage. Pilots when flying for us, had never had to think about putting the wheels back down before landing in the past. Our airline pilot should have been firmly in the habit, but I guess, even then, airliners had all sorts of electronic gizmos and warnings which the old Dove did not.

As the aircraft made its final approach, with its wheels up, all hell broke loose, the Landrover was despatched, bouncing and careering wildly across the field to try and get to the runway first and force the pilot to abort, whilst staff and club members also sprinted in the same direction, arms waving frantically. At the last moment the aircraft lifted and began to circle, then we saw the undercarriage descend. It was as we'd surmised, brain lock, not mechanical failure! What the pilot thought seeing the melee beneath him I can only surmise, what the…. Followed by oops I imagine. We gave him a hard time, but not for too long, pilots are a valuable commodity at a parachute club and one way or another it's not a mistake you're likely to make twice.

Spotting, is getting the aircraft in the right place so that you can leave it, confident that you can land safely on the drop zone. It's a bit of an art. Sport parachutes are opened, under normal circumstances, at just over 2,000 feet, say 2,200 feet, in my day anyway. So at 2,200 feet on the way up we'd throw out a wind drift indicator. This device is a length of crepe paper, half orange and half white, in order that it should be visible in all weather and light conditions, with a weight at the end. It flutters down at the same speed as a parachutist under a canopy. It is thrown from the aircraft directly over the target in the centre of the drop zone.

The aircraft then circles to the right so the jumpmaster can watch the WDI, widdie in parachute slang until it lands. If the WDI lands 500 yards downwind then the correct opening point is 500 yards up wind. It gives you an accurate heading and drift distance. It's important to get the aircraft over the target to throw it, which is done by the jumpmaster, or spotter sticking his head out and looking straight down, then correcting the pilot's path five degrees at a time, by tapping him on the shoulder in a small aircraft, or with buttons operating lights in the cockpit for larger aircraft. From altitude you only need to be looking a few degrees off from vertical to be a long way off target on the ground. This is bad enough at 2,200 feet, when throwing the WDI, but when jumping from 12,000 feet you also have to allow for freefall drift, and the time it takes everyone to get ready in the doorway and other considerations.

One day on a staff jump my good friend Ken managed to get himself hooked up on the wheel. We adopted all sorts of postures, hanging outside the aeroplane to try and minimise separation and ensure we all went together. On this occasion Ken had asked Jamie, the pilot to make sure the brakes were on as he intended putting one, or both feet on the wheel. We climbed out, Ken put his weight on the wheel, Jamie forgot the brakes, the wheel went round, Ken slid down the strut and got hung up. We all left, Ken didn't. Ken tried to climb back up, Jamie started to descend in long circles. Ken wasn't making progress, but as the ground got closer, being unable to run at eighty miles an hour the urgency of his struggle increased. Eventually he managed to climb up enough to unhook whatever was caught up, stick his head inside the cockpit and swear at Jamie, who nearly died of shock. Unable to climb right in and kill Jamie, I think they exchanged a few words, Ken then let go and opened his canopy.

For years at the parachute club we had small aircraft and a limited number of people skilful enough to build an eight way formation. I remember a visit from, the then, Chief Coach and Safety Officer Charlie Shea Simmonds. It was decided to fly two aircraft in formation and put together an eight way. Most parachute clubs today have large aircraft and this is not such a big thing, but for us it was. For six of us it would be the first time we'd been in an eight way. Due to the fact that the larger a formation is, the slower it falls, it gets progressively harder to join. Number eight is last out of the aircraft and has the greatest separation to make up, both vertical and horizontal, but he dare not risk going below as he's unlikely to get back up. As National Coach, Charlie was given the honour of going number eight. The formation built to seven. What more can I say?

Later when I was Chief Instructor I organised a competition at Thruxton. For this event we had four way relative work teams and style and accuracy events. We hired in an

Islander for the occasion and a later National Coach came down for the event. It's the only time I've had to use the words "emergency up and out". It wasn't a life threatening incident really, we had plenty of altitude, although there was some cloud around, when one of the engines failed. I asked the pilot if he wanted us out, he said yes and I gave the command. I watched everyone out until it was just me and the National Coach, he looked at me and I gave him a look which I hope said it's my show you go first. He went and I followed.

Sadly for me, that evening I had the only migraine I've had since my acupuncture years before. As a result I missed the evening's shenanigans and the prize giving. The competition took a lot of organising and of course there were rivalries, and some politicking. On the whole though it was a great success. The prizes were given out by a beautiful lady called Beth Taylor, who, in style and accuracy I believe, had represented the UK at the World Championships, I think in Yugoslavia that year. I was also told that due to the cost of training and the event itself, she'd had to sell her kit afterwards to get home again. Parachuting has never been a spectator sport and I doubt there's sponsorship money in it even now. If only it could be an Olympic Sport. The filming technology is so much better these days.

One of the instructors at the club was a lady called Sue Lear, now Sue Dixon. I did my first and only kiss pass with her. My girlfriend at the time, Sue, was not amused, but it's not an erotic experience kissing in a freezing hurricane, but if you can do it without cracking heads it does show you're both in control. Sue is now a top international judge and a very successful business woman to boot. She married another parachute instructor Tony Dixon from the Royal Electrical and Mechanical Engineers. After Tony left the army they toured the canals of Britain and France on a narrow boat, before settling near Poitiers, on a small-holding to lead the good life, like the television programme of the same name. Sue however, is too dynamic for that and built up a substantial estate agency, selling to other Brits primarily, wishing to escape to France. Papillion Properties if you're looking for a property in France. Two more, wonderful, interesting, exciting people, living life to the full.

Another club member who stands out for me is a guy called Paul Williams. He had been a Royal Navy diver and when he started frequenting the parachute club he was diving on the North Sea oil rigs as a saturation diver for one of the big specialist companies called Comex. Paul would do a stint on the rigs, then get a period of time off, during which he would come back south and live at the parachute club for maybe a week or two, getting in as many jumps as possible, winter or summer.

Such are the risks of diving in the North Sea that companies like Comex have their own medical teams, decompression chambers and facilities for life saving in emergency situations and for undertaking medical checks on their personnel. Since Paul was spending extended periods at the parachute club including mid week when things were less busy I got to know him pretty well and we became firm friends. Paul confided in me that he was in love with a lady called Stephanie, who everyone called Steve apparently, who was the nursing sister at the medical centre for Comex. Steve had apparently rebuffed his proposals of marriage, on the grounds that she was quite a lot older than him. Clearly the age difference mattered not a jot to him and he was sensible enough to know that one day advancing years could make problems that other couples might not face. Paul knew Steve was the girl he wanted to spend his life with and that was that. Not that he didn't have at least one adoring fan down at the club!

One mid winters night, when the snow lay deep and crisp and even, and was still falling, I received a telephone call from Paul. He was on his way down to the club and had got to somewhere near Oxford and his car had broken down, oh and he had Steve with him and they were freezing, was there any chance I could bring the club Landrover out and tow them in? Of course I would. It took some time to get there and find them so I got to them in the early hours of the morning. Since Paul's car wouldn't run there was no heating, so Steve sat in the cab of the pickup style Landrover with me. I'd heard all about her, but never met her before, nonetheless we got along as though we'd known one another all our lives.

Ken and Jacqui.

It wasn't long before she said to me, "you know Paul's asked me to marry him don't you?" "Yes" I replied cautiously, "well what do you think?" she asked. I said that I understood she had turned him down because of the age difference, but I expressed the view that none of us knows what life has in store for us despite the best laid plans, they may have two good years together, five, fifty, who could tell, and what constitutes a successful marriage these days anyway. If she loved him as he loved her, I opined, she shouldn't turn away from the chance of happiness. Shortly afterward they announced their engagement and not long after I had to take time away from parachuting to drive to Aberdeen for the wedding.

One other anecdote about Paul, the expert diver, from before his marriage. He took Cindy, myself and another lady from Thruxton village down to Lulworth Cove, again in winter, to teach me to dive. It was blowing a gale and hailstones were pouring down as we descended the cliff to the bay, carrying all the gear down treacherous muddy paths a goat would have eschewed. "Don't drop your air tank" Paul told me jovially, "it could explode, with the force of three hand grenades." I particularly remember changing into the wet suit he provided, I stripped off in the freezing conditions and Cindy held it open for me to step into, as she did so it filled with hailstones.

Then I saw Paul putting on an extra pullover. "What are you doing?" I asked. "Oh, I've got a dry suit" he said. "It seals at the neck, wrists and ankles, so you can wear normal clothes underneath. I had never heard of such a thing, outrageous. Paul briefed me and we entered the freezing water. In those gale conditions you couldn't see your hand in front of your face. With some difficulty I could just see how much air I had on the gauge. Pretty soon we were separated but not knowing any better I stayed down, grubbing around on the bottom where bizarrely I found an old, mollusc encrusted, partly eaten away diving knife. It's now a treasured memento. When my air gauge was approaching the red I came to the surface and swam in to the beach. If my friends were relieved they didn't show it. Paul helped me out of my gear, but had great difficulty removing the weight belt, a quick release item in an emergency, supposedly, I don't know quite what had happened I can only surmise that one of the weights had become lodged against the buckle and was interfering with its operation.

Years later in preparation for living on a boat and exploring the world I took a Padi dive course and bought a full set of diving kit, to enable me to examine the hull of my boat, or rescue an anchor. If I knew then what I know now!

Sadly I lost touch with Paul and Steve, albeit after many years and several visits to them in Aberdeen. I don't know if it went wrong when I moved or when they did, but several attempts to trace them have yielded nothing. While I was doing my yacht up in preparation for my trip I came across another ex Comex diver living in South Dock Marina London. He knew Paul and Steve, but like me had lost touch, he thought Norfolk but wasn't sure and the people in the old house thought Devon. One day they'll turn up.

One of our club members had flown Vulcan bombers and gone on to be a director of Wilkinson Sword, another who was a brilliant mechanic and helped me re-build the suspension on my Austin Healey Sprite is still jumping. Maybe the only one of us who still is. I visited the Joint Services Parachute Club just before setting off around the world and there was Micky Doyle, now a much sought after freefall cameraman. One of my students from Bristol University, became known as Carrots, around the club, not because of red hair. A group of jumpers were standing around discussing a malfunction and someone said, "well I suppose it's character building!" Neil, on the fringe of the conversation miss-heard, "carrots?" he said, "what's carrots got to do with it?" From then on he was Carrots. I'm not in touch, but I'm told he's now a cosmetic dentist to the stars in Hollywood.

Inevitably there are many more anecdotes about everyday

life at the parachute club during those magical years. From used car dealers, to top company directors, from an El Al Security chief and the bodyguard of an Air Vice Marshall, to high ranking military personnel, all life was there. To those characters I've omitted I humbly apologise.

One final person who didn't become a regular, but who does stand out to me, is a lady called Paddy Parry. She and her charming husband Mike have two wonderful daughters Francesca and Zoe, but they sadly also had a son who was a victim of cot death; despite the fact that Mike was a GP and Paddy a nurse. Paddy was making a sponsored jump to raise money for cot death research when I met her. We became friends, Paddy is as mad as I am, the rest of the family eminently sensible, mother and daughters quite beautiful. Paddy had crossed the Sahara on foot in her youth and after making her parachute jump successfully, she wanted to come up with another money making stunt for the cause.

At the time I was doing some hang gliding on Mondays! I know, incorrigible. Paddy had me up on the roof of her daughter's private school, equally incorrigible, to see if it would be possible for her to hang glide off it, sponsored again of course, at the school fete. My opinion was that it wasn't a good bet and thankfully she didn't do it. I'm still in touch with the family and visited them in Spain recently whilst sailing my yacht around the Mediterranean. The girls were bridesmaids at my first wedding and the whole family came to my first motor race. I used to visit them by motorbike occasionally, now Paddy and some of her friends are ardent bikers too, my kind of people.

Just to complete the picture, my hang gliding career was not long. I couldn't afford to buy one and the parachute club didn't afford me much time, but as a skydiving instructor it was obviously a subject of natural interest. There were two, rival national associations, the NHGA and the BHGA (National and British Hang Gliding Associations). I joined both and studied their magazines. I then approached my nearest club.

The Chief Instructor of which was a guy named James Bond, well you can't forget that can you? I offered him a deal, a parachute course for a hang gliding course. I thought he'd love that, but no, he really didn't want to throw himself out of an aeroplane, he preferred having something open above him at the same time his feet left terra firma, and no later. I was disappointed, until, realising that we had much in common and that I was on a very low income, he taught me to hang glide anyway, for free. What a great guy. I embarrassed myself very badly there one day. Hang gliders weren't as sophisticated and efficient then as they are now and taking off with no wind was terribly difficult. On this particular day a group of us was sat at the top of a hill hoping for a breeze, just the opposite of skydiving really. James wouldn't let the students fly in those conditions but said to me "you can go if you want Malcolm". I did, but I got it wrong.

In a sailing boat, if you face into wind, the wind passes over both sides of the sail, which then does nothing except flap. This is called 'being in irons'. Equally with the hang glider you have to get the angle of attack right, if the nose is too high, there will be too much drag, you'll never run fast enough to take off, nose too low and it will have the air on top of the wing and push the nose into the ground. The angle has to be perfect air under the sail to fill it, but not so much as will stop it. I had it nearly right, but a little too low, air was passing over and under the fabric, it was in irons. I pushed forward to raise the nose but was already running full tilt and instead of rotating the glider I just got it further in front of me, until I sprawled down the hill. Over confidence, and I paid the price though thankfully without doing too much damage. Of course I flew again after that, like falling off a horse, you have to, but parachuting six days and hang gliding on the seventh, even if the weather permitted, was a bit too much really. I'm very grateful for the experience though.

CHAPTER 9

An End To The Skydiving Life

As WITH MANY experiences in life, the early part is often the best. The first couple of years at the parachute club were one adventure after another, one lesson after another, always a new goal to strive for and parties and girls. When I became chief instructor it was still wonderful, but things changed subtly. For example my old pal Ken became the second person to threaten to kill me when I told him it was his turn to clean the loos! As CCI you have to lead by example, although cleaning the loos was no longer a part of the job description, hence the ill feeling from Ken!

Difficult decisions, they say, are the privilege of rank and so it was. Having total responsibility for everything that went on made a difference. When I started, as I mentioned before, I earned £11 per week. However, there were opportunities to supplement this. My test jumps bought me a music centre which ate all my tape cassettes, despite going back under guarantee several times, and taught me that material possessions aren't everything in life.

Nonetheless, most of us want more than we have and I had two further options for extra income. The parachute club was very proactive. I hate that word, but you'll understand what I mean. We could only run three courses per week at our own premises, but if we went out to colleges, universities and hospitals with social clubs, then we could train people at their own premises, and they would simply phone the club for weather information, and come down on a good day to collect their jump. The weather could change between phone call and arrival, and forecasts aren't always accurate, but on the whole it worked well.

One club member, Tony Rolfe, was already running such training courses for Bob and there was another aspect to it. We would offer the university and hospital social clubs a free film show and talk on skydiving, and at the film show and talk we'd sign up as many of the audience as possible for a course. We had a couple of really great, for that time, American made skydiving films, one was called Masters of The Sky, the other title I've forgotten, sometimes we'd just put them on at the club when the weather was bad, turn off the soundtrack, listen to Pink Floyd and dream. Bob paid, I can't remember how much, but he paid, every time I went out to give a talk or to teach.

Sometimes I'd go along with Tony when he was running a course, particularly in winter if there wasn't much else on. On one occasion I went along with Tony to a hospital social club training session. I sat at the back for a while, I knew the patter by heart and I'd heard the jokes before so I went outside for a walk. I met this rather lovely off duty nurse. Her name was Suki, we got on rather well. I went along to Tony's second night training there and met her again, we got on even better. I lost track of the time until I heard Tony wandering around the corridors shouting for me as he wanted to go home. I couldn't resist it, "in here Tony", he opened the door to what was a bathroom in the nurses home and there I was in the bath with this gorgeous girl. No wonder he threatened to kill me when I went after Cindy.

I've had some of the best times of my life in nurses homes, years later I had a friendship with a nurse in Tunbridge Wells and nurses came to the club from Winchester and London and elsewhere. I already mentioned the party at a nurses home in London, the one that caused my parents to wait up all night. My final adventure in a nurses home was with a nurse called Sandra from University College Hospital. I've been very lucky, especially in my youth, to date some beautiful girls and arguably Sandra was the most beautiful. Paul Young the chief instructor at the time rarely passed any personal comment, but he commented on Sandra. My father never said anything about my girlfriends, but he likewise was bowled over. She was simply amazingly beautiful.

I met her when I did a free film show at University College Hospital. She took the course and stayed with me at the club a few times. We also went to a concert and spent the night at my fathers house. On one of our last dates I stayed at the nurses home. We had a bath there and again there were communal bathrooms dotted around the building. Suddenly she got out, grabbed my clothes and ran off. I half expected her to return, but no. I hadn't even made a careful note of the way back to her room, so I had to wander about the nurses home stark naked asking for directions. Nothing bothers nurses it seems. I couldn't see a girl like that moving into the comparative squalor of the parachute club. The buildings had been temporary in the war and the water pipes lay above ground, so they froze every winter. So it was, she took a Mediterranean holiday and met someone else.

I ran many training courses away from the club, in the evenings to supplement my lowly income. Sometimes it was too much. I'd teach, or work on the drop zone all day, then drive a hire car possibly a hundred miles to a university or college, teach until possibly eleven pm, then pack up and drive back, and, if necessary, be back up good and early to pack rigs. On one of these occasions I lost concentration driving back from Oxford in fog. I hit the central barrier and smashed the side window of the car with my head, losing consciousness. When I woke up the car was in the middle of a field. It wasn't running but the ignition was still on. I could tell where the road was from the sound of an occasional passing car. However, I wasn't visible from the road due to the fog. It was a sobering experience, I realised that if the car had caught fire I'd be dead and if I'd been seriously injured no one would have found me until the fog burned off, hopefully the next day!

The car restarted and miraculously all the lights worked. I was probably concussed, but the broken window ensured plenty off fresh air. I autocrossed back onto the road and made it home to the parachute club. I was worried about the potential reaction of the Ford Dealer when I returned the car somewhat damaged the following day. They were fine, I was fully insured and hired from them so often that they wanted my business at any price.

Mostly though, teaching out was a joy. The most memorable course was at Bristol University. It was a large course and there was a time limit on the availability of the room we were using. By the end of the second evening we'd completed everything, except that they hadn't had anything like enough practice at parachute landing falls. This is a way of falling over so as to spread the impact and absorb it gradually and generally speaking avoid any injury, depends what you land on of course! Bearing in mind that in my day students jumped on ordinary round canopies which didn't allow for gentle stand up landings and we didn't want to be breaking too many of our customers' legs; the deficiency couldn't be ignored.

Therefore, I took the whole lot of them outside and we did our parachute landing falls on a large grass roundabout in the middle of the Bristol traffic. I was about the same age as my university students and we all had a bit of a devil may care attitude, but it worked and none of the bemused motorists seeing ranks of teenagers fall over by numbers actually crashed! One of those students Kevin, went on to be a British Champion and attend the World Championships. When I was Chief Instructor we didn't always see eye to eye, he was one of those guys who would want to jump when conditions were borderline, always wanted to be last in a formation and that sort of thing, however, his passion and determination were undeniable and his attitude took him to the top. Ultimately he was and possibly still is an asset to the sport. I believe he may still be jumping somewhere in France.

My closest friend at the parachute club was John Field who joined the staff shortly after me. Technically I was his boss for a while but our relationship was never like that. I have to say that he made it very easy for me. At that time, square parachutes were still in their infancy and the sport was governed by people who were mostly military or ex military. They'd been taught always to keep space between one another in the sky, and it's a fact that if one round parachute gets itself on top of another then like a yacht that's had its wind stolen by another the top one will lose the air controlling its descent and will collapse into the canopy below with disastrous consequences.

These days everyone has seen displays with square canopies stacked up. This can be done because square parachutes are really gliders and the dead air is mostly behind them not directly above. Linking and stacking canopies became known as canopy relative work. It started in the USA and there was much debate in the British Parachute Association, and amongst parachutists generally in the UK, about it. It was considered dangerous, which it can be, and there were moves to ban it. It may even have actually been banned for a while. John and I used to practice it during the week when there was no one else around, until it became acceptable, putting us in the vanguard, although a stack of two is still the biggest I've been in. We'd also read somewhere that a grapefruit will fall at the same terminal velocity as a freefalling parachutist and that therefore you can play catch in freefall. We tried it, over an open field, so as not to kill anyone if we dropped it! It was fine until one of us missed it, I won't say who, but it wasn't me. Left to its own devices it out ran us even though we dived after it!

John and I knew so much about one another, and could sound so alike, that one evening we sat at the bar in the White Horse with the pay phone on the counter. I rang John's girlfriend and talked dirty to her, John did the same with Cindy, they never found out they'd been talking to the wrong guy, until now possibly.

When the parachute club days were over for John and I, he emigrated to New Zealand, where he now runs a successful air conditioning business. Prior to being a parachute instructor John was one of the original Rockers. His picture appears in the book Rockers. The photograph was taken at the Ace café on the North Circular Road. John was heavily into motorcycles, he had a Norton Commando during his time at the club, but had previously built a Triton, a marriage of Norton Featherbed frame and Triumph Bonneville engine. He was, and I'm sure still is, a hell of an engineer. In fact his Commando must have been the most pampered bike in existence. John, popularly known by his initials JF, stripped it completely and rebuilt it each winter, he even chrome plated the hose clips (John is very cross that I wrote this and denies he ever chrome plated a hose clip even if it is possible, so it was probably something we just joked about at the time). His Commando was however far better than when it left the factory, and was a real credit to him, how he ever parted with it is a mystery to me. Paul had a Kawasaki KH400, one of the iconic two stroke triples of the era, I love them, they sound amazing and remind me so much of those days. Many of the club members also came down on motorbikes. My first ride on a proper motorcycle was one borrowed from one of the club members and I took every opportunity I could to have a go. I say proper motorcycle, because when I was about twelve I found I could start my Dad's old Quickly moped without the key and churn up the lawn on it!

One of the club regulars, by the name of Rick Shilabeer, had a Triumph Trident, another triple, but a four stroke. I remember I rode it around Thruxton circuit a day after a race meeting. Racing cars running on slicks leave little pieces of rubber which have literally rolled off the tyre when hot and molten , they lie just off the racing line. In motor racing jargon they are known as marbles, because when you accidentally get on them they generally send you off the track. For some reason I chose to ride the wrong way round the circuit which means a different line, actually the line for bikes and cars is a bit different anyway. Well, whatever the excuse I got on to the marbles and was excruciatingly close to writing Rick's bike off. I certainly couldn't afford to replace it. Having somehow caught the slide, I very carefully pottered back and told him what a wonderful bike it was!

Luckily for me, the club then invested in a little two stroke Suzuki 175 trail or 'off road' bike as a speedy means of getting about the airfield without using our great big thirsty Landrover all the time. I had some great fun on that bike, there were plenty of earth banks and loose stuff on which to hone my motorcycling skills. I had no plans or ideas then that I'd ever race motorcycles. I still hankered after racing in single seater racing cars.

If John was my best friend at the parachute club then Paul, who was chief instructor when I joined, was my mentor. He taught me pretty much everything I know about skydiving, about teaching, about self discipline and about leadership. He's a hell of a guy and post parachute club he went on to work for British Aerospace full time, and at the time of writing he still does. He married his girlfriend from the parachute club era, a very smart, beautiful and sophisticated lady, the daughter of an Admiral. I heard the Admiral wasn't too pleased that his daughter married a deserter from the Foreign Legion. He should have been proud, Paul is an incredibly talented and resourceful man.

Thruxton airfield wasn't only home to the parachute club, the flying club, The British Automobile Racing Club and the gliding club. There was, and still is a small industrial park there, very small, but it too had its fascinating characters. The first one I met was a former racing driver by the name of Tony Shaw. Tony had, and at the time of writing still has, although he's semi retired now, a workshop for car repairs and tuning. It's an ancient wooden and corrugated steel building, with a pit for getting under a vehicle. Not much in the way of mod cons here. Tony, though, is an artist with cars. His particular passion is Jaguars and he used to race an E-Type with considerable success. If he'd started younger and had the backing who knows what he could have achieved, but that's racing as I now know only too well myself. Tony is married to a wonderful lady by the name of Anne, her nickname is Figgins, don't know why, but Figgins she is. For years she was a journalist on the local paper. She's a powerful character and a match for Tony. I'd say they're a match made in heaven, both a bit wild, but they look out for each other.

Tony's arch rival in racing was a local millionaire John Burbidge who had a small bakery and supermarket in Andover. He lived, possibly still does, in a big house just outside Thruxton village. Despite their rivalry Tony prepared John's E-Type as well as his own and I'm sure he did an equally good job on it, he'd want to beat John on a level playing field, and clearly John trusted him with the job. It says a great deal about trust and the character of both men in such a competitive environment I think.

One evening I went on a bit of a pub crawl with this lot Tony, Figgins, John, myself and I think either Ken or Tony from the parachute club. We ended up in the basement of John's house, where he has a bar with the autographs of many famous racing drivers on the walls. Honestly now, I'd had the least to drink, I've always been quite cautious in that regard, even though drinking and driving didn't carry quite the stigma then that it does now. I'm not coming out in support of drinking and driving, quite the reverse, it's just the way things were. Figgins asked me if I'd drive her and Tony home, as she thought I was OK to drive and they certainly weren't. I agreed and put them both in my old Morris Minor GPO van. In his drunken state Tony said to me "bring this thing down to my workshop tomorrow and I'll make it the fastest post office van there's ever been". This appealed greatly to me, I figured he meant for free and I didn't forget.

Next day, somewhat hung over, Tony swore he couldn't remember saying any such thing and he probably couldn't. However, he did the job and only charged me for parts he had to buy. That was the start of a much valued friendship and when I got my next car, an Austin Healey Sprite I spent all my spare cash with Tony tuning that car in all sorts of ways.

I kept the Sprite for donkey's years and when I finally

achieved my ambition and bought my first single seater racing car I towed it around the country with the Sprite. Hardly ideal, given the size and weight of the Sprite but it happened, without accident. The Sprite had Janspeed inlet and exhaust manifolds, electronic ignition, a gas flowed, polished and ported cylinder head and the rear suspension was stiffened up with Koni shock absorbers, I had Dunlop SP Sport radial tyres all round. As far as my budget allowed it was state of the art for the time. With those shock absorbers on the back and the extra power it was possible to slide the thing under control and driving this car I learned about opposite lock and heeling and toeing. It was fun with a capital F.

The nearest it ever came to being destroyed was after one of my joint birthday parties with John. Despite being late April there were blizzard conditions. I gave one of the girls a lift home to an outlying village. We were doing about ten miles an hour trying to see ahead, when the wind blew a tree down. The tree brought the power lines down. The tree trunk was a couple of yards behind us and the telegraph pole a couple of yards in front. All we had over our heads was a convertible soft top. Someone up there was looking after me, or more probably her!

Other characters I remember fondly are John Thorne, who had an electronics business on the estate and sadly died far too young, Baz Knight who still runs an engineering business at the airfield, but who used to be an engineer for the Norton motorcycle race team in its early days of greatness, (not to be confused with the later Rotary engined bikes) Norman White a famous motorcycle racer from the days of the Thruxton 500 and many others. One of the BARC guys, John Wickham, went on to run a Formula One team. 'Plastic Graham' and his wife made a fortune as early importers of Tupperware and now run a lovely pub. Pilots from Thruxton parachute club are now Captains with major airlines, the whole place was simply alive and buzzing with amazing people.

After six years my time as a parachute instructor was coming to an end. I'd had the option at one stage of going to Kent to be Chief Instructor at Headcorn, a new full time parachute centre which was started by a friend of mine one Dave Parker. Dave and I progressed through the British parachutist category system at the same time in 1975. In the UK there are ten categories, with category ten being the highest qualification, before going on to be an instructor, although category eight qualifies you for most things you'd want to do. There are also four internationally recognised qualifications, A,B,C,and D licences category ten in the UK, more or less qualifies a jumper for an international D Licence.

Dave was a merchant banker from London. He was a student at the same time as me. I joined the staff and jumped six days a week to race up to category ten and D Licence. However, staff jumps were not unlimited, or we'd make no money. Dave would be around every weekend, money no object and he'd pack as many jumps in as possible. We progressed through the system with a friendly rivalry at about the same dynamic rate. The only difference was that Dave stopped at D Licence, while I went on to Advanced Instructor. Therefore, when Dave decided he wanted to quit banking and start a parachute club he asked me to be his Chief Instructor.

There was a time when Dave and I dated a couple of Bunny Girls from the famous Playboy Club in London. Dave managed to hang on to his for quite a while, but mine went off to be a croupier on a cruise ship based in the USA where she doubtless married an American millionaire. Anyway, around about 1978 Dave asked me to be his CCI, I was not yet CCI at Thruxton so it would have been a good career move, further, not having the qualifications himself (although he later got them and a pilot's licence) he was prepared to talk about shares in the business. By then however I was in love with Cindy and relocating to Kent would have been the end of that, my amateur dramatics and all my friends at Thruxton. I couldn't do it.

When recession and Bob's financial adventure with the

adventure school dragged his business down I had my first taste of redundancy. By then I was on a proper salary, with a mortgage and others were only too keen to do the job for less. The opportunity at Headcorn was by now ancient history and anyway I was too proud to make enquiries in that direction. Despite making changes Bob ultimately had to sell the club anyway. It changed hands one more time I believe, before a terrible tragedy brought it all to an end. For me the parachute club was liberating, exciting and a learning and growing experience. The low point was when I gave it up briefly for my then fiancee, the highs were many.

I alluded to the fact that my fiancee's family conspired to get rid of me. Cindy's sister was married to a sales rep. By comparison with me he made a lot of money. This is before I was CCI. Cindy felt that if we were going to get married I should get a proper job, be more like Andy, her brother in law. In my heart, I suppose I thought she was right, in reality I was probably earning between twenty and thirty pounds per week by this time, plus my accommodation in a hut! Hardly ideal for getting married. And, if you're going to make that kind of commitment to someone, you have to take account of their desires and needs. I found a job as a sales rep with a company that sold welding consumables and equipment. I gave my notice to the club and rented a flat in the nearby village of Appleshaw, together with my friend John Field, for the time being. I started the new job one week before Cindy's eighteenth birthday. We'd already become engaged. For that first week I had to go away on a residential training course. It would be the first real separation from Cindy since our first date on her sixteenth birthday. Neither of us were looking forward to it. Cindy's family suggested she stay with her sister and brother in law that week, they would entertain her and help pass the time, and I could collect her on my way back.

At the end of my training I drove back to Cindy's sister's house, laden with presents for Cindy's eighteenth. Cindy answered the door, but instead of giving me a hug and a kiss she gave me my engagement ring back. I was totally bewildered, shocked, heartbroken, confused. I drove back to Appleshaw in a daze. I was hoping to discuss it all with John, but John wasn't there, just a cold empty flat. Was this what I'd given up the parachute club for, a career that didn't inspire me, a flat that didn't feel like home and no fiancee, wife, family. I got out my address book and wondered who to call, who to talk to.

I rang a couple of friends but they were out and then I rang a lady called Faye in Andover. She wasn't a close friend, but she was close geographically. She used to have a wing walking act and was a tough cookie, I thought she might help me pull myself together. I rang her number and a girl answered, but she had a French accent. I asked for Faye and she said Faye was out. I asked her who she was and she explained that her name was Francine, she was from France, obviously, and she was staying with Faye for a while, but she'd arrived that day and Faye had a previous engagement so she was there alone. I was totally straight with her, I told her I was a friend of Faye's and exactly what had happened to me. I said I needed someone to talk to and I might not be the best of company, but if she would help me, I would buy her dinner and show her around Andover, so at least she'd know where everything was. Not difficult, given the size of the town!

She said yes, I jumped into my new company car and drove over there, after washing my face anyway. Now Francine could have been anyone, but, as it turned out, she was young and beautiful with fabulous hair down to the bottom of her spine, the sort of girl you'd notice in a crowded room. Strangely my first impulse was not to seduce her! I really was in love with Lucinda. I took Francine for a meal and managed to talk about some other subjects as well but probably mostly about what had happened to me. I was getting it off my chest and although the future looked bleak, selling welding rods when I should be jumping out of aeroplanes, nonetheless my spirits lifted. After the meal and a stroll around town, I asked her if she would like to go to Andover's only night spot at the time, the Town Mill.

This was an old water mill with a disco come nightclub inside. You had to be a member or signed in by a member, but I was a member so no problem. We went and I was about to sign the book when I saw the signatures of Cindy, her sister and brother in law. Hell, Cindy was celebrating her eighteenth in there, I hadn't expected that, I'd left her in Old Basing, some miles away. There was another signature too, that looked like it was with the other three, so Cindy had a new man and she was in there with him. Life rarely gives you opportunities like the one I squandered that night. Andover is a small town, certainly at that time I would have known many of the people in there and mostly everyone knew everyone. Not Francine though, no one knew her, and she was a crowd stopper. Of course I should have walked in with this stunning girl. All the guys would be wanting to know who she was, Cindy would be somewhat amazed at least, jealous at best, I mean this was just hours after she'd returned my ring.

Sadly I was too shaken up, emotionally wrecked, so distraught at the thought that I'd given up my life to make a future for Cindy and I and yet after one week away, she was out clubbing with a new man. I felt physically sick. I told Francine I couldn't go in with Cindy there and I took her lamely back to Faye's. Later I sat in my new car in the Town Mill car park, in the pouring rain, waiting until chucking out time and watched Cindy emerge arm in arm with her new lover. For a while after that I sold welding rods. Of course word got around. Not long after I became single I started dating Janet, who eventually married Bob. She played the Commandant's tart at Butlitz. Later still Janet became a mountaineer, she's one of those 'free climbers' who won't use ropes or artificial aids. How it was that Thruxton attracted so many incredible people in the seventies is a mystery to me still.

Thank goodness my career selling welding kit didn't last. Bob invited me round to his house one evening and announced he was starting the Adventure School, Paul would be Chief instructor there, which would leave the parachute club in need of a new chief instructor, did I want the job, did I! John and I gave up the flat in Appleshaw and the three of us, that is John, myself and Artos the cat moved home. Artos was a gorgeous, huge black cat who'd been a gift to me from Tony Rolfe.

When he first brought him to the club Artos would fit in the palm of your hand. We had a rat or two at the club in those days and I'd expressed the view that we needed a cat, I'd been brought up with one and have always had a soft spot for them. When Artos first arrived I was terrified that a rat would kill him, before he was big enough to defend himself. One day, soon after, at the end of the day's skydiving I came home to find what looked like a dead rat and a dead kitten. Artos had a huge gash in his chest and was not moving, the rat was dead. I hurried with Artos to the vet and obviously had to leave him there. I really didn't have much hope. In a few days however Artos was fine. He grew up to be huge, and hugely popular with the club members. He had a lifelong hatred of rats and killed more than a few around the airfield, but he was a bit of a monster, he'd take on fully grown hares, and then walking backwards he'd drag them all the way from the airfield to the clubhouse as a present for us.

I'd not been chief instructor long when Cindy came to see me. She told me that when she went to stay with her sister that week I was away training for my salesman's job, Andy her brother in law, had brought a colleague home to stay, for the whole week. She'd fallen for him, which she said, she realised now, was what her family had intended all along. This guy apparently had a reputation at work, that he could 'pull' any girl. Cindy's version of events was that Andy must have said something to him along the lines that his wife's younger sister was getting married, either too young, or to someone the family didn't approve of and would he like to stay with them for a week and try to get in her knickers. A challenge he duly rose to. He kept it up for a while too!

However it wasn't meant to be, nor was it likely to become a permanent relationship under such circumstances. Unfortunately, of course Cindy found out, or realised that she'd been set up. Now she was full of remorse and wanted to get back to the way things were before. Bob was paying me a living wage as CCI so I didn't need to sell welding rods and I bought a house in Andover. Foolishly I took Cindy back. I reserved most of my anger for Andy, Cindy's brother in law. He'd been the one to interfere in my life, I felt, and yet he didn't even know me, certainly I'd done nothing to him. Bizarrely, and I really do mean under bizarre circumstances Andy popped up in my life again very briefly twenty years later, he didn't recognise me, but I've never forgotten him. I bought the house in Andover in joint names with Cindy although I paid. Of course it didn't work out second time around and then I had to buy Cindy out of 'my' house.

My final girlfriend of the parachute club era was a local lady called Sian. She was smart, sexy, loyal and kind. Again my mother, who met her when we went sailing together, thought she was wonderful. So she was, and so of course I didn't hold on to her. I probably sound a bit promiscuous and for a short time I was, immediately after leaving home, it was like opening the candy box of freedom. Since then I've really been a serial monogamist, still hoping to one day make a relationship work. I've always gone my own way so my mother's approval of Sian may have been the kiss of death. Sometimes I wonder though about the wisdom of arranged marriages, because with hindsight I've been involved with some wonderful ladies and my own judgement has been seriously lacking.

My relationship with Sian survived my redundancy from the parachute club, but not for long. Which was in no way her fault. I wasn't very happy, or nice to be around, but I did take stock and decided to turn the crisis into an opportunity. Having a mortgage I went on to state benefit of some sort, but only for about a fortnight. I had plenty of confidence in my ability with people and seemed able to make the right impression at interviews. I had no shortage of energy either. In the short term I needed a job, in the longer term I needed a strategy for a new form of fulfilment. I knew what would kick start me, the long cherished ambition to be a racing driver. Of course I was about twenty five now, too old to make it to the top by today's standards, at the time of writing they've just crowned a new World Champion, Fernando Alonso, he's twenty four I think. However, I wasn't concerned about age, I just had to go racing before it was too late altogether.

CHAPTER 10

Making Money In The Real World

I GOT A job in pretty short order as a sales rep for Thorn EMI, selling, of all things, catering equipment. Primarily this consisted of potato peelers and chippers for fish and chip shops, industrial sized food mixers, cold meat slicing machines and that sort of thing. My next adventure was not of my own making and I can't use the names of those involved for reasons you'll understand shortly. My boss was a large Scottish fellow, living in a respectable part of Surrey as I recall, but really more of a London suburb. My 'territory' was down in the Hampshire, Dorset area, so I continued to live in my house in Andover. One Friday, soon after I joined the company, we had a sales meeting, as frequently happens in this kind of business. I was very much the new kid on the block. At the end of the meeting as everyone was leaving, my boss invited me to go home with him, meet his wife and go out for a meal or a drink. It was one of those invitations you can't say no to really, so instead of heading home for a weekend of my making I followed my boss to his house, where he collected his wife and took us out. A pub crawl was really what he had in mind. I used every bit of cunning I could to appear to join in but not get drunk and disgrace myself, I ordered shandys with the weakest beers and avoided finishing them, whatever it took, I was determined to remain sober. My boss was too busy drinking to really notice my abstinence.

When the pubs closed I breathed a sigh of relief and prepared to go home, but my car was outside my bosses' house and I had no idea where I was! I was reliant on him to get me back there. To my horror my boss said "Auch, ya must meet……." I would love to use the names as I misunderstood exactly what he said and it was quite hilarious with hindsight. However, since I'm going to talk about what could be construed as attempted murder, and since I decided against pressing charges at the time, I can't tell you. My boss took me to his friends' house. There turned out to be a party going on. My boss introduced me to his friend, in a drunken slurred voice, as a parachutist, clearly he thought this would be of interest to his friend. His friend it transpired had been bodyguard to an important middle eastern figure, now living in exile. His friend had married an English lady and settled here. I knew I was in trouble when, his reply, clearly based on the erroneous impression that I'd been in the parachute regiment, was "Think you're hard then do you?" I tried to make a joke of it, "er no, not particularly" I tried to explain I was a sport parachutist. He clearly wasn't getting it. I followed my boss into the party. All I really wanted to do was get home. My boss clearly intended to stay. There was a mixture of ordinary suburban professionals of both sexes there. Popular music was playing, there was food laid out, savoury and sweet with knives for cutting cheese, cakes and so on.

I decided to make the most of it, I couldn't get out of it. I had some food to soak up what alcohol I'd had to drink earlier and some orange juice to dilute it, I still sensed I should have my wits about me. People were dancing, the way they did in the early eighties, all quite separate, no contact, just jigging about in whatever way they interpreted the music. The hell with it, I joined in. I was facing my hosts' wife, but she was on the opposite side of the living room and I certainly wasn't making eyes at her. Suddenly I found myself down on one knee as someone jammed a foot hard into the back of my leg. I looked around and up, in time to see a large fist descending into my face. Being very sober by now, and with that familiar adrenalin rush, I removed my face swiftly out of the way. The punch never landed, but my host wasn't about to stop. He picked up a knife from the table, I dodged that once too and removed myself out of range. My boss, drunk as he was must have thought …… is attacking Malcolm, Malcolm works for me, he punched his friend. As far as I was concerned this was out of hand, even before my boss joined in. There were kids sleeping upstairs too. No mobile phones then, so I went to the hall in search of a phone, didn't spot one and since I was obviously the object of my hosts' anger I decided discretion was the better part of valour and left the house.

I found myself in a quiet suburban street in goodness knows where. All neat lawns and hedges, and very middle class. I was still dressed in my work suit. I hurried down the street until I saw a light on. It was by now the early hours of the morning. I rang the bell and a well spoken middle aged lady came to the door. I said "excuse me, do you think I could possibly use your phone to call the police, there's a bit of a fight going on up the road and there are children in the house". "Of course dear" she said "it's not that Iranian fellow is it? I called there the other day collecting for charity and he was very strange". "Actually it is" I said. I dialled 999, got through to the police and told them what had happened, the lady of the house furnished the street name and the number of the house up the road. I thanked her profusely and hung around until a few minutes later I saw a police car draw up. I approached them and explained it was me that had called them. They then knocked and were admitted, probably by the lady of the house or by one of the guests. By some miracle my boss had knocked his friend out, and then pretty much collapsed himself. The police asked me if I wanted to press charges. I hadn't even thought about that side of things. I had to think fast and make a decision. How much would my boss remember, he was currently unconscious, would the other guests, none of whom I knew be witnesses, what would my boss make of me accusing his friend of attempted murder, or assault with a deadly weapon, or even just assault. "No" I didn't think I wanted to press charges.

Since the violence was over and I didn't want to press charges, the police left. My boss's wife asked me to help her get her comatose and rather heavy husband into the car, which we achieved. I drove them home under her direction and helped her lug my boss into the living room where we dumped him unceremoniously on the settee. Taking him upstairs and undressing him wasn't on my agenda. My boss's wife said I should stay with her. Was I imagining it or was there more to the invitation than just, you must be tired why don't you stay. She wasn't unattractive. Hell no. I didn't want that, not even the thought of it, no temptation, no suspicion, no nothing. I was already concerned about just what my boss would remember, without being caught, innocent or not, effectively alone in his house with his wife. Goodbye.

Goodness knows what the time was now three am, four am, five maybe. By the time I was halfway home and the adrenalin was worn off the tiredness hit me like a sledgehammer. I was on the M3. I'd learned about the perils of driving when tired at the parachute club, but I didn't think it was allowed to stop on the hard shoulder, just to sleep. I had to make Fleet services. I didn't, I fell asleep and crashed my new company car. Well, I hit the central reservation and spun the Escort estate several times, potato peeling machines and ham slicers flying about inside. That woke me up! Enough to get to Fleet anyway, where I dosed up on coffee and assessed the damage. There were dents and scratches all down the offside, but no lights out, punctures, burst radiators, or noticeably out of alignment wheels. I felt I could drive home. I was really looking forward to phoning in on Monday!

When Monday came I set out on my pre-arranged appointments. Mid morning I telephoned my boss. How much he remembered and how much he'd been told by his wife I have no idea, but thankfully I was still in a job and he was all apologies for what had happened. After receiving his profuse apologies I told him I'd crashed the car on the way home. What could he say? He told me not to worry.

At the end of the day it was just a job. I had no ambition to spend the rest of my days visiting fish and chip shops and cafes. I was still doing amateur dramatics with Thruxton Players and we had a forthcoming panto in which I would be Father Christmas. I had a demo to organise. I parachuted into a local school as Father Christmas to publicise this, my last production with them, as it turned out. To date it was my last parachute jump too.

I only had one other memorable adventure during my short time selling catering equipment, but it was far more enjoyable. I called at a nice restaurant in a well to do seaside town. I tried to get the waitress to talk business, or introduce me to someone who would or could. I wasn't getting anywhere. I liked her though, she was petite, sexy and rather sweet. I decided to have lunch there. After I'd eaten she refused to take any money from me. I didn't want to make it obvious by arguing with her, in case she lost her job or something, so I accepted. Later I went back and gave her a bunch of flowers. I didn't see her for some time after that, but next time I was in the area I called in. It was probably too soon for a follow up business call, but I was my own boss, out on the road at least. We met for a drink that evening and dated for a while. It transpired she owned the restaurant and the shop next door and a couple of flats which she let out. She was sexy, loaded and into classic cars, it was too good to be true, or at least to last, so it didn't!

In fact she was probably a pioneer of sex tourism, although the term hadn't been coined then I think. She told me she really liked young black men. She took holidays to warmer climates, where she would find young black men only too willing to play ball. I think I amused her for a short while, and for me at least the sex was wonderful. At the end of the day though, I doubt she wanted a steady relationship with anyone, she knew what she wanted and she went out and got it. She was honest with me and I remember her fondly as a result.

The experience could have dented my self confidence, but in fact I was a little below par at that time anyway. People tend to judge people in a number of ways. Job title, wealth, the house you live in, the car you drive. It's a crazy way to value someone, but we've all thought along those lines, or been judged that way ourselves, at sometime. For me it was difficult to tell people I was a sales rep. It was quite different from saying "I'm a skydiving instructor", or later, "I'm Chief Instructor at a skydiving club". I always felt it was as if I was saying "I'm only a sales rep." I recognise that a successful sales rep can earn a lot, that it's a vital skill, which many companies value highly, with good reason, that later the titles Sales Manager and Sales Director can even have some kudos. Some of the best friends I've made during my advertising career have been sales reps. who visited the companies I worked for, but it wasn't for me, I needed to take control and set myself on a path that would inspire me.

I decided, having looked at various trade magazines, that a career in advertising would be the thing for me. People in advertising were being paid large sums according to the advertisements in Campaign magazine. It had the appearance, from the outside at least, of being a fun industry to work in, and, if I could get to work on a car account it just might help me get on, when I started racing. As you know, I'd realised, whilst still at school, that the only way I was ever going to get on the starting grid was to fund it myself. The only problem was, I knew nothing about advertising. What did fmcg mean in the recruitment advertisements? I began reading Campaign regularly and Marketing Week. I discovered that fmcg meant fast moving consumer goods. I learned some more jargon too, but it wasn't going to be enough. Further I had a mortgage to fund, I wasn't going to go to college now, not with that and rates and electricity and all the usual bills to cover, so a formal qualification wasn't an option. I would have to bluff my way in.

The advertisement that set me on the path to fulfilling my aim, came not from Campaign, but from my father's Waltham Forest Guardian, which I happened to look at when paying him a visit. A company called Westex Fiat Promotions was looking for people to manage promotional events for Fiat, Lancia and Ferrari. They were based in a small industrial estate, just along from the Speedway stadium at Hackney. Not really the area where you'd expect to find a successful company and a good career, but I had to find out. I applied and got an interview. It was actually a fun and challenging job, with a reasonable salary, not dependent on commission. What's more it really could open doors. Westex was basically a small transport company, running delivery vans, they delivered Fiat and Lancia brochures to the dealers. They had then won a contract to run promotional vehicles. This meant outside events units, which could go to all sorts of events; golf tournaments, show jumping competitions, county shows, car racing, you name it. The vehicles were as large as you could drive without a heavy goods vehicle licence. There were several of them, the Lancia outside events unit was like a horsebox that unfolded into a promotional stage, with a hospitality area as well. For Fiat there were units with hydraulic legs that would stand up clear of the lorry's chassis, the lorry itself could then be driven out from underneath and the unit lowered to the ground. These units had a rooftop viewing area as well.

In addition to driving the unit, setting it up and liaising with the local dealer the operator really ended up running the promotion, nine times out of ten. There were also indoor promotions, regional motor shows, dealer launches, new model launches. For these we would have a panel van of about three tons, with a stage, sound system, lights and whatever else was needed for the particular event. What Westex needed was operators who could be relied upon, not just to get there on time, but who would make the event run smoothly. When the technology went wrong they needed to have an operator on site who would display some initiative, sort the problem, hire another sound system if necessary, whatever it took. To preserve the contract they needed the promotions to be well run, for dealers to report back favourably to Fiat and Lancia, for Fiat and Lancia's area and national managers to be impressed when they attended, and so on. I convinced Westex, that having run a parachute club, with all the Civil Aviation Authority considerations and red tape, plus all the responsibility for training, maintaining equipment, safety and so on I could manage promotions, sort problems, display initiative and get on well with their clients, the managers of Fiat and Lancia and their dealers.

I got the job and I supplemented my income by taking lodgers in Andover. The new job, for the most part meant living out of a suitcase anyway, I'd be travelling all over the British Isles. When I did have to spend time at base I'd stay at my father's house. My income went up, my living costs went down, at last I could start saving money towards my goal of becoming a racing driver, whilst potentially looking for a way into advertising proper. I found myself rubbing shoulders with people like Fiat's regional promotion managers, employed by Fiat's above the line advertising agency. Above the line is jargon for proper advertising, press, radio, TV and posters primarily. Agencies describe themselves as above the line, below the line, through the line, all sorts of things, it's a bizarre world.

The new job really was the start of a new and better time for me. The parachute club had been wonderful, but if I'd spent my entire working life as a skydiving instructor I'd have missed out on so many other experiences. The best part of the new job, was probably the Lancia promotions. Lancia were involved heavily in the World Sportscar Championship, with drivers of the stature of Riccardo Patrese and Eddie Cheever. They were also involved in rallying. There was a two wheel drive rally car which was basically the same shape as the little Monte Carlo sports car, but this was a real beast and it won the World Rally Championship. We took one to various promotions. Life was starting to be fun again.

I had a couple of important relationships during the period. One was with a married woman, which is not something I'm terribly proud of. Possibly her husband should have paid more attention to her, in which case I might never have met her. Nonetheless, I was a bad lad and I know it, although I still value her friendship. The more serious relationship, in the sense of long term potential, was with a lovely and single lady from Glasgow. Angela was the love of my life. I guess everyone has one. The relationship got off to a strange start.

Angela was the receptionist at the hotel I stayed at on a trip to Glasgow, where we were putting on a fashion show at a large dealership, which also had the Ferrari franchise. When I checked in I thought wow the receptionist is a bit gorgeous, but I didn't have time to flirt, I had someone I had to meet. That evening I went out for a drink with Fiat's Regional Promotions Manager for Scotland. There was a very attractive barmaid at the last bar we went to and I asked her what she was doing after closing time. She told me she was going to a party and invited me to join her. Having said goodbye to Martin I went back and met her.

She was casually dressed in jeans and carried a tiny handbag. We went to a private house in a Glasgow suburb, where there was indeed a party going on. As we were admitted my new friend excused herself and said she had to go upstairs and change. I assumed she must have left some clothes at the house earlier and proceeded into the living room, where I was engaged in conversation by another single guy. He turned out to be a mechanic at the Fiat Dealership where I'd be setting up the fashion show. He enquired how come I'd been invited to the party, if it was my first time in Glasgow and I didn't know anyone.

In fact I'd only been in town a few hours. I explained how I'd met this girl and that she was upstairs changing. At that moment the living room door opened and in walked Heather. There was a moment of silence as everyone turned to look. "Is that her?" my mechanic friend whispered, "er yes" I replied. "Bloody hell" he said "I've lived in Glasgow all my life and I've never seen a bird like that". It transpired that the dress, if it's fair to call it that, had been in her handbag all the time. There was nothing to it and what a body. Later I took her back to the hotel. I still sort of thought of myself as a playboy parachute instructor, and I was intent on playing the field and taking whatever opportunities came along. A bird in the hand then. I still had designs on the hotel receptionist and I figured taking Heather back to the hotel would blow any chance there clean away, but I couldn't resist.

Heather's existing commitments, and mine, meant I wouldn't be able to see her again on that trip anyway. What the hell, she could only say no. I asked the hotel receptionist if she'd like to come to the fashion show. I was surprised, but not counting chickens when she said yes. She told me later, she'd intended to put me in my place, after seeing me bring that other girl back to the hotel, but we got along really well. She was beautiful. There's a really corny song, which I hate, and therefore it always comes to mind when I think of Angela. The line goes, "if the angels ask me to recall the thrill of them all, I will tell them I remember you". It's true. I was no gentleman in those days and in fact I'm far more responsible, as you'd hope, now I approach double the age I was then. There's no getting away from it though if there's one girl I'll never forget it's Angela. She was a virgin when I met her and we dated for some time before that changed.

I took every job I could get, worked every weekend and bank holiday I possibly could, in order to build a bank of time off I could spend in Glasgow. Angela worked every shift she could get at the hotel and banked her time off too. If I had a promotion to do anywhere in Scotland she'd take time off. We met in London, Birmingham, Andover, anywhere and everywhere we could. We took holidays together, including a trip to Rhiconich of course.

We went there in my Austin Healey Sprite. There was no compulsory seatbelt law then, or if there was Angela ignored it, often sitting with her back to the dashboard legs crossed, or one foot straying to my lap. We were passionate, young, optimistic. I fervently believed we had a relationship that would last forever. I mean forever too. I felt that if there is a hereafter we would find one another. We telephoned all the time. I took risks, taking her on jobs, Fiat's most senior manager for the North of England and Scotland at the time turned a blind eye. He was a lovely man, very professional but human too. I liked him obviously. I think he liked both of us, and so long as the job got done, which it always did, seeing Angela's face in the background didn't bother him.

Angela and I talked about getting married. At first she said yes. Then we talked about where we'd live and how we'd live. I still had a burning ambition to be a racing driver. One of the most beguiling things about Angela was that despite being the most beautiful girl in the world at that moment, she couldn't see it. She was modest, kind, sweet, innocent yet sexy, and a home bird. She simply wouldn't leave her family and friends to live in England. I love Scotland, but I didn't think I could launch my racing career there. I know, Jim Clark and Jackie Stewart and all that, but nearly all the circuits were in England. I said to her "just a few years, just while we see if I can make it, then we can live anywhere you like, I love Scotland, I'd love to live here, but I have to do this first". She wasn't having any of it. I couldn't believe she'd hold out. I felt she loved me and that she'd come round to my way of thinking, after all it really wouldn't be forever. I felt so strongly that we were inseparable that it just had to work out. However, back in Glasgow Angela had another fan. He was local, with no ambition to move away and he was persistent. No matter what hours I worked I couldn't be in Glasgow all the time.

By now I'd purchased my first racing car. Angela couldn't get to my first race, but she got to the second one. She didn't like it, or she didn't like the way I was when I was racing. I was so focussed on getting everything ready, qualifying, what were my times, checking everything on the car between qualifying and the race. It wasn't fun or glamorous for her, she wasn't into it, and I wasn't even paying her any attention. We were pulling apart.

I got in touch with an advertising poster firm and had a forty eight sheet, one off poster made asking her again to marry me. It went up in a street near her home. How extravagantly romantic can you get? For a while, I thought, from telephone conversations we had, that she was going to say yes after all. Then the media got involved, who was Angela the local press and radio wanted to know. Someone gave the game away. A photographer came to see me, and took, frankly, the worst picture I've ever seen of myself. I didn't see it though until it was published in the paper, it was enough to put anyone off. I'd like to wring his neck.

Whatever the picture had been like however, the last thing Angela wanted was fame or notoriety. No matter how fleeting or localised. In the end it was the final nail in the coffin, and the best thing that had ever happened to me came to an end. Of course I didn't deserve her, and ultimately I went back to playing the field, although there was a long period of grieving I would say, and a sense of regret that lasts to this day. However, I wouldn't have had my car racing career, my motorcycle racing career and I wouldn't now be living on a yacht sailing about the world and writing this book, if I'd married Angela. And, as they say, life goes on, it certainly has.

My life at Westex Fiat Promotions created some other adventures too. Living in hotels was a whole new way of life. No cooking, no washing up, no making beds. Downsides are the disruption to your social life, never being in one place long enough to really get to know people, missing your old friends. On the whole I think the advantages outweighed the disadvantages, provided one didn't do it for too long. I really got to know my way about the UK and discovered lots of interesting places, I'd never have visited. I was in two hotels which caught fire. Fortunately no one was injured in either and some of the events were comical.

The first time I heard a fire alarm I was in the Station Hotel at Ayr. It was, and I hope still is a big, old, grand hotel from the heyday of the railways, lots of wood and brass, old fashioned lifts, high ceilings. I'd booked an early morning call. It came. I groaned and really didn't want to get up. Snow had been forecast and at best it was going to be cold. I was telling myself I had work to do and I'd better shift when the phone started ringing again. I picked it up, but the ringing went on.

I was less than half awake when I realised it wasn't the phone it was the fire alarm.

It's always a false alarm isn't it? I got out of bed, rubbing my eyes and yawning, as I strolled across the very large room to the door. I opened it and stuck my head out into a long corridor. I looked left and right, in a Wimbledon grandstand kind of a way, but all I saw were other heads doing the same. Tortoise like I pulled my head back into the room and turned around. Through the thick drapes I thought I could make out something flashing. I stuck my head round the curtain. Yes, there was no mistaking the approaching fire engine. Sod it, it's not a false alarm. I was dressed, bounded down the stairs and was outside in the darkness and snow in double time, but something was missing. Flames, yes that was it, there were no flames, or smoke. There was in fact a fire, just a teeny weeny one in the kitchen, so that was alright then.

The next hotel fire was also in Scotland, somewhere in Dumfriesshire, on the way to the Larne ferry. About two a.m. the phone rang. I must have taken some while to wake up, for as I reached for it, it stopped. Who the hell is ringing me at this time I thought, not unnaturally. I needed to pee now, so I went to the bathroom. I was just getting that aah feeling of relief when the damn phone started again. It can be difficult to stop, with a full bladder in full flow, but I wasn't going to let the bastard get away with it again. I put the brakes on, hurried back to the bedside and grabbed the phone. "Yes". "Is that Mr Snook?". "Yes" "This is the hotel reception, I'm afraid the hotel is on fire, will you please evacuate". "Why hasn't the fire alarm gone off then" I retorted, "what kind of a system is it phoning people individually?" "Well sir the fire's limited to your wing and there are only a few guests in your wing, whilst the other wing is full, so we thought it best to just phone the few people affected". "OK" I said "I'm coming". I still found it hard to take seriously, hadn't I been in a situation like this at Ayr? It seemed unreal somehow and I needed to finish that pee, which I did and then got dressed. By the time I opened the door there was smoke coming up through the floorboards in the corridor. Bugger. I legged it, but it was soon put out, thankfully.

Northern Ireland was a revelation. I'd lost a wonderful friend from the parachute club there and consequently I wasn't particularly keen to go, but I wasn't going to be put off either. My friend had been a physical training instructor in the army. He was based at the Royal Military Academy at Sandhurst. Not a dangerous posting. When he was at the club and the weather didn't allow for jumping, we'd run around the racing circuit together. He was offered a promotion, but it meant a posting to Germany. He took it. He was only in Germany about two weeks, I think, when his unit was re-posted to Ireland. He'd hardly been in Ireland two minutes and he was dead. He stopped his Landrover to help someone injured in a road traffic accident I'm told. I don't know if it was a genuine accident or a put up job, but when he got out of the vehicle to help, he was shot.

I don't know which period is considered to be the height of the troubles, but I went several times in the eighties. It was a strange thing, for me, seeing armed troops and convoys on the roads. Having an English accent and being alone it would have been very easy to become paranoid. I avoided that pitfall, if that's what it was, with the attitude most of us have to flying accidents, that is the voice in the back of the head that says, it'll never happen to me.

Different hotels had different levels of security. From none at all, to one hotel in Belfast, which had previously been bombed and now had a perimeter fence, with a hut set into it, where your luggage was searched before you crossed several yards of open ground to the hotel doors. That night, my first and only night in that particular hotel, I went to the hotel bar for a drink. Or was I looking for an unattached lady? Whatever, I sat alone at the bar and ordered. My accent, very English. A couple of guys approached me. It turned out they were 'loyalists,' that is nominally protestant. There was a bit of a do going on in one of the hotel function rooms. I don't know if it was a wedding reception or what, but it was a catholic bit of a do. These guys had some more friends with them and they were itching to have a fight with the catholics, but they didn't want to be seen to start it. So why didn't I gatecrash the do, they suggested, and as soon as I opened my mouth there'd be trouble, "but don't worry we'll be good and ready to come and rescue you and sort them buggers out".

If I told them what I really thought, they'd be wanting to sort me out. "Great idea" I said, "I'm just going to take a leak while you get ready and I'll see you in a mo". Back to my room it was, door locked and there I stayed until checkout.

At another hotel, way out in the countryside they had sliding glass doors, operated by a button behind reception. I've no idea if it was armoured glass, but anyway, they could let you in, or not, depending on whether they liked the look of what they saw, or not. So some sort of security anyway. I checked in and enquired at what time breakfast would be available. "Seven thirty" I was told and I booked a morning call for seven. In the morning, by the time I'd washed, shaved, dressed and got downstairs it was about seven thirty five. No problem, I marched into the dining room, pushed open the door, there was a step down into the room and as I stepped down the door closed behind me, and it was pitch black, no lights, heavy curtains and having come from a brightly lit area, you couldn't see your hand in front of your face. I turned around, put my foot on the step and felt for the door handle. I found it, and opened the door just as the first waiter, coming on duty pushed from the other side. He literally fell into the room and screamed. For some reason he thought his end had come.

I opened the door again, and this time held it open, with the light coming in from outside I found the light switch and turned it on. The waiter seemed to have regained his composure somewhat, so in case I'd been misinformed I asked him what time breakfast started. "Seven thirty sir" he said. It must have been approaching seven forty by now, I pointedly looked at my watch. "Ah but I'll get you something now sir if you like", he said.

I did some fun events in Ireland, but aspects of it were disturbing. One of my colleagues noticed some holes in the signage of either some shops or the Fiat dealership. I'm not sure which, when he enquired about their origin he was told they were bullet holes from an automatic weapon, but the youngster holding it hadn't been accustomed to the recoil, so instead of shooting down into the street, at the soldiers, he'd ended in shooting up the signage along the top. Of course stories like that could have grown with the telling, but I do hope they find a permanent peace in Ireland and indeed everywhere.

My immediate boss Paul was planning to leave Westex, he didn't see eye to eye with the directors there and although Fiat were clearly happy with the job we were doing, at the shop floor level so to speak, there was some uncertainty as to how it would all pan out. Paul wanted Dave, one of the other promotions operators, and myself to become partners with him in a new venture. I decided to hedge my bets. For one thing I felt there could be legal action if Paul poached his employer's client and I didn't want to be involved. However, I didn't really want to give the job up either, so I told Paul that if he got the new business going I would invest in it and come to work in it, but in the meantime I was leaving.

I easily got a job as a salesman at my local Fiat dealership in Andover. They also had the Mercedes franchise which made it more interesting. For a while I got to spend increased time with my friends at home too. I had by now purchased my first racing car. For my first race I was still employed at Westex, but with the car being prepared near Andover, and kept in a lock up in the town, there were several advantages to being based at home. The major disadvantage was that I wouldn't be travelling to Scotland on business and I would have less time off. I still believed Angela would want to be with me and would move south. It was at this time that I had my advertising poster made and I was in the dealership when the newspaper photographer found me. Angela did visit me in Andover. It was the last time we were together as a couple. I felt it in my heart when she got on the train, but in my head I still believed in us. Or was it the other way around? It was an emotional time.

There is one quite amusing anecdote from those few months that I sold cars. In all the years that I've jumped out of aeroplanes, raced cars, raced motorcycles, sailed, skied, snowboarded, rode horses I never once broke a bone. Some cuts and some very horrible bruises, but no broken bones. On one occasion about twenty percent of my body was black from a motorcycle racing accident, I've been knocked out and concussed, but still, never a broken bone. However, we're now up to 1985 and while I was working as a car salesman in Andover we had the amazing Live Aid concert. I imagine that like Kennedy's assassination and other major events, most of us can remember where we were that day and what we did.

I'd made good friends with a lady called Rachel who worked at one of the other garages in the group. She was not my girlfriend but I liked her a lot. She played hockey. On the evening of Live Aid there was to be a charity roller skating race around the streets of Bracknell. Teams of six were required and Rachel only had five. So of course I said yes. Only then did she tell me it was in fancy dress. Her team were to be parrots, could I make myself a parrot costume from coloured crepe paper. "Yes of course". She kept the last condition to herself until the day of the event. I spent most of the day listening to the concert in my garden and basking in the sun. In the evening I took my costume, skates and a sleeping bag off to Rachel's parent's house. Once it was clear that I wasn't going to be able to back out Rachel told me that there were several pubs en route, and that each member, of each team, had to down a pint in each pub before continuing. As I've said before, I'm not much of a drinker so this stipulation was a bit of a blow to me. I really can't drink a pint that quickly and it was a race, and I have always been a bit competitive.

As luck would have it, the heavens opened as we set off around the streets of Bracknell. We were actually roller skating on closed roads in front of an audience. The dye from the crepe paper started to run, so I had multicoloured legs, the paper itself lasted quite well, but ultimately it started to disintegrate too. At each pub I had my drink, but accidentally spilt as much as I dared, with the torrential rain and my t shirt and shorts already ruined by crepe paper dye a little beer couldn't do much harm! Nonetheless, by the last pub I was starting to get a little unsteady on my legs, which of course had wheels on the end of them instead of feet.

Within sight of the finish was a small, white gleaming dome, known to all of us as a mini roundabout. Somehow, in the melee I hit it. I remember it in slow motion, I remember seeing my feet go up and into the air, they were in front of me, that was wrong I thought, then they were above me and I was twisting in the air and then, finally, after what seemed like many seconds I was descending. Crunch, I landed right shoulder down. Even through the alcohol induced anaesthetic I knew I was in great pain.

I had to finish for Rachel's sake and the rest of the team and I did. I said to Rachel "I think I'm really in trouble here, I think I've done some damage". "Oh nonsense you'll be alright, anyway there's a party at the Hockey Club". She wouldn't take no for an answer so I went to the party and sat in a corner to nurse my injury. "Oh no you don't, you've got to dance, stop being such a wimp". Maybe she was right, maybe I was being a wimp, I did my best to dance and smile, but I couldn't wait for it to be over. Back at Rachel's parent's house I slept, or tried to in my sleeping bag on the settee. The pain didn't seem to be getting much better.

The next day, as previously arranged I drove to my mother's maisonette in Loughton for lunch with her, her second husband to be (my Uncle Eric!) and my sister. I told them the story and they took me to the local hospital where I was x-rayed and the hospital duly announced that I had broken my collar bone. I took great delight in phoning Rachel and telling her that I wasn't exaggerating, or being a wimp.

CHAPTER 11

Early Adventures With Car Racing

THE FIRST RACING car I bought was a Merlyn Mk17A. It was built about 1970 or 71 and was eligible for the British Racing and Sportscar Club pre '74 Formula Ford Championship. This must have been about 1982. Money for racing was hard earned and saved, I had to figure out how best to utilise my meagre resources. It wasn't compulsory to have training then, but I decided to have one lesson only, at the Ian Taylor Racing Driver's School at Thruxton. My instructor was James Weaver, very well known in motor racing circles, then and since. Initially we went out in my Sprite. I'd been driving it and heeling and toeing and opposite locking around Andover's many roundabouts for some years. He was impressed with my car control he said, but not with my lines and he started to give me a better understanding of lines, braking points, the importance of exit speed rather than entry speed, and how to go quicker rather than to look spectacular!

I had my first taste of an open wheeled single seater racing car in one of the school's Formula Ford 1600 Tigas and I got to have a drive in a Sports 2000. This is like a mini Le Mans car, open top, with slick tyres and a two litre racing engine. It was fabulous to drive and had so much more grip than the Formula Ford. Single seaters were my dream though and an old Formula Ford was all I could afford. I'd considered other things, particularly modified sports cars since I had the Sprite, but for the cost of adding a roll bar, fire extinguisher system, safety fuel tank and other things I could buy an old Formula Ford outright, which had all those required features and would be more the sort of thing I wanted to race.

After my one lesson it was in at the deep end. Basically I had a local specialist check the Merlyn over to make sure I'd get through scrutineering. Then the plan was to do several races with the car exactly as it came, just to get some experience.

Meantime I would have a second engine built up, and after the first half dozen races I'd put the new engine in and try to make some headway. It was a strategy of sorts, largely borne out of poverty, but it would get me to the grid after all these years, and that was an achievement in itself.

My first race was at Castle Combe in Wiltshire. My colleague and good friend David O'Brien, from Westex came to help and so did Paul, my boss at Westex. I was also supported by some friends from the parachute club, who I've already mentioned these were Mike and Paddy Parry and their two gorgeous little girls Francesca and Zoe. One thing I didn't say about Mike was, that amongst other things he was one of the GPs covering the Grace and Favour apartments at Hampton Court Palace. He said something to me once which has remained with me ever since. He told me that he's had to watch many elderly people pass away and that almost all of them had unfulfilled ambitions, yet they were leaving plenty of money behind. Money which would have enabled them to fulfil those ambitions in many cases, if they'd been prepared to part with it a little earlier in life, instead of keeping it back for security.

I'd had strong ideas about how I wanted to lead my life right back in school. However, there are times when the idea of a bit of financial security seems very appealing. It's a conundrum I weigh in my mind very often indeed. At the moment though I'm still taking risks and remembering Mike's comments about unnecessary regrets.

Scrutineering is the first major task to get through when you arrive as a competitor at a race circuit to race. It often starts quite early, perhaps seven or eight a.m. depending on the time of year. First is the formality of signing on, showing your licence and so on. Then you wheel your car to the scrutineering bay, where suitably qualified officials check it over. Primarily for safety, but also for obvious infringements of the rules. At club level, the stripping of engines and so on would only be done in the event of a protest, or possibly at the end of the season. There is often a queue for scrutineering and should they wish you to change something you could end up queuing again. It can be nerve wracking, because you have to pass scrutineering before you can go out on the circuit, and each race has a specified time for practice laps, and the practice times provide qualifying or grid positions. Miss practice, no race.

Fortunately and as a result of taking great care, we never failed scrutineering. Then would come the practice laps, fifteen or twenty minutes to familiarise yourself with the circuit if it was new to you, and to familiarise yourself with the conditions at that time, so that you can, by the end of the session, set a time which will hopefully put you as far up the grid as possible. Drivers with a proper budget will go testing, ahead of racing, at circuits where they plan to race during the season. At these test sessions drivers can experiment with different suspension set ups and different gear ratios. They can get to know the circuit and make notes for future reference, they can scrub in tyres, bed in new engines, there are many benefits to a proper programme of testing.

In Formula Ford everyone has to use the same engine and the same 'control' tyres. Even so having a bigger budget than your competitors helps. Properly equipped teams would have heavily worn, almost slick tyres for dry days and newish tyres, just scrubbed in, but with plenty of tread, for wet days. As well as all the right gear ratios for all the circuits, they may well have different springs and roll bars for different circuits, or for different weather conditions. Two engines, built identically, so that measure them as you may you cannot see a difference, will still have different characteristics, one may have better top end power or rev just a little harder, another may have more low down grunt. I've been told that the top works teams would actually select different engines from their collection, to suit the needs of the particular circuit. And this is not Formula One were talking about here.

Even in pre '74 Formula Ford some people took it very seriously indeed, and frankly I'd have done everything I could do, to win within the rules, if I'd had the money to do it. My little team rolled up with the Merlyn on an open trailer, a jerry can of petrol, a can of engine oil, some spare tyres for punctures, a spare nosecone (the most vulnerable bit of bodywork) and some tools. I planned to learn the circuits by racing at them. I budgeted for one test session only, to accomplish the vital task of running in my new engine after the first six races. I chose my gear ratios from books. Initially I had only a single layer Nomex (fire resistant) suit and some Nomex underwear, gloves and boots. I had a legal, but not top of the range helmet. The costs of getting involved in car racing are considerable. I think I did it about as cheaply as is possible. You need club memberships, licence fee, medical, clothing and crash helmet, the car itself, spares, transportation, fuel, entry fees. At the event you have to feed yourself and your helpers, it goes on and on. Even if you pay for a drive with a team, all these costs are built in, plus they want to make a profit, so it's no less expensive.

The first time I drove around Castle Combe circuit, ever, was in qualifying for my first race. Unsurprisingly I qualified on the back row of the grid. However, I'd been sensible, started slow and was getting quicker with every lap, I felt I could possibly finish better than last and that was my aim, given the circumstances. If you've never raced you may have the idea that the bravest wins and that it's something to do with who has the bottle to push down furthest on the loud pedal, but it's not like that. Everyone is absolutely flat out on the straights, pedal to the metal as they say, and to some extent how quick your car is will play a part. However, the performance differences are minimised in Formula Ford, as far as you can go; apart from putting everyone in identical cars all prepared to the same standard by the same organisation. That happens these days in some events and I think it is a wonderful way to find talent.

Where the talent comes in, is largely in the corners. There are some very high speed bends or kinks where it's touch and go whether you can get through flat, as the jargon goes. That is without, lifting off or braking at all. These require a certain amount of bravery, or confidence anyway, and a car that is set up well enough to stay on the tarmac ribbon when you do. Most corners require some braking, some down shifting through the gearbox, and then accelerating through. Exit speed from a corner, or from every corner is the key to a quick lap. Corners are generally followed by straights. If there are two corners in quick succession it may pay to compromise the first, if it helps you to get out of the second one, and on to the straight following it, at a higher speed. The reason for this is fairly simple logic, the cars accelerate at the same rate pretty much, so if I leave a corner 5mph faster than the car following me then I will remain 5 mph faster right along the following straight, or until both cars are going as fast as their potential allows. Few straights are long enough to allow that to happen, so in the real world if I exit the corner faster than my competitor I'll be faster than him all down the straight, be it stretching my lead or hauling him in.

Usually, the best way to get out of a corner quickly is to go wide on the entry and get your braking over fairly early, so you're set up to get on the gas early, coming out with more speed and with the engine on the cam, that is pulling hard within its power band. If you are under threat from someone close behind, then going wide on the approach to the corner and braking early, leaves the door open for the other guy to nip up the inside block the apex and overtake, so you have to drive defensively, brake later and not leave him space. This makes you slower and it's the reason why two cars dicing with each other will often let the leader get away if he's on his own, or why they may get caught by someone behind who's not involved in a tussle at that moment.

Understanding the theory and putting it into practice are two different things. Practice is of course the key, if you go and test at a circuit you can experiment with different lines and braking points. You can try different compromises, and see which has the greatest effect on the overall lap time.

To my way of thinking, there are two phases to learning a circuit you've never been to before. The first phase consists of pretty much just learning where it goes. Is the next corner a left or a right, does it have a blind crest, what gear will I take it in, roughly where is the line and the braking point. In other words you've memorised enough that you have a certain mental picture of the corner, long before you get there, no doubts at all. You know whether it starts looking tight but actually opens out, or perhaps looks wide open but tightens up as you get into it, basic stuff. This may sound obvious and if you take the short circuit at Brands it doesn't take long to memorise that much. At a more twisty, complex circuit like Cadwell Park it will take longer and circuits with several corners that look similar when you're just inches from the ground at 120mph can catch you out too!

Having completed phase one, then you can start to experiment and push, you can try braking a bit later to see what you can get away with under pressure, you can start putting the power on earlier and see if you can stay on, or whether you run out of road. Usually sliding around a corner scrubs off speed and is wasteful, but sometimes, just sometimes it may be a better way to control your speed if it means you keep the engine in the power band. Non racers may think that pounding around the same bit of tarmac, going over the same corners again and again is crazy, but what circuit racers are seeking is the perfect lap and it is a rewarding challenge. To learn the short circuit at Brands at level one is easy, to get the most out of it takes a lot longer. In fact I don't think I've ever achieved anything like the perfect lap there, in a car, or on a motorcycle and I've driven and ridden more laps there than anywhere else.

The major difficulty with my strategy, which was to learn the circuits by racing on them, was that qualifying and racing are short, maybe fifteen laps of qualifying if you're lucky and a ten lap race. Further, most of the learning is restricted to qualifying, where people want to spread out and have clear laps in order to get a good grid position; they don't want their times compromised by dicing with one another. In the heat of battle, during racing, you don't start experimenting you basically go as fast as you can with the knowledge you have and drive defensively when necessary. Occasionally you may be far enough ahead of whoever is behind you to experiment a little, or you could be last! The point is, that unless you've got space and time to think, you're not going to learn a great deal about the circuit. Racecraft comes from racing, but understanding a circuit is best achieved through testing. Go testing for a day and you could get in a hundred or more laps, then you can really try different things, and time them too, because what feels fast doesn't always turn out to be, but the stop watch rarely lies.

On the occasion of my first race at Castle Combe I just about completed phase one of learning the circuit during qualifying. Then I had to go and race. A Formula Ford of the time would accelerate to a hundred miles an hour, I was told, there's no speedometer, in under nine seconds. Not nought to sixty, nought to one hundred. The first time you experience this kind of performance, in a car that is light and skittish, with narrow tyres it feels exhilarating. When twenty to thirty of you are on the grid just a few feet apart and you're all accelerating at that rate, with the bottleneck of the first corner just ahead it is a real thrill.

Later, when you're more accustomed to the performance you'll drop the clutch and accelerate just as hard, but you'll be gripping the steering wheel tightly, whilst mentally saying to yourself come on, come on, faster, get those revs up, I want to change up. Like most things when you get used to it, it seems very different. Nonetheless, a mass of open wheel racing cars hurtling into that first corner is always going to be a great adrenalin pumping thrill. I stress open wheelers, because with open wheelers it's possible to touch wheels, or interlock them in a way that's impossible with sports cars or saloon cars. The consequences of which can involve flight.

At Castle Combe there's a long run from the starting grid to the first corner at Quarry. Long enough to reach one hundred and twenty miles per hour, but on lap one all of you will still be in very close company. Further, there is a blind crest, well blind in a low slung single seater anyway, just before the braking point. As you crest the rise you want to brake for the corner, but the car goes very light before settling back down. It's tricky, but wonderful too. When the lights went green I got away well, not too much wheel-spin and from the back row I found I had two cars behind me. I was determined to keep them there, that would be a fantastic result for me, I didn't know how many miles my engine had done, I was on second hand tyres, I'd never raced, nor even driven the circuit before qualifying. For a couple of laps I did hold that position, but a little further round from Quarry is one of those kinks, which can be taken flat out. Given a perfect line and a perfect set up, with the car working well. I was lifting, I admit it, but with each passing lap I was trying to lift off less, or not at all, until I spun off into the field on the infield. I didn't hit anything, or do any substantial damage. I was able to rejoin the circuit and finish, in last place though.

My friends all rallied around and congratulated me for finishing and for making a race of it. They clearly enjoyed it, especially while I was doing ok so to speak. Hell, so did I. It was a lot of years since I first stood on the bank at Crystal Palace, it was a long time since I played truant to go to the racing car show, and finally I'd been in a motor race, a public one, at a real circuit, in a real single seater, people had paid to watch and it had been exciting, very exciting, and the car was still in one piece, so there'd be another. It felt like that too, it felt like I was just going to live race to race, for racing. If I had a big accident I may not be able to afford to rebuild the car, it could mean a year off, two while I saved up again. I felt good. One of Paddy's little girls gave me a Mars bar as a prize. I grinned for a week.

My Merlyn Mk17A after my first race at Castle Combe. Seated in the car is Zoe and stood beside me is her elder sister Francesca. The girls are daughters of a lady I trained to parachute and they would later become my bridesmaids.

I was never going to be a winner doing it like this, but I could get out there and have fun. I loved that Merlyn. It had character and in fact they're quite collectible now. Being pre '74 it looked like the sort of racing cars I'd lusted after as an adolescent. I polished it, I scoured the magazines for second hand parts, spare bodywork and suspension, all the vulnerable bits, and I did those first six races without disgracing myself, but always towards the back. With hindsight I may have learned more by going testing, but you just never know what is around the corner so to speak. My biggest investment that year was in a second hand engine, which I had rebuilt by the best known engine builder around at that time. The local specialist fitted it and I booked a test day at Silverstone, primarily to bed the new engine in, but also to learn a new circuit.

I towed the Merlyn to the circuit, with the Sprite. I was on my own, none of my friends could make it, Angela had by now left me for the other guy. It was wet. Didn't matter to me though, I wasn't going to take any chances, just learn the circuit in a basic sense and pound around gradually increasing the revs until the engine was at its best. I met some other racing people there, and it was quite sociable, none of the pressure of a race day. I pounded round all day, running the engine in and increasing the revs. It felt good and strong. I don't know if I was kidding myself because of the money I'd spent, but I told myself it was faster than the old engine. So like an idiot, at the very end of the day I decided to just do one more lap, just one fairly quick one. There's one of those fast kinks there again, not so unlike the one that caught me out in my first race at Castle Combe, a corner poetically named Maggots. Yes, I came off at speed, but this time I hit the barrier hard with one back corner, which got wiped off, and the gearbox? Broken casing. Engine? stopped instantly, probably shocked. Chassis? Twisted, and oh yes, I was unconscious.

At major motor races the television cameras sometimes show you the medical facilities, interview the chief medical officer, that sort of thing. At club level races, when I raced, the facilities were somewhat less. I'm not knocking, or complaining, there were always doctors, marshals, St John's Ambulance and they did a marvellous job, but on a different scale. I don't know what it's like these days at the grass roots level, or if there even is a grass roots level for anyone other than the mega rich, now that short term money seems to be the main concern of the circuit owners. This however, was not a public race meeting, this was a test day. The car came to rest in the middle of the tarmac. Those pretty colours you get when oil spreads out on water were spreading rainbow like across the wet tarmac. Being unconscious I was unaware. A marshal came across and shook my shoulder. I was coming round now and all I cared about was the state of my precious racing car, bones and bruises heal, racing cars take years of hard work to save for.

"You're leaking fuel mate". What he meant was get the hell out of there, it may be raining but everything's still hot and there's explosive petrol vapour around. Being concussed I wasn't thinking too clearly. "It's alright" I said "I won't need it now". What happened next is a bit of a blur. I did get out of the car and a recovery truck with a crane turned up. They asked me where I was in the pits and I was just about compos mentis enough to tell them. They took the wreckage back and craned it on to the trailer, where some of the people I'd met during the day expressed their sympathy, "oh well, that's racing" and helped me strap the wreck on. I was still well concussed. It was about this time that I realised that my left arm wasn't working. It wasn't broken, just wouldn't respond to commands from my brain. My brain didn't care though, it was in mourning for the Merlyn and anyway it had taken one hell of a bump.

With the use of one arm only I drove back to Andover towing what was left of my dream. I only had the use of my right hand, so I took it off the steering wheel and reached across to change gear. It was like a waking dream, it wasn't irresponsibility on my part. The accident happened towards the end of the test day. I don't know if there were any medical facilities. I think someone may have said "are you alright mate", to which I would have said "yes", partly because I was more concerned for my car, partly because I was concussed, and partly, because it's a bit like when someone says "how are you?" It's sort of a convention, or human nature to say "fine thanks". There was simply nothing in place to stop me, or check me out, so I drove home in a concussed daze.

I opened the lock up and somehow reversed the trailer in and unhitched it. Then I drove back to my house in The Crescent and knocked on the door. I still had my racing overalls on and I couldn't be bothered looking for my door keys, when I had a lodger.

My lodger was a beautiful, and very intelligent, woman. She worked for a major electronics company, she'd been head hunted to another major electronics company and had sold up and moved away from Andover. The company she left in

Andover missed her so much they'd made her an offer she couldn't refuse, so she'd come back and was living with me until she found the right place to buy. She was an incredible woman, who wrote instruction manuals and fault finding guides and that sort of thing for the electronic gizmos on nuclear submarines. I worshipped her from afar.

Well at that moment I was very close to her, but she had two boyfriends already she told me. One was a fellow scientist, who satisfied her intellectually, with whom she could enjoy cultural activities and conversation on her own level, but who bluntly wasn't too hot in the sack. The other was a soldier, fit and muscled and red hot in bed, but, well, not on her intellectual plane. I've lost touch with her now, but I felt a bit sorry for her dilemma, although she seemed happy enough. Perhaps I should have suggested she look for someone more in the middle, you know, like me, me, me. I never did though, I don't think she fancied me, I guess you can sense these things, but she was a lovely friend to have.

Luckily she answered the door, took one look at me and said "are you alright?" Honesty seemed like the best policy at this stage, "No I don't think I am, I've had a bit of an accident". She took me straight to hospital and explained what had happened. They did some tests and kept me in overnight for observation. At some stage my left arm just came back to life, and sometime the next day they let me go home, told me to take it easy and come back if I had any problems. So that was that.

When I could face it I went to the lock up and examined the wreckage. I spoke to the company who had done the basic set up on the car. It looked as though it might cost as much to repair as it had to buy. If I'd known then what they were going to be worth I might have hung on to it, but if it would cost as much to repair it as to buy another, then anything I could sell it for was a start towards saving for a new car. Also, in my cold, damp, lock up things would only deteriorate further. If I sold it to someone who wanted to rebuild it then the car would be saved for posterity, there were few enough Merlyn Mk 17A's around and I wanted it to survive. I sold it to a fellow from the west country who loved Merlyns and promised to restore it. I had £900 as a start towards saving for the next car. It was a knock back, but I wasn't giving up on the dream.

I knew also that I needed to be better organised. I needed to find someone who could make repairs when necessary, at a reasonable cost. Accidents being inevitable, once you start to explore the edge of the envelope. By the time I was ready to buy my second racing car my career had moved on somewhat, and I was actually working for a genuine above the line advertising agency on a major account, but we'll come back to the advertising business later. I was living in Andover and commuting by car to the agency, which was then based in Richmond, pretty much to the west of London and not too difficult a commute. Living not far from me was an old acquaintance from my parachute club days.

John Schofield was an interesting character. This is not the same John Schofield that was supposed to meet me in Madagascar, it's just coincidence, but he is the one who used to share a house with Bob. Like me John had wanted to race cars as a youngster. He'd got as far, apparently, as doing one Formula Three race and had met Colin Chapman of Lotus, possibly it was Chapman who gave him the one race, I'm not sure. When I met John he was running crop spraying aircraft from Thruxton airfield. I was told he'd won an award from the Times Newspaper, as Britain's most promising young businessman, or something along those lines. It must have been the kiss of death, because he got into the crop spraying business just as everyone started turning green, organic and anti chemical. I was even told that sometime in his youth John had trained as a novice monk, or priest. I've always wondered if that was a wind up, but I believe there's a grain of truth in it! I do know he was in the Merchant Navy for a while and worked with lumber jacks in Canada when his ship was awaiting repairs there. Another wonderful, whacky character however, that crossed my path through life as a result of the parachute club years. He was best man at my first wedding.

What was particularly interesting about John at that moment, for me, was that he was running a guy called Ringo Hine in Formula Ford. That is to say, in the main Formula Ford Championships and the Formula Ford Festival, at national level.

Ringo finished as high as sixth in the Festival, which was really a Formula Ford World Championship at Brands Hatch; competitors attended literally from all over the world and the Festival helped launch several famous F1 drivers. I particularly remember Johnny Herbert winning it, but I also remember watching Eddie Irvine and David Coulthard there. Ringo came from a pretty well off family, and clearly had a decent budget, but he was getting results in a car which wasn't considered to be the best at that time. He'd opted for a new Reynard, but that year the Van Dieman turned out to be the chassis to have. John Schofield had helped Ringo modify the Reynard to make it work. It didn't look as pretty, but it certainly handled better. John agreed to help me and he charged me a very reasonable rate. He also came to most, if not all of my races, which was wonderful. That year, after buying my second Formula Ford I also raised about two thousand pounds, in my first ever sponsorship arrangement. It was not a fortune, but it sure helped.

The second car was a Royale RP21. This was slightly newer than the Merlyn had been. It was eligible for the British Automobile Racing Club '74 to '78 Championship. There was also a new championship called Formula E. Formula E was for Formula Fords with outboard suspension. These championships kept a lot of older Formula Fords racing as the technology marched on. The more modern Formula Fords were typified by inboard suspension, where the shock absorbers are removed from the airflow around the car. Outboard suspension cars had more drag and weren't really competitive with the latest models. For me, those two championships, and the one circuit championships, meant there would be lots of opportunities to race during the year. The one circuit championships were called Champion of Castle Combe, Champion of Brands and so on. Brands Hatch is quite a popular circuit and there were some 'monied' drivers in that championship, but although these championships were open to the latest cars, there were quite a few like minded amateurs; in Champion of Castle Combe particularly.

The Royale was advertised for sale a long way north from home, but it sounded good. John, my then girlfriend Juliet and I went up to take a look, met Brain Cooke and his wife and decided they were jolly decent people, whom I could trust. I bought the car as much for that reason as for the car itself, but it proved a good decision and I stayed in touch with Brian for quite a long while afterwards.

I actually campaigned that car for quite a long time and entered races in the four different championships mentioned above. I had some spills and occasionally hit something solid, but now I had someone who could fix things at a sensible cost. John's workshop was a former chapel or church hall in a village near Marlborough. Some American soldiers had been billeted there during World War Two and some of their graffiti still existed. It had character.

Usually Ringo's car was in there and now John had a Formula Three car in there quite often too. The F3 belonged to someone from Swindon Racing Engines I believe. The other car that was taking shape in the workshop was a Ford GT40 replica. The Ford GT40 won Le Mans four times and John Schofield had some old connection with John Wyer, the original team manager for the Ford works team. John Wyer was responsible for Fords' last two wins at Le Mans after failing to win initially and losing the contract to Carroll Shelby. John Schofield had always wanted to own a GT40, and since he couldn't afford to buy one he'd resorted to building a replica. Some purists denigrate 'kit' cars, but when they're built by really good engineers they can be very good indeed, and they allow many more people to have the experience of driving such a car than would otherwise be the case.

CHAPTER 12

The SEAT Works Team Soap Opera

AT THIS JUNCTURE I have to mention my career, since it and racing became mixed up together briefly. The advertising agency I was working for handled SEAT business, the Spanish car manufacturer, which had recently launched itself, with our help, on to the UK market. The SEAT Ibiza had an engine designed, for the company, by Porsche of Germany. Of course Porsche are sports car manufacturers with a fabulous racing pedigree. Much was made in the Ibiza advertising of the System Porsche engine. The company importing SEAT into the UK was part of the Lonrho group. My boss at the agency was, like me, a fan of racing. He'd been to several of my races and he'd met John Schofield. We weren't the only agency working on SEAT business, and their budget was not infinite, so the more projects we could get hold of the better; for our turnover and profit. We suggested to Paul Evans, the marketing manager for SEAT in the UK that competing in Group N saloon car racing would add to the credibility of the System Porsche claim and therefore to the appeal.

I wasn't totally convinced that John's little set up in a church hall in Wiltshire had the credibility we were looking for and I had another contact. Roy Baker is the brother of Derek Baker who produced the Thruxton Players plays. I'd helped Roy with some design work and print for his racing team through the good offices of other friends in the printing game, and so I knew him reasonably well. Roy Baker Racing competed in the World Sportscar Championship. A quantum leap up from Formula Ford, or even Formula Three. In fact Roy had invited me to join him and the team at Le Mans one year, but it clashed with a Formula Ford race I'd already entered and I always preferred doing rather than watching, so I didn't go. I brought Roy Baker to meet my boss Richard and ultimately our client. SEAT agreed to provide an Ibiza for testing and developing as a race car, plus an initial budget of about £10,000, just to put in a full roll cage, seam weld the body or whatever was allowed by the regulations and do a couple of test sessions, with Carlos Loss, one of Roy's sports-car drivers, and me!

The new team, when and if it got off the ground, was to be called Dealer Team SEAT. Roy did a good job of stripping out the car, having the roll cage fitted, and other modifications to make it legal to race. I don't think anything was done to the engine, but the car was lighter and stiffer for sure. We tested it at Silverstone then at Donington Park, where we invited the key managers from SEAT, and from the public relations agency to come and see it in action. I managed not to crash it! The car looked great, some of the budget at least had gone on the Dealer Team SEAT livery and we'd used some very good graphic designers, the little hatchback looked fabulous. Carlos and I were lifting one rear wheel off the ground in a couple of the corners, and the handling needed some sorting for this kind of use, but it looked dramatic. Even by my Formula Ford standards it was a little on the slow side, but I didn't care, it was a chance to race professionally, to get known.

I had by now done enough races and got enough signatures that I had an international racing licence, so I was eligible to race this thing at national level for sure. For Carlos the whole experience was a bit bemusing I think, especially after having raced down the Mulsanne straight at close to two hundred miles and hour! He said to me "I can't believe people actually race this slowly!" I just shrugged, I'd have killed for the chance to race at Le Mans. I believe Carlos is the son of a Greek shipping magnate, not Onassis, but you know, not short of a bob. Carlos wasn't really a professional racing driver he'd paid to race at that level, but I'm not knocking, I'd have done exactly the same given the chance.

SEAT provisionally agreed to fund a season of racing. We had to put a proposal together. I could feel all those years of planning, trying to get in the right place at the right time, finally paying off. OK I was too old to make it into F1, but there are professional racing drivers in a variety of Formulae and saloon car racing is very important to manufacturers. I felt I was on the brink of the big time. At this juncture our agreement with Roy Baker Racing was technically over and people in advertising are used to having to pitch for business. Richard, and I think Paul Evans of SEAT, felt we should receive pitches, if you like to call it that, from a number of teams, saying how they would handle the project and what their costs would be and so on.

All ready to test the racing SEAT Ibiza at Silverstone. At the time it looked like all my hard work, career change and planning were about to pay off and I'd get my shot at the big time.

Naturally Roy Baker Racing was in pole position to get the job, but it wasn't a done deal. I think Roy was dismayed at having to compete for the job having done the work thus far, even though he expected to win. Naturally, I wanted to make sure my position as one of the drivers wasn't threatened, by someone coming in completely from outside. I introduced John Schofield into the equation and one other, another racing contact from my years at Thruxton, in fact the same guy who helped me check over the Merlyn when I first got it, a chap called Mike Eastick. The three team managers made their pitches.

John Schofield didn't have the credibility of Roy Baker in many ways. Both these guys were my friends and so was Mike to a lesser extent. I knew that John, Roy or both of them was going to be very upset if they didn't get the job. Mike was interested I think, but not so excited by the opportunity as the other two. They both thought they had someone on the inside helping them i.e. me. In fact all three of the managers might well have thought that. Given my level of seniority, I could, in fact only put in a good word here or there, and I'd also stressed to all of them that I was impartial, that it wasn't my decision. All I wanted was that the winner would back me as a team driver. I can't remember exactly why John Schofield was chosen. Probably the main reason was that for John this was going to be a huge opportunity, one that he'd put all his effort in to, while for Roy it would be a side issue so to speak, second fiddle to World Sportscar Racing. Probably John's rates were lower too. Roy was furious and couldn't believe the job was going to someone else, someone with so little pedigree alongside his. Ironically he was probably considered to have too good a pedigree for the reason given above.

It was very tough telling Roy that the deal had gone to John. Of course Roy knew that John prepared my old Formula Ford and I'm sure he must have thought I'd stabbed him in the back. Sadly I haven't spoken to him in years. It wasn't like that though. Given that the guys with the real power wanted to look at options it made sense for me to introduce people who would support my case as a driver. They couldn't all win. Of course as sad as I was about Roy, I was happy for John. Just as this was a big opportunity for me to become known as a driver, so it was an opportunity for him to make a name as a team manager. The car was handed over to John and went to reside in the workshop at Burbage in Wiltshire. It was decided that there would be a ceremony to mark the handing over of the cheque for the racing budget, at SEAT's head office in Reading. The car would be taken there and shown to all the staff, John would be introduced by the agency and the cheque formally handed over, so that the car could be further developed and we could enter the championship.

The race car that never was, the Dealer Team SEAT Ibiza and my chance to turn pro.

The great day dawned and we all trooped off to Reading, with the car. When we got to SEAT's offices we were ushered into a side office and left to our own devices for quite a while. We could see lots of people bustling about, furtive conversations and it was obvious something strange was going on, but what? Eventually we were told. Lonrho had decided to replace the Managing Director that very morning. That very morning, the news came through. The company was momentarily paralysed, they couldn't spend any money, or enter any new agreements, Lonrho were going to put their own man in there to run things. If the ceremony had been scheduled just twenty four hours earlier we'd have had a contract in place and the cheque in our hands. As it was SEAT took possession of the car and we went away empty handed. The new

Managing Director had no interest in racing. The whole thing was shelved indefinitely. I've never come so close to pulling off the big deal as that one, twenty four hours earlier, that's all it needed, just twenty four little hours.

My only other opportunity to get in with a major manufacturer was with something called the Ford Fiesta Challenge. I don't remember now which year it was, even whether it was before or after the SEAT debacle. I do remember what happened though. I entered this competition and along with a few hundred other hopefuls I went along to a day out in the Essex countryside somewhere and we were all put through various tests, to ascertain our aptitude as racing drivers. The highlight of the day, and I think the main deciding factor, was to drive a rally prepared Fiesta around a course. It was like a mini rally cross course, but it crossed over itself, and frankly wasn't that well marked out. Still we were all given the opportunity to walk the course in the morning. First thing in the morning.

Then there was some sort of lottery I think, to decide who went first, second, third, two hundredth etc. Lucky old me was virtually last. I waited all day for my go, went as hard as I could of course, but went the wrong way round one of the loops where the track crossed itself and got disqualified. Crazy, annoying, but it was impossible to memorise it from one walk round about eight hours earlier, when it was such a confusing layout to begin with. Well it was impossible for me anyway, perhaps that was part of the test, but I'm sure it would have been a lot easier if I'd gone earlier in the day. The prize was a test in a Formula One car. What a prize!

After these two disappointments I still wasn't ready to throw in the towel. I still wanted to find a professional role for myself within racing. Some people never learn! I wrote to a whole host of major teams, including Williams, Jordan and March. The once mighty March Team was past its heyday in Formula One, but was one of several teams, the others being Penske, Lola and Reynard, to have enjoyed a run of good fortune in Indycars, the premier category in the USA, which has the Indianapolis 500 as its blue riband event. Even in this arena things were no longer looking so bright for them, but there was a new car on the drawing board.

I was seeking after a position where I would be responsible for helping to win sponsors and liaise with them. My qualifications: my love and knowledge of racing, combined with my experience in advertising and marketing, my ability to speak, present and get along with people from many different backgrounds. Mostly I got letters declining. Jordan left the door open a little for a future approach but Dave Reeves, Managing Director of March agreed to see me. In fact I saw him a couple of times and visited the factory. He even took me to the home of, and introduced me to Robin Herd, one of the founders of March, back in nineteen sixty nine or seventy, the 701, seventy being the year and one being the formula, was their first F1 car. They even gave me a book on the history of the company. It seemed they liked me, but in the event I did not secure the position. I'm not sure anyone else did either and I think my failure had more to do with their financial situation than with any flaw on my part. Had I obtained the job I would have been back on the employment market not long afterwards. What contacts I might have made in that short time I know not, where I might be as a result will be forever unanswered. March went to the wall, and sadly the great name of March, like other great names, Lotus to name but one other, is no longer a current part of the on going story of motorsport and Formula 1.

CHAPTER 13

Happiness and Pain

Not so very long after failing to go racing with SEAT or join March, my career took another turn. I was planning to marry Juliet my first wife, when a job became available at an advertising agency called Newton and Godin. The client was Fiat, right up my street, and it was a much bigger agency and a much better paid job. Juliet wanted me to take it, assuming it was offered to me, because she liked the idea of a fresh start in Tunbridge Wells. In addition Roland Long Advertising, my current employer, and the SEAT dealer agency had relocated just a little further east, making the commute a bit more of a hassle from Andover. I went for the job and was duly offered it and accepted. It was a disaster from start to finish, I'll go back to my career path in the next chapter, but suffice to say my stay at the new agency lasted only a few months and in those few months Juliet and I were preparing for our big white wedding and a honeymoon in Italy. Planning a big wedding is tough enough, but I had another problem. My mother had left home, years before, about the same time I did. Way back when I was nineteen in fact. I'd fallen in love with the parachute club. She'd fallen in love with the husband of my father's sister. That is to say her brother in law. It was all a bit close.

Dad, being a devout Christian, felt that his marriage vows held good until death and he never really accepted it. Not even when mother divorced him and married Eric. There was nothing he could do of course, the law allowed her to divorce him whether he liked it or not, once she'd been apart from him long enough. My sister and I worked hard to stay close to both our parents without taking sides. I believe Eric saw rather less of his kids as a result of the break up, and the fact that Mum retained hers so to speak may have rankled. My sister Margaret and I managed to walk the tightrope and stay on good terms with both parents, right up until the advent of my wedding.

By this time Mum had married Eric, she intended bringing him to the wedding. Not unnatural, but this wasn't just any old divorce that had happened. It had riven the family apart, because of the close nature of the relationships between the main characters so to speak. Dad had fallen out with his sister, ostensibly over Grandad's will, but I think the fact that Dad's wife had gone off with my Aunt's husband certainly didn't help their relationship. Basically my father said he would not attend the wedding if Eric was to be there. Mum stated that she wouldn't come, unless Eric could be there. My fiancée said she didn't care how I did it, but she wanted both of my parents at the wedding. This last ultimatum gave Mum the opportunity to blame Juliet for the problem, which suited her better than blaming her only son. However, I decided I had to back my wife to be. As a result, what I said to my parents was that I had never taken sides, had always loved them both and that I wanted both of them at the wedding. I didn't care how they sorted it out, but they were both grown ups and they owed it to me to sort it out, so that this once they could both be in the same place at the same time. For me.

A game of brinkmanship ensued. Mum wrote a not very nice letter to Juliet blaming her for the stand off. At the eleventh hour Mum came alone, with Eric scheduled to collect her later, but right up to about a week before the wedding I didn't know what would occur. Not only were Juliet and I planning a wedding, but that other very stressful thing, a relocation was going on. I'd made an offer on a house in Tunbridge Wells and it had been accepted. Then suddenly the seller started showing reluctance to exchange contracts, although no reason was given. I decided that I would have to sell in Andover and put my belongings in storage. That way I wouldn't lose my buyer, I could move into rented accommodation in Tunbridge Wells in order to get on with the new job and as a cash buyer I could say to the lady selling the house I wanted, either exchange as agreed or I'll take my cash elsewhere.

I duly moved into rented accommodation in Tunbridge Wells, sharing with one of my new colleagues. Most of my possessions went into storage on the mezzanine floor of John Schofield's workshop, in the old chapel at Burbage. Rather than lose the deal the seller in Tunbridge Wells finally exchanged contracts, so just a few weeks before the wedding I finally took possession of the new house. Two weeks before the wedding I still didn't know whether my parents would resolve their differences and both attend. Before I could get my possessions out of the workshop in Burbage a tramp broke into one of the out buildings and started a fire to keep warm. The fire got out of hand. Inside the workshop at the time were three racing cars, my Royale, Ringo's Reynard and the Formula Three car, the race model SEAT Ibiza had been returned to SEAT by now, thank goodness.

Tragically though, also in there was John's GT40 replica, now completed, but only a few weeks old as a finished project. They would all have had some fuel in them and there were gas welding cylinders. The chapel was completely destroyed, along with its historic graffiti. All four cars were of course completely lost. Where the two cars which had a lot of aluminium in their construction had been, there was just a shadow in the ashes more or less. The steel space frames of the Formula Fords were twisted by the intense heat, as were the huge girders that had held the building up. I'd lost not only my racing car, but all my spares, my trailer, my clothing, stop watches and crash helmet. Everything I'd built up for racing; pit signal board, jerry cans everything you can think of gone. And most of my other worldly possessions had been on the mezzanine.

Then I lost my job, with two weeks to the wedding. The job had been a disaster from start to finish, but it was my income. It was one problem too many. The fire and the loss of so many material things, the stress of the move, the stress of the wedding and the problem over parents and now no job.

I probably could have coped with any three of those things coming at once, but the four together were too much. That's really an excuse, but it's the only way I can make sense of it. I went into the garage closed the door and started the engines of the Sprite and my motorbike. The garage quickly filled with fumes. I thought it would be easy. I thought it would be just like falling asleep. It wasn't.

The smell was awful, it was choking, my eyes stung and watered. I was starting to think I couldn't stay in there much longer when Juliet hammered on the door. I came out. Considering I've not attempted suicide since, you could say it was the lowest point of my life. Of course it's not something I'm proud of, other people have been through far worse and not given in. It has taught me a lesson though and made me stronger, probably. I've handled equally tough times since, just a little better as a result. There's that old cliché, that what doesn't kill you, makes you stronger. I know now that suicide can never be right. I've had some very hard times since then, very hard, two divorces and my daughter living away from me, bereavement and more job and income worries. On the other hand I've had some wonderful experiences too, experiences which of course I'd not have had if I'd succeeded in killing myself. My wonderful daughter may not live with me, but she wouldn't be here at all if I wasn't. When I hear what people went through in Sarajevo and in other conflicts, or in terrorist attacks (indeed, what my own grandfathers endured in World War One) I'm ashamed that I gave in, with, comparatively speaking, so little reason. It is never right to take your own life, except possibly, just possibly, in the case of certain illnesses, and even then the effect on those around you must be considered.

The wedding itself went off rather well. We had the full church service, the gowns, the flowers and lots of guests, a sit down meal afterwards and then an even larger party with a buffet in the evening, during which Juliet and I set off on honeymoon. We had a professional photographer, a professional video and a wonderful old 1930's Buick wedding car with running boards. Juliet's parents paid for part of the reception. I paid for everything else.

CHAPTER 14

Racing a Van Dieman – The Final Throw

THE VAN DIEMAN company is probably the most successful builder of Formula Fords in the long and varied history of this, in my view, most interesting of all the grass roots formulae. Formula Ford has certainly lasted many years, evolved dramatically, helped many a great driver get started, and has given pleasure to millions. Johnny Herbert, Damon Hill, David Coulthard and many others made names for themselves in Formula Ford. I've always thought it sad Ford didn't do more to protect their position and let in Formula Renault, Formula this, that and the other. Thus allowing the whole arena to become diluted, talented drivers appearing in different championships when they should possibly have been racing one another. Nonetheless, if the Formula Ford story is written, Van Dieman will run through much of it, generally at the front of the pack.

After the fire destroyed my Royale and trailer, tyres and equipment and most of my furniture too I started to regroup. My household contents insurance covered the goods lost from the house as they'd been in storage pending a move. There was no insurance on the racing car, or the equipment however. It is possible to insure a racing car but as you'd imagine it's a bit pricey. I'd calculated that if the car survived six races the premiums would have been enough to buy another car. Well, racing does destroy a few cars every year, so you can understand the insurer's point of view for once! Of course I'd not anticipated the car being destroyed in anything other than a racing accident and I hadn't anticipated the loss of all my equipment at all.

I saved and saved and bought new three layer overalls, which looked much more professional, new helmet, gloves, boots, watches, tools, pit-board and of course a new racing car. The new car was a Van Dieman RF85/6. I raced the car in 1989 and 1990. The numbers which Van Dieman give their cars refer to the year. So a Van Dieman RF85 is the 1985 car, mine was called an 85/6 because it was possible to bolt the 1986 wide track front suspension to the 1985 chassis, which the previous owner had done. I tested the car at Brands Hatch, just as I bought it and did the best lap times I've ever done there. Nonetheless, I decided to hedge my bets engine wise, not knowing quite what I had in the back, or how many races it had done. I had the engine from the car rebuilt by an engine builder who was relatively new to Formula Ford at the time, and whose engines seemed to be making a name. I also bought an old engine which had been rebuilt by Swindon Racing Engines.

Once I'd replaced everything and started racing again I had two wonderful years. Van Dieman were just about the most successful of all the various Formula Ford builders down the years, and although not new, this was the closest I would come to racing a competitive, contemporary, single seater racing car. Albeit four years old! With the loss of John's workshop, the Van Dieman resided in the garage alongside my semi detached in Tunbridge Wells. I'd chosen the house with racing in mind. Very few small houses have a double garage, but this one did. One of the previous owners had extended the garage backwards to add storage for his business. The garage then was double length not width, with a drive in font. The trailer for the racing car lived on the drive, and we lived on the side of a hill so there was a drop beside the drive and anything placed at the back of the garage was pretty inaccessible. Nonetheless, I had space for everything, and I wouldn't have to collect the car from somewhere else before race day, so I had control. For major repairs I would have to take the car away to a specialist, but with several seasons experience behind me I decided to do as much as possible myself.

I placed advertisements in the press looking for someone to help me on race days. The deal was that I would provide free entry to the race and food on the day plus I would transport said helper, who would also have the fun of being in the pits and being involved. For the helper it would mean a long day and possibly helping to load up the night before, followed by an early start and a late finish unloading everything. For long distance races it meant going the day before and camping. I had several replies to my advertisements and ended up with two brilliant guys to help me.

The first of my new team members was Howard. He was a young lad, still at college and his father came with him to meet me, to see what he was getting into. Howard was bright, keen to learn, very enthusiastic and had all the energy of youth. Early starts and late finishes would not dim his enthusiasm and he had that competitive spirit, he cared how we fared, really cared.

Equally committed was Ken, somewhat older and more mature he was solid and reliable. What a combination, their assistance was priceless and their friendship added a new dimension to racing. My girlfriends had never liked me much on race days because I was a different person, totally focussed on the job in hand. Howard and Ken got it, so no problem. It's probably a boy thing! I was of course married to Juliet by now. She came less and less, then not at all.

The Van Dieman, was too new to be eligible for championships the previous cars had been entered in. Technically it was eligible for national level events, but it wasn't likely to be a winner at that level, although I did try my hand at the annual Formula Ford Festival. Primarily I raced the Van Dieman in Champion of Brands and Champion of Castle Combe events. These one circuit championships allowed competitors to really get to know a particular circuit. If you raced mainly at your local circuit, then it allowed you to cut down on travel costs and staying away expenses too. These series also gave amateurs the chance to actually win something as well. Of course there are amateurs and amateurs and I was still pretty low down the food chain in terms of budget, although I did raise another couple of thousand pounds in sponsorship.

Brands Hatch was my local circuit, so it made sense to race there, however, of all the one circuit championships the one at Brands was the best supported and the most competitive, often with enough entrants to require more than one race. Castle Combe was a long way away, but it was where it all started for me, I knew the circuit well and loved its high speed nature. Castle Combe was the only place where I ever scraped into the points and then only once, but it sure felt good! We tended to camp at Castle Combe and in good summer weather it was idyllic. My neighbour in Tunbridge Wells came to many of my races in those seasons with her daughters, and often various friends would come to Brands to support me, another advantage of racing locally.

Racing is very competitive but I met another driver by the name of Chris Nowobilski who was from Poland. We became friends and helped one another out from time to time, which also added to the enjoyment. Chris's car was one year newer than mine and he was generally just a fraction faster than me. I remember overtaking him once in qualifying but he still managed to be one place ahead of me on the grid!

Around October or November each year was the end of season Formula Ford Festival and World Cup. This event had started life at Snetterton before moving to Brands Hatch. Three days of racing with heats, quarter finals, semi finals and a grand final for the main event effectively created a Formula Ford 1600 World Champion. There were also supporting races for older Formula Fords, pre 1974 and Formula E as mentioned before, plus Formula Ford 2000, Ford engined Sports 2000 and in later years Formula First and Formula Forward. For me this was the ultimate event of the year. I'd gone as a spectator for as long as I could remember. Many times races were televised on Grandstand and I recorded them and watched them over and over again. The Van Dieman would allow me to compete in the main event!

I'd entered the Royale in the Formula E supporting race one year. Naturally I'd been well down the grid, everyone tried extra hard at the Festival and the entry list was always impressive. That year even the Formula E race was televised. From the start at Brand Hatch there's a relatively short run into the first corner, named Paddock Hill Bend. It's a right hander that sweeps away down into the bottom of a valley. It can be a little bit visually intimidating, especially in a single seater racing car where the driver is just a couple of inches above the ground, and where the visibility forward is somewhat compromised. You can get a nasty surprise if someone loses control just in front of you, but whilst I have seen cars come off on the inside, most spinners get thrown off into the gravel trap on the outside, out of the way.

I love that corner, once you know where it goes, where to turn in and so on you can really attack it. The sensation as you swoop down that hill, the exhilaration lifts the spirit in the same way skydiving did on occasions. It makes me think of the Spitfire pilot John Magee's poem when he says 'I've chased the shouting wind along, and flung my eager craft through footless halls of air'. These feelings are shattered as the car bottoms out in the valley and your bones jar as your backside all but hits the tarmac. Your right foot is pressed hard to the floor, you look in your mirrors for the opposition, can I take a wide line in and brake that tiny bit earlier to come out fast, or do I need to protect the inside and brake at the last, last, last possible moment to protect my position?

In later laps you may only have one or two other cars to worry about, but Formula Ford 1600s, with their control tyres and similar power outputs, don't get strung out too quickly. The run up to the second corner, Druids, the hairpin is crowded to say the least and especially from a completely full grid. Two gear changes down and hard on the brakes, the car on the edge of adhesion wants to snake or slide. On this occasion we were three abreast. My right hand wheels were interlocked with someone trying to get up the inside, but he had two wheels on the kerb or even the grass. Our wheels touched and suddenly I was flying. I thought the car would roll, it started to, after all it had been flung up on one side only, for all that all four wheels were up in the air. I landed in the gravel trap left side first then right. Gravel traps work on the whole though and coming down on one like that pretty much guarantees you're going to dig in and be brought up short with the breath knocked out of you.

Rounding Paddock Hill bend in my Van Dieman RF 85/6, my favourite corner and one before my nemesis. The circuit of course one of the world's best, Brands Hatch, in Kent, southern England.

I jumped out of the car and climbed over the tyre wall to watch the rest of the race from the sidelines. When I saw the video of the television coverage they showed my car in the gravel and the aftermath but they'd missed my only ever flight in a racing car. After the race the car was dragged out of the gravel and I was able to restart it. Although the suspension wasn't quite right, it was driveable, so off I went to the exit slip back to the paddock. John Schofield, Juliet, at that stage my girlfriend not my wife, and other friends were waiting for me at the first available spot. I stopped the car and looked at them. I can't remember if I said anything or just shrugged, "oh well, that's racing". Clearly I was unhurt, which was their main concern. As I pulled away, probably a little faster than I needed, I heard them all laugh, even over the noise of the engine. The car had deposited a little pile of gravel behind me in disgust.

When it came to racing the Van Dieman at the Festival my goal was just to get beyond the heats. Having been competing in Champion of Brands at least I knew the circuit. I wasn't optimistic though, there was a pretty full grid of mostly even newer cars and monied drivers. I qualified at the back of the grid. Oh well. On race day it was wet though. Some of the drivers wouldn't have experience of Brands in the wet. I felt I could do well for once. Paddock Hill Bend is different on lap one, you're not up to speed and it's crowded, but most drivers seem to take it just the same way as they do on every other lap. Round the outside for me, it was a gamble, anyone spinning off would likely come my way, but by avoiding the traffic jam on the apex I could make up places. I did too, several of them. Then I was hammering up to Druids, but I wasn't at the back of the field, I was back in the melee. I knew what I had to do and I knew I had to brake early, but in trying to watch everyone else and not lose that which I'd gained I locked my wheels and sailed off in to my old friend the Druids Hill gravel trap! That corner was starting to look like my Achilles heel. I've driven around it hundreds of times by now and ridden motorcycles around it at least as often without getting it wrong, but the exasperation of those two times, both on lap one lingers to this day. I've had better races of course.

As I mentioned before, getting into the points at Castle Combe was pretty fantastic for our little team, without even a caravan, or a closed trailer, our poverty was palpable! On that occasion I was in the last points scoring position for much of the race, when an incident brought out waved yellow flags. Yellow flags are a caution, often there are marshals working to get someone out of a car or some such thing at the side of the circuit. Overtaking is banned. Waved yellows are more serious, maybe a car is in a dangerous position, with marshals on the track even, not only is overtaking forbidden, but drivers should back off, in order to avoid exacerbating the situation with another accident, or worse hitting a marshal.

I backed off and was promptly overtaken. I'm sure the driver concerned hadn't seen the yellows, people simply don't do it. I got hauled over the coals once for not backing off quickly enough in a motorcycle race when the yellows came out. In fact I was leading that race and several spectators assured me that when the yellows initially came out they were behind me. They're not necessarily put out all around the circuit. So that was, I believe, a genuine mistake by the officials and a pretty rare one. Everyone involved in racing at club level is there for the love of it and I've never met a Clerk of the Course I didn't have time for.

When the green flag was shown and we were racing again I tried as hard as I could to get that position back. It didn't happen and the guy in front, if he hadn't seen the yellows immediately, in the red mist of racing, must of thought he'd overtaken me before they were shown. I was disappointed but I didn't want to raise a protest it would seem like sour grapes and this wasn't Formula 1, or even Formula 3. Shortly after the race I was summoned to see the Clerk of the Course, Howard Strawford. One of the best, great character and strict, would have made a great parachute instructor I think. The other driver was already there, one of the marshals must have reported an overtaking incident under yellows. Under the circumstances I told the truth, saw the other guy's face fall and knew how he felt, but not protesting is quite different from contradicting the marshal's report. Naturally that reinstated my previous position in the official results.

One final race in the Van Dieman that stands out in my memory was on the Grand Prix circuit at Brands Hatch. The full Grand Prix circuit is not used very often as it goes much closer to local houses than the short 'club' circuit. The locals don't like the noise and a compromise was reached so that it can only be used for a few days a year. Therefore getting the chance to race on it is a real privilege. That said I wonder how many people bought houses there, knowing there was a racing circuit nearby. Some of the most vocal noise protesters near the parachute club had only just moved into the area, in the full knowledge that there was an active airfield next door, which they then wanted closed down.

Anyhow, with just two laps or so of this race, on the grand prix circuit, to go I was far enough in front of the car behind that all I had to do was keep going, and I was too far behind the car in front to catch him. With no distractions I could brake in the comfort zone, take the optimum line through each corner and that would be that. The grand prix circuit has some very long straights and although you're going very fast there's time to think. The last time I'd had the opportunity to race on the G .P. circuit my distributor drive had broken and cut my day short. On this day I'd completed qualifying and now the race was nearly over. I knew that I couldn't keep putting hard earned money into racing year after year. I expected to have children one day and I had other unfulfilled ambitions. A little voice in my head said to me, "you won't be able to do this forever you know, one day all this will be nothing more than a memory, here you are fulfilling your dream of racing single seaters, on one of the greatest circuits in the world, in front of a paying audience and you're thinking of backing off, you're crazy, these could be your last ever laps on this circuit, GO FOR IT."

I did go for it too. The result of which was that I spun off at a tricky chicane like corner round the back, one that's not on the club circuit and which accordingly I didn't know so well. Luckily no harm came to the car or to me and I was able to finish the race, albeit one place down from where I should have finished, what a gift for the guy behind!

That was the final throw of the dice. I'd loved motorcycles since I first rode them at the parachute club. A new client at work sent me in a new direction I got heavily involved in the world of motorcycles and motorcycle racing. The Van Dieman was put up for sale along with my entire equipe: tyres, spares and spare engine. The Merlyn had been sold as a crashed and un-repaired car, The Royale had tragically gone up in smoke, I said goodbye to the Van Dieman intact and in good working order. I would miss the sensation of the tight cockpit, small steering wheel and full harness, even the view of the two front wheels. There will always be a magic about real racing cars for me. Still it was good to see it go to a good home, in one piece.

The car was bought by a charming Frenchman and sometime later I went to the South of France to see him race it. Club racing there was very different. They had motorcycle racing and car racing at the same event for one thing, which I though was a fabulous thing for competitors and spectators alike. I hate to say it, since car racing was my first love, but in Britain it is a bit snobby compared with bike racing. In the French paddock the atmosphere was much more like that in the paddock at a UK club level bike meet, regardless of whether you were involved with the cars or the bikes.

In the French car racing championship, all the competitors, their wives, girlfriends, helpers and supporters sat down to a meal together the night before the race in a local chateau which they took over for the evening. What a wonderful concept, all amateur sportsmen and women with a common interest enjoying themselves together. I'm sure the racing was no less competitive as a result. I can't quite imagine it happening at home. The French competitors made me feel incredibly welcome, despite my poor French and I'm most grateful.

CHAPTER 15

Life As An Advertising Executive

THE ADVERTISING INDUSTRY can be a lot of fun, but as I mentioned previously that wasn't its primary appeal to me. After my years as a parachute instructor all I really wanted to do was to earn sufficient money, quickly enough, to go motor racing while I was still feasibly young enough to have some chance of making the big time. In a nutshell what happened was that I talked my way into a promotions job and then used those skills to talk my way into a proper advertising agency. When Westex Fiat Promotions started to get too political I went and sold cars in Andover for a while, but when my old boss set up PPS – Publicity and Promotional Support Ltd I invested in it, and joined the new company as Sales & Marketing Director.

There were three directors to begin with; Paul my old boss, David O'Brien who had been doing the same job as me at Westex, although he'd been there slightly longer, and myself. The new company was based in Middlesex, I was living back in my house in Andover and was back to commuting, this time by car. To begin with it was great fun. As before, we distributed Fiat's promotional materials and brochures, and ran promotional events for them. Job titles weren't entirely meaningless but we all joined in to do whatever was needed and there was a real esprit de corps.

Unfortunately the bonhomie didn't last. Paul had his ideas and Dave and I had ours. Paul had a controlling interest and made his girlfriend a director too. Relationships became tense. I still felt I wanted to get into advertising proper so it was back to Campaign and Marketing Week magazines to see what I could find. What I did find was Roland Long Advertising Ltd. SEAT, the Spanish car company, previously owned by Fiat, but now, effectively being run by the Spanish government was about to launch in the UK, and they had appointed three agencies. Burson Marstellar to handle PR, TBWA to handle the brand and RLA – Roland Long Advertising to handle dealer advertising.

I knew about car dealers, I'd been dealing with them for some years now running Fiat and Lancia promotions, and I'd even worked for one for a short time. Not only that, but as the dealer agency RLA would have to take care of all the franchise launches. This would be a huge job. SEAT were starting from scratch and may well need, or want, a network of two hundred or more outlets, each one to be launched in a blaze of glory so to speak. RLA was strong on advertising expertise, they had a superb director in place and already had some good ideas regarding the launches, but still, they needed help.

I applied for the job of Account Manager (Account Director designate). RLA, whose head office was in Bournemouth, not as crazy as it sounds, since there's a college there pumping out advertising and artistic talent, had set up a London office solely to handle SEAT, arguably, and certainly potentially its most profitable piece of business at the time. Launching a car brand and dealer network from scratch is a huge undertaking, with a budget to match. The SEAT company in the UK was owned by Tiny Rowland's Lonrho organisation and they would have to spend heavily to get it going. It is rare to have such an opportunity and to start with a clean sheet of paper.

After two interviews there were two candidates left in the race, myself and Martin Shead, who had been a Regional Promotions Manager with Fiat's above the line agency, a more prestigious position than the one I'd held. Complicated and incestuous relationships abound in this industry, but it meant he was one of the people Westex and PPS had been, if not directly responsible to, then certainly one who we'd want to impress. Technically, although he worked for a different organisation he could claim to have a degree of seniority in the Fiat hierarchy, and he held a formal marketing qualification, although we both knew that broadly speaking, in practice we had a lot of very similar and relevant experience. To complicate matters further, in the course of working on Fiat promotions over several years Martin and I had become very firm friends. Before he got married, Martin and I had some great bachelor nights out.

Not a happy situation and I knew that if I were making the decision then on paper I'd make Martin first choice, and I knew he'd have given a good interview. The only extra thing I could offer, was that I knew I was more hungry for the job, not enough of an argument, really, to win the day though. Predictably, Richard Lancaster who was Managing Director of RLA London offered the job to Martin. Fortunately for me Martin had other irons in the fire and decided RLA wasn't to be his destiny, he turned the job down. Richard was totally honest with me when he offered me the job, a mark of the man. I told him I would be very happy to join RLA and that by the end of my probationary period he would know he'd got the right person.

I sold my investment in PPS back to Paul for a small profit and invested the money in another venture. I worked out some notice at PPS, we were friends after all and then joined RLA. After I'd gone, David's relationships with Paul and the new Director, Paul's girlfriend, worsened and when Dave finally left, it was, sadly, a rather bitter split. Dave decided to take total control of his working life and from being a company director in a business with a healthy turnover and good prospects he went off and did 'The Knowledge' to become a London cabbie. It was a smart move I think. Now he can work when he wants to and take it easy when it suits. Whenever he needs money he can go out and earn it and get paid straight away, no invoices to write and no two month wait for the cash. Best of all, no boss or partners to worry about. Dave is a great guy and a wonderful friend still. My current adventure would be very much more difficult without his help. My relationship with Paul didn't deteriorate to the same extent as David's, nonetheless, I have lost contact.

Joining Richard at RLA was fabulous for me. Richard was a

true professional and he knew the advertising business inside out, everything good I know about the business, how to do it right, I learned from Richard. My next position would show me the other side of the coin, everything bad I know about the business and how not to do it I learned at my second advertising agency, but that was another two years plus down the line. In effect my time at RLA taught me about above the line advertising, we were involved in television and cinema production and media buying, radio and press campaigns and not just through contact with TBWA, the brand agency. RLA produced all of the above on behalf of the dealer network. Which first of all I had to launch!

I can't take the credit for the creative concept, it may have come from Richard, or from Creative Café, a resource used by RLA, particularly for creation of our television campaign. The basic idea existed before I joined the company, all I had to do was make it a reality. The plan was to hold launch events at the newly appointed SEAT dealers, with Spanish food and wine, nothing earth shattering there, and to have a presentation, which purported to come from SEAT's Marketing Director. In fact he was to be played by a wonderful actor named Michael Kilgariff. We commissioned a portable stage with a Spanish town backdrop and some graphics paying homage to the main brand advertising. There was also a reception desk and we employed roadies to transport everything and set it up, plus we took a stunning promotions girl to act as hostess.

The stroke of genius in the show was in the final ingredient, the recruitment of Andrew Sachs, the actor who played Manuel in Fawlty Towers. My job, having set everything up, liaised with the dealers, arranged local advertising and invitations, was also to oversee the events, ensure they ran smoothly, sort any problems and evaluate. The presentation started with Michael introducing himself as SEAT's Marketing Director. He would talk briefly about the company and the cars, about Giugaro design and System Porsche engines, all the kinds of things you'd expect, but a little staid. Until that is a Spanish waiter pushing a broom appeared at the back of the room saying "No, No, ees no tonight ees tomorrow, you no be here, get out, get out". The whole place would collapse with laughter, sometimes to the point of tears as the 'marketing director' tried to explain to the waiter that he was wrong.

With forty or so dealers to launch in the first tranche, Bridget, Michael, Andrew and myself went on the road for several weeks. We shared a car quite often, with our two hard working roadies in a large van following along. We stayed in the same hotels together and we were a happy team. We all got along well and the show was terrific fun. I'm sure also that it stuck in the memory of everyone who saw it and played its part in establishing SEAT in Britain. I stayed in contact with Andrew and Bridget in particular for some time although sadly one can't stay in touch with everyone for ever.

When it came to the second series of launches Andrew was not available, at least not for all the dates, and cost was also an issue by this time, so we decided to try and put on a show with a Spanish flavour, but with only one celebrity or actor. Bridget wasn't available for all the dates either so another promotions girl was employed for some of the launches. The two roadies were the same and this time we employed Geoff Durham, The Great Soprendo, an Englishman with a terrific Spanish magician act. The team then was slightly different, but again it was great fun.

Andrew had told us stories about his family background as we travelled and Geoff told us about living in Madrid and about becoming a performer and magician. I don't know if he felt overshadowed by his more famous spouse, but he struck me as a lovely man and as a superb performer live. Television dilutes the impact of conjuring because we all know what special effects can do. When Geoff made a large portable stereo, which was making a loud noise vanish instantly, despite being only two feet from the front row of the audience, people were stunned. The instantaneous silence emphasised the disappearance. He told me he could make a car disappear from a crowded room and I believed him. The cost of the props though was prohibitive.

When I wasn't involved with the road show I was involved with every other aspect of the work RLA London was doing with SEAT. The real Marketing Director at SEAT was a man called Paul Evans. He was in the position of launching SEAT, with that clean sheet of paper I referred to, such a different situation from, say, taking over a similar position at Ford or Vauxhall. Paul wanted his dealers to be more professional than those of the opposition and he was able to dictate certain conditions in the franchise dealer agreement. As a result, all would-be dealers had to agree to take our launch event and our local advertising and so on. This gave SEAT consistency of message, and to ensure everyone sang from the same song sheet as it were, there were regular coordination meetings between the three agencies.

Whilst we all had specific responsibilities we were of course, in reality competing to get hold of as much of the SEAT UK budget as possible. This is partly why the agency embraced my car racing proposal! The money can only be spent once so the more of it that was spent with RLA the better, but that meant less to spend with TBWA, the main brand agency, or Burson Marstellar on PR.

On the basis that SEAT Dealers were supposed to be a cut above the rest we created local radio commercials and regional television campaigns. Dealers were obliged to contribute to this 'dealer' advertising. Richard was very clever. He and I negotiated very beneficial rates for the television slots, by showing the TV broadcasters that this was dealer money and therefore over and above the brand advertising budget, therefore this space or time, should be sold to us at the lower rates applicable to local and regional businesses.

In effect the dealer campaign, as well as conveying the message that SEAT dealers were more professional than their other counterparts, a claim with dubious credibility in my mind, also put the SEAT Ibiza on television screens across the country, cheaply. In other words the campaign did a job for the brand too. TBWA, the main agency must have hated us. I'm sure that behind the scenes they were struggling to restrict us, invoking contracts and so on. Paul Evans however, knew he was getting good value, he also appreciated Richard's genius. Ultimately TBWA would get their way and take Richard and my successor from RLA, but that day was some way off. My involvement in those coordination meetings, our private meetings with our client and with our suppliers, being involved in the planning, creative briefing process and being on set, when TV and cinema commercials were shot, taught me far more than a couple of years in college and I was getting paid.

After around two years at RLA and with the company having moved from Richmond a couple of miles east, which made a surprisingly big time difference to my daily commute from Andover, I started to think about looking for a more senior position somewhere else. I had no desire, nor the experience to supplant Richard so it was hard to see an upward career path within RLA. However, I was armed with all the knowledge and experience I'd gained courtesy of Richard. I also had a new fiancee who was keen for a fresh start.

It came to my ears that Newton and Godin, just about a top fifty agency at the time, located in Tunbridge Wells and with my old friends Fiat as clients, were looking for a new Account Director, and on the Fiat account to boot. I made contact and arranged a meeting with one Billy Hart a group account director on the main board. It looked like a match made in heaven. The previous account director had left to join Vauxhall on the client side, so nothing particularly sinister there, or so it appeared. N & G had been working for Fiat for years, particularly on the designing, writing and printing of the very brochures Westex and PPS had distributed. So I knew very well who N & G were and how profitable the Fiat account was for them. They offered me the seniority I was looking for and a far higher salary than RLA.

This would be offset by the need for a far bigger mortgage on a property in Tunbridge Wells rather than Andover, but there was a relocation package to help with the cost of the move itself and I thought a house in Tunbridge Wells might well prove to be a better investment. Of course house prices subsequently crashed. It hurt to tell Richard I was off. He'd effectively mentored me after taking me on as his second choice. I'd repaid him with hard work and loyalty, but there was no denying he'd given me a good break and allowed me every opportunity. I would soon appreciate just what a rare animal he was.

What Billy Hart hadn't told me at my interviews, was that a break away agency called BBB, basically led by ex N & G employees had taken the brochure business away from them! To all intents and purposes, as I saw it, I was account director in charge of a non existent account. It wasn't quite that bad, N & G were getting some small jobs from Fiat and after seventeen years or so doing business together the door was open to us to go and present ideas. I pulled out all the stops to build relationships at Fiat and not without some success. I worked long hours and over much of Christmas.

BBB were of course anxious not to allow N & G back in, they were working hard too, and the momentum was very clearly with them. The new agency was the one in favour. David Batten, one of the Bs in BBB had good solid relationships within Fiat. He could also stomach one or two of the self important individuals within the marketing department a little better than I could I imagine. Not that I let my feelings show of course, but the atmosphere was not like that at SEAT, where what you achieved was more important than whether your face fitted politically, or the lunch culture. I speak from my own observations and it's a personal opinion. I managed to win quite significant parts and servicing promotional business and as such I think I was a thorn in the side of BBB who didn't want N & G to have so much as a toe hold. From N &

G's point of view the parts and service business was a poor substitute for the very profitable brochure business. Certainly not enough to warrant a highly paid account director with company car and benefits package.

It was clear to me that Billy Hart had not painted, for me, anything like the whole picture, before I joined the company. With hindsight I would have to think that he was closing the stable door after the horse had bolted and possibly trying to cover his own backside with a fall guy, if he, that is to say me, failed to win the account back. Mentally I congratulated my predecessor for getting out, and even considered telephoning to see if there were any other positions going at Vauxhall!

There were some very good, professional and decent people working both at N & G and at Fiat, but it's the only time in my life I've worked for a company where I had zero respect for the top management of the agency and little more for two of the key decision makers at the client. At the time Fiat were number two in Europe, they'd been number one before dropping SEAT, which was subsequently rescued by the Spanish Government and then sold to VW. This loss to Fiat and gain by VW made VW number one in Europe. I'm very fond of Fiat cars and Lancia and Alfa Romeo, they're sporty and have character, but where are they in the league table today? A friend of mine in research and development at Peugeot tells me that (sadly from my point of view) they're not even in the top four or five today, if some of the UK managers from my days there were representative....

There were some very good creative people working at N & G. I didn't like all their ideas and we had some battles, but on the whole I felt they could produce good work. I did have a big problem with jovial Jeremy the Creative Director, judgement is a personal thing and human beings will not all see things the same way. Very often though an advertising agency's success rests on the judgement of its creative director.

I found out as much as I could about my new employer and the history of the company. It seemed to me from what I gleaned, that historically the genius and powerhouse behind the agency was one of the original partners, Reg Godin. He had brought the agency up to top fifty status and moved it from London into the garden of England. On his retirement it seemed he'd sold the agency to Gray Advertising, one of the largest international advertising agencies in the world. It appeared, although I don't know what share holdings they had, or their terms and conditions, that the senior managers or directors that Reg Godin had around him at the time did rather nicely out of it. Certainly my immediate boss flew everywhere first class, ate at the best restaurants and led the rich man's lifestyle. I doubt the other board members were any different. Right place, right time? It's not for me to say, but it's a plausible possibility.

An account manager or account director is basically involved in what is known as account handling. These managers provide the link, or conduit, between the client and agency. A large part of the job is to maintain good personal relationships and N & G understood the value of wining and dining. Their generosity was probably appreciated in one or two quarters, and possibly helped keep the door ajar longer than would otherwise be the case. The other important aspect of the account handlers' job is to take hold of the client's aims and aspirations, understand them and the product. Grasp the benefits and the message and translate that requirement into a concise and, if possible, inspiring creative brief. The capable account handler will then appreciate whether the creative work presented to him by his own people meets his brief, veto it if necessary and when it is right, it's his job to go and sell it to the client. When it is successfully sold he will oversee the production and in some agencies the billing.

The crunch came when Fiat launched a car called the Tipo. Various agencies, including N & G and BBB were invited to pitch for the business. That being advertising jargon for, compete for the job. I knew in my heart that if I failed to win this business my job would probably be gone. The agency wanted the job badly too. Not least Billy Hart and the other directors still smarting from BBB's success. Creative Director Jeremy decided the job was too important to trust to his own team. If that's not an admission I don't know what is. Billy got involved in the briefings by the client, wonderfully undermining my position. Jeremy put the brief out to an old friend of his. I was told that this was not a freelancer, but someone working at another large agency, I was also told his fee was in the region of ten thousand pounds. I can't vouch for the veracity of either claim that was simply what Jeremy told me, by way of reassuring me about the efforts being made I suppose. I was anything but reassured by the way they were going about things.

Like many other car manufacturers Fiat had produced models in the past which rusted badly. The brief to us was that the Tipo bodyshell was 100% galvanised with zinc against rust. There were lots of other things too, about interior space in the class, performance and economy, and about its styling suggesting a strong hand pushing it along. It's small wonder ordinary people hold marketing in such high regard! From the entire brief Billy and Jeremy latched on to one thing. The galvanising. Very often it's best to have one strong clear message, but this wasn't the time, the product or the right benefit in my opinion.

Now I appreciate that it was necessary to bury any reputation for rust. However, by this time in the development of the motorcar, customers weren't going to buy a car just on the basis that it shouldn't rust. They didn't expect the opposition's cars to rust badly either. We would never persuade the general public that the new Fiat was the best car to buy solely on the basis that it wouldn't rust. Further, it would be an unrealistic expectation, given the history, to think we could persuade people that the new Fiat would outlast everything else on the road. As I saw it we would have to sell the benefits of the car first and foremost, at the same time as reassuring people that the rust problem was a thing of the past.

Jeremy briefed his buddy and then came back with his presentation. They would liken the Tipo to a submarine! I know nothing about submarine design, but according to Jeremy's friend they don't rust, despite prolonged exposure to corrosive sea water because they are galvanised with zinc. That was it, buy a Tipo because it's like a submarine. That was the one idea. I asked what else did he come up with? Nothing, and what's more in Jeremy's judgement this idea would win us the campaign. In my judgement the idea was crass. If only someone would pay me thousands of pounds for rubbish like that.

I had nothing to lose, I knew in my heart that the job was on its last legs, after only about six months, and anyway I didn't want to work for people like them. The problem was I was stressed out with the relocation to Tunbridge Wells, which had not gone smoothly, there was only a month or so to the big white wedding and honeymoon, most of which I was funding, since my wife-to-be was in debt and my future 'in laws' were, shall we say, careful. Now of course I also had a huge mortgage, up about three hundred percent from the one I'd had in Andover. I didn't want to stay at N & G but I certainly didn't want to be jobless either. I wanted to protect my position long enough to make some financial sense of it all and if possible, to make my leaving look like a rational career decision.

I dug my heels in. I made all the arguments about people requiring that a car shouldn't rust and pointing out that since that should be a given, the new Fiat needed to have its real benefits spelt out. They weren't having any of it. I'm sure they'd have loved to sack me right then, but with the big presentation coming up, internal discord wouldn't look good. "I won't present it" I ventured. As an employee I should really present the agency's work and do my best to sell it, but I knew Fiat well enough to know we'd be laughed out of the room. "At least we should have some other concepts I said, what about our own people?" No Jeremy wasn't going to muddy his water with other ideas to distract from his wonderful account-saving idea. "I'll present it myself" said the Creative Director, "but you'll have to be there, it would look odd if you weren't."

And so, come the big day I sat at the table and watched. I listened to the stifled laughs, I observed the incredulous looks. I heard the "what else have you got Jeremy?" or was it "where is the real presentation?" Then we were out. After the post mortem, Jeremy and Billy retained their highly paid positions, my slightly less well paid position was apparently redundant. Well that's how Billy put it anyway.

CHAPTER 16

Romeo and Juliet

IN WHICH CHAPTER I am Romeo and Juliet is, well Juliet, my first wife. When I met Juliet she was the PA to the Marketing Director of SEAT, Paul Evans. It was the era of Dallas, Dynasty, power dressing and padded shoulders. For the girls that is, as well as the American Football stars. It was also a time of white stilettos, spray on jeans and see through blouses.

Juliet went to work in power suits, with tight slit skirts and plunging neckline jackets, over high neckline, but slightly transparent shirts, with lacy cut away bras. She didn't wear the same thing to the office every day of course, but she had a tendency towards sexy figure hugging clothes and tall shoes, and quite frankly I fancied the pants off her.

Dating the client's PA, now that I'd finally made it into a proper advertising agency with a thoroughly decent boss, was an enormous risk. So naturally I asked her out. It was a risk for her too, so I can only assume she fancied me equally. Our first date was on a Friday night and we stayed together for the whole weekend. Sex on a first date? I'm afraid so. It wasn't casual though, we both felt strongly and it wasn't a case of wham bam thank you mam either, we started seeing each other at every opportunity, whilst keeping our feelings secret at work.

At the end of my probationary period at RLA Richard gave a very complimentary summing up of my performance. I remember him telling me "and you've established very good relationships at SEAT". He meant of course with Paul, Jeremy and David our main day to day contacts, as well as a few others, I doubt he even thought of the client's personal assistant.

Juliet was living in shared rented accommodation, she also had a nice SEAT Ibiza leased from her employers and an active social life. She was, like so many young people, living beyond her means and running up debts. We were having fun, lots of fun, but there seemed little sense in the travelling and if Juliet lived with me, I could support her while she got out of debt. Furthermore it would only be a matter of time before word got around. Getting found out so to speak would be worse than telling our respective bosses ourselves. Especially if we wanted to take obviously simultaneous holidays together.

Juliet came with me when I purchased the Royale Formula Ford and supported me at races. In her spray on jeans, tall shoes and see through blouses she almost distracted me from the job in hand, but not quite, even when she leant over the pit wall with the board!

It came to the point where I had to propose to this girl. Since Juliet could hardly go to work sporting an engagement ring, without being asked questions, we decided to break the news to Richard and Paul simultaneously one morning. It was a nerve-racking moment and there are sound business reasons why such a liaison could be a problem, but since both Richard and Paul are decent human beings who trusted us, they both simply congratulated us and we carried on in our former positions and now everyone could know.

Juliet was fun, lively, sexy and she joined in, with everything. All of which changed when we got married. Shortly before the wedding Juliet asked me whether I intended to carry on racing. It had never even occurred to me that I might not. Aside from my relationship with Juliet, racing was what my whole life was about at that point. I'd spent years working as hard as I could, just to get on a grid at a genuine race meeting. Juliet expressed some concern about the costs getting out of hand, and clearly she wanted to make sure we had enough money for making the house nice, holidays and so on. Really alarm bells should have gone off. In fact to some extent they did, but not enough to make me back out of the wedding.

I didn't pay Juliet's debts for her, but I did support her while she paid them off and I found myself paying for most of the wedding expenses. Not that I expected, or wanted, greater generosity from Juliet's parents, they paid for a sit down meal after the wedding. I paid for the wedding itself, flowers, car, photographer, video, dresses, evening party with music and buffet, and a honeymoon in Italy. Many thousands of pounds all told.

Before the big day I made an agreement with Juliet regarding money. It was basically an upper limit per month to go from my wages to the racing budget, all else would have to come from sponsorship. Furthermore I would match every pound I personally put into racing with a pound set aside for holidays or home improvements. The fact that I'd had to make this deal, after helping Juliet with her financial difficulties and paying most of the wedding expenses stung me a little. In another way though it was reassuring, a potential problem dealt with and put to bed, before we took our vows.

On honeymoon no less, Juliet announced that she wanted me to give up racing. I couldn't believe what I was hearing. "But we discussed this before the wedding" I said "and we reached an agreement that I'm going to stick to." "Yes" she said "that was before the wedding, you're married now, you've got responsibilities." "Look we discussed this before we got married, precisely so that it wouldn't come between us once we were married" I said, but she was having none of it. I went out for a walk, on my own, in something of a daze.

Once back from honeymoon we started our new lives, not without some stresses, for me I was starting a second new job in a little over six months. Juliet had a new job too. She came to a few races, but grudgingly now, no longer the happy-go-lucky supporter. There were other changes too, she still went to work in sexy tailored suits, but as soon as she was home in the evening it was mumsy, shapeless tracksuits and slippers. Then she started missing races and finally stopped coming altogether. Our sex life suffered. She still had a fabulous body, but somehow I didn't want to make love to her anymore and I certainly didn't want to bring a child into a marriage that wasn't working. Then came the first ultimatum "give up racing or I'm going home to my parents". I told her I was sticking to the agreement we made, until such time as I decided I was ready to give up racing.

Home she went to mum. About six weeks later she came back. "Did you miss me?" "Yes I did." "Are you going to give up racing then?" "No I'm not." She stayed for a few weeks, then went home again. This time she stayed away a little longer before coming back. "Did you miss me?" "Yes I did." "Are you going to give up racing then?" "No I'm not." "I tell you what, why don't you go back to your mum and this time stay there." Well that did it. My conscience tormented me, when I made my wedding vows I meant them and I thought we would make it. For a long time I was very angry with Juliet for moving the goalposts.

Ultimately I decided to move for a divorce and Juliet decided on revenge, she told me she would take every penny I had. The court disagreed. On the day of the hearing her legal people asked me if I'd like to settle for rather less than they'd been asking, in fact they said they would accept my last offer, which they'd previously rejected out of hand, but now I decided to go through with the hearing. I'd made what I thought was a perfectly reasonable offer and in rejecting it they'd made my costs significantly greater, now we were at court and I'd be paying the QC no matter what happened, therefore we might as well see what the court had to say. The court awarded Juliet half the amount I'd voluntarily offered, so that justified my decision and I felt it demonstrated that I'd tried to be reasonable, even generous, in the first place.

From Juliet's point of view it must surely have felt like a defeat. However, once it was over her hatred seemed to diminish. We stayed in touch for a while. She told me when she remarried and told me also, how she nearly died from pre-eclampsia when she had her first child. I was glad she made it and glad she was happy with a family too.

Looking back now, with greater experience, I realise that I probably didn't love her enough. She probably didn't love me enough either, or she wouldn't have tried to change me. So there we are, both of us to blame really. Hindsight doesn't always provide answers, but I can't help feeling that upbringing has a lot to do with how we turn out. Juliet's father was an NCO in the RAF. He was quite a big man, not one you would call a wimp. Nonetheless, it appeared to me looking in from the outside, that my mother-in-law ruled the roost. If she said be home by a certain time for Sunday lunch, he'd be there, one suspects, even if it meant leaving his buddies on the eighteenth tee. Now you can look at that in a number ways, he loves his wife, he sets store by punctuality, or he doesn't dare to be ten minutes late. I can't help myself feeling that Juliet grew up partaking in a family life in which mum was boss, and that not unnaturally, even if sub-consciously, she thought that once she'd caught her man and had him sign on the dotted line, life would be like that for her too.

The stresses of the wedding, my parent's inability to put their differences aside even temporarily, moving, changing jobs and in my case losing mine, none of those things helped. Juliet's new job in Tunbridge Wells was pretty awful too. With her SEAT experience she got a job at Mazda's head office, but handling customer complaints. Which means being shouted at, and sworn at, over things she had nothing to do with, by people she was trying to help. The move to Tunbridge Wells really marked the end of a fairy tale life in some ways and I felt sometimes I was cursed. I bounced back and had some very good times there, but there were more bad ones over the horizon too. I have never felt at home in Kent the way I did in Essex and particularly in Hampshire.

Juliet and I lived together for thirteen mostly happy months before we got married. Within about three months of being married Juliet was heading home for the first time. Thirteen months or so after getting married we were getting divorced. One telling anecdote concerns the engagement ring, a sapphire with diamonds around it. Juliet chose it, but later decided it wasn't grand enough, she went out and bought a ring with an enormous cubic zircona, which she passed off as a diamond and which she told everyone I'd bought for her. Consequentially, her real, and far more valuable engagement ring was at home when the house was burgled, how she loved that ring once it was gone. If she'd loved it enough to wear it she'd still have it. I stood by Juliet when my mother accused her of things which really weren't her fault and we came through many tribulations, including my attempted suicide. A bitter sweet chapter or rather sweet and then bitter. Better now to remember the good times and learn from the bad. Juliet and I lost contact years ago now.

CHAPTER 17

Forwards and Back Again

WHEN I WAS made 'redundant' from Newton & Godin I naturally went back to Campaign magazine and Marketing Week and started making calls and sending out CVs. Within two weeks however I got a call I did not expect. It was from BBB – Barker, Baker, Batten. "We've heard you've left N & G and wondered if you'd like to have a meeting?" Of course I was interested. There's actually quite an advertising community in Tunbridge Wells, with one really large agency in the town, a lot of the sort of companies who provide services to advertising agencies, print and production companies for example flourished. Then there were breakaways from N & G and breakaways from the breakaways and quite a few individuals who'd decided to go freelance.

I didn't fully appreciate this, at that time, even if I had, any lead for a job in the industry, which wouldn't involve another relocation had to be looked at. BBB were looking for an Account Director to work on Wiggins Teape Paper business. They already had a full and good team working on Fiat unsurprisingly, but since I'd obviously been something of a worry to them when I worked for the opposition, they must have figured I was worth having on board. They knew the problems I'd had to deal with at N & G too, mostly having worked there themselves, so they appreciated as well as anyone that I'd done a good job at N & G with one hand tied behind my back.

I met the three directors, Colin Barker was the director I would be responsible to if I took the job on the Wiggins Teape account, then there was David Batten, also on the account handling side, the most senior guy on their team dealing with Fiat, and Chris Baker Creative Director. They were all personalities I could identify with better than those of the directors at N & G. It wasn't as professional a set up as RLA had been, nor was there anyone there of Richard's calibre. However, there was a sense of entrepreneurial flair, enthusiasm and most of the people working there had a sense of fun too. It wasn't a totally happy ship however, some of the guys who were there when I joined, went off and started their own business partnership. And two of the B's in BBB subsequently ousted the other B. It's a funny business advertising.

To begin with though things looked more rosy than they had for a long time. Colin Barker introduced me to the Marketing Director and Marketing Manager at Wiggins Teape's carbonless paper division, the two Neils. After working on cars, which I clearly have a strong interest in, carbonless copying paper was obviously going to be both thrilling and stimulating! The more senior of the two Neils was clearly a very bright man, but my goodness he liked to talk. It wasn't that he wouldn't let you get a word in edgeways at all. He was quite prepared to listen too, he just enjoyed the debate so much that decisions took forever. One of my colleagues described it as intellectual wanking.

The other Neil was more pragmatic and together we actually got things done. I never could find the subject matter exciting, some products just are as dull as dishwater; which is why I suggested creative briefs should only aspire to be inspirational, sometimes there are limits. And carbonless copy paper is close to the limit. The more senior Neil actually seemed to believe that what he was doing was important in the world! What was interesting about the job was the international nature of it. We had to produce campaigns in every language under the sun, including Chinese, Japanese, Arabic, Russian, Greek, Finnish and many others. As you can see many of the languages we had to work in don't even use the same alphabet as ours and copy checking Chinese and Japanese characters is a time consuming business.

One of the perennial debates in advertising is about the pros and cons of international campaigns, a sort of one message suits all philosophy, as against local advertising differentiated by country and by cultural considerations. In an age where air travel has shrunk the world, different messages all around the globe can have disadvantages. There's also the cost issue, the words may need translating, but the one campaign, one brand approach, does mean the same visual elements can be used, which controls costs marvellously. And when people see the same advertisement abroad, that they've seen at home, they will recall the message even if they don't understand the language being used. Strong arguments for that approach then and ones often put forward by the world's biggest agencies with branches all over the world. The campaign can be decided upon in the client's home country and be produced and placed by local offices in each country who will also take care of the translation. A badly translated campaign will make the advertiser look very amateur, in which case they'd really be spending money to make themselves look bad!

On the other side of the coin, we do all have different cultures and frankly what works with one audience may be a real turn off elsewhere. I've never actually got used to calling a Marathon bar a Snickers bar personally. There are pitfalls too, particularly linguistic. Yamaha insisted on giving one of their motorcycles the nomenclature TDM, many Brits started calling it the Tedium. Yamaha named another bike a Diversion, with the idea that a diversion is a recreation I suppose, but to drivers and riders a diversion is a pain in the backside as a rule! Campaigns created locally may be more expensive, they may also be more effective and avoid pitfalls borne out of too shallow an understanding of language, culture, tradition or local conditions. Swings and roundabouts then.

However, if the benefits of a product are pretty universal, whether you live in London or Beijing, if the visual images are not going to cause offence anywhere, and if the client has to control costs and wants creative control too, then the international, one message suits all campaign logically wins the day. That anyway was the route we and our client chose for

Idem, Wiggins Teape's carbonless copy paper, used for business forms and invoices and so on.

BBB was not a big international agency with local offices in every market, so the big thing for us was to have the translations done in such a way that they would have credibility in every location. Even in one country, one culture, one language, different people will have their own subjective views about an advertising campaign or message. There are countries though with several languages, like Switzerland and Belgium. It's a minefield because the second thing one has to do is bring the directors and managers of all the national offices on side too. This is of considerable importance to both client and agency. Take the marketing director, if his colleagues overseas hate his chosen campaign the political situation is not bright, and if he goes the agency may well follow, if indeed they're not made the fall guys in the first place. Very often, if sales do not meet or exceed targets, the marketing department and the sales department get a bit tetchy with one another and fingers start to be pointed.

I found a translation agency with a network of writers working in every country we were active in. Having finally gotten a decision out of Neil senior I briefed our collaborators to take the UK advertisements and to use them as a brief only. In other words, to have a local, native writer rewrite the advertisements to suit the local audience. Perfect grammar and local style was to be a given. A degree of creative latitude was given too, but the visuals could not be altered, nor branding, and the key benefits had to be communicated.

When I had everything in place I then had to sell the campaign to all the senior people in all the country offices of any significance. Some places were visited individually, in some cases conferences were set up. Generally we pulled it off. Some of the directors or managers overseas may not have liked the campaign, but that was just because they had their own ideas. Everyone seems to have opinions in advertising, whether they understand the principles or not. If you have enough people in the room you'll have someone who doesn't like something, no matter if it's popular with the majority.

In the final analysis it was a big challenge. It meant a lot of hard work, a lot of travel and a lot of pressures, but on the whole I loved it and learned a lot as well. Two of the managers from Wiggins Teape at that time became friends, one still is a very dear friend indeed. Wiggins Teape was taken over by a French company called Arjomarie during the time I worked on the account. The new name became ArjoWiggins, now that's one to conjure with!

One small moment of joy for me was when I organised a UK based conference and used the conference facilities at the Williams Formula One Team Headquarters. At last I'd got myself through the door, even if it was only as a client!

On the home front I was earning enough money to race, Juliet left and after a short while I had a couple of lovely girlfriends, in quick succession Paula and Melanie. I wasn't a good boyfriend to have straight after my divorce, but I'm glad to say they're both still friends. At work there were other things going on. Some of the creative bods decided to leave and start a new agency Oxberry, Webb, Miller and Moss otherwise known, as like so many agencies, by their initials, OWM&M was born. Of the three Bs in BBB I suppose I identified best with David Batten. We're not out of the same mould, but he was a bit of a lad and we shared an interest in cars and motorcycles. I didn't always respect the way he went about things, but I quite liked him. Chris Baker always appeared a bit out of it. He rolled in late every day, and yet, even though he pissed me off mightily in the end I'd have to say that somehow he did manage to produce some first rate creative work. Colin Barker, bizarrely, had been to the same senior school as me, back in Walthamstow. He was older than me and we weren't there at the same time, but that shared heritage should have stood us in good stead.

Colin was good for me in that he gave me a free rein and as stated I enjoyed the challenge. Colin did spend a lot of time on the phone at the office, managing his money, stocks and shares. It lead to trouble later. First however, we had a splendid account win. With the Fiat business another car account would have meant a clash of interest. David Batten and I decided to go after a motorcycle account. We made several overtures and managed to make a presentation to Yamaha. A big name and a great product, even if the motorcycle industry is a cottage industry, compared with cars. A comment made to me once by Jeff Turner, in charge at that time of marketing and racing activities. It's true that what motorcycle companies spend on marketing compared with car companies is tiny, but that didn't interfere with our euphoria when we won the account.

Soon after winning the business David and I paid a visit to the Isle of Man for the TT races. We had a great time there and I got to ride the course on a Yamaha FZR1000. This was a state of the art sports bike at the time and would still be considered a quick machine today. An old friend of mine from Andover was there too, competing. Sadly he coasted to a halt with mechanical failure right where David and I happened to be viewing one of the very major races.

For a while things were good again, the Wiggins Teape account was challenging and involved international travel and Yamaha was right up my street . I switched to motorcycle racing, but more of that later. The chapter is called 'Forwards and then Back Again' for a reason. With me pretty much running the Wiggins Teape business single-handedly, from a managerial perspective, Chris's people still did the creative work of course, Colin's contribution started to look a little thin, to some members of staff and to the other two directors. Colin didn't help the situation, by spending much of the day on the phone, checking his shares or tinkering with his investments.

I'm not passing any kind of judgement on what happened next. I wasn't around in the early days of the business to know what contribution Colin made towards setting it up and making it successful, and certainly I didn't see much evidence that

David or Chris tried to help Colin raise his game or become inspired again. What they did do was conspire to get rid of him. There was much shouting and Colin removed lots of files. The other two had voted him off the board as I understood it, though they couldn't vote him out of his shares naturally. And so, inevitably a legal battle took shape. Whatever David and Chris had to pay Colin it doubtless hurt them and put the business under a financial strain.

The upshot was that they sold the business to Gray Advertising, who merged it back into Newton & Godin and just as in a childhood game of snakes and ladders I found myself back in Union House, in the agency that had given me the worst time of my life.

Clearly I would have to leave, a decision made easier by a memo from Chris Baker telling me to give up motorcycle racing, since I was too highly paid and too important to their success to be laid up injured. Cheeky bastard, this is the man never in work before 10:30am. I kept the memo framed in my toilet at home for years.

CHAPTER 18

The Switch To Motorcycle Racing

WHILE I WAS living in Andover in the early eighties, I met a guy called Colin Gable; the friend David Batten and I later watched coast to a halt on the 'Mountain' section of the TT Course, just after we won the Yamaha business. By then I'd known Colin for several years and had attended his first ever motorcycle race. Back then I was racing my first car, the Merlyn. Colin was a regular working guy, not rich and living with his parents still when I met him. He owned a Kawasaki GPZ900R, a fabulous motorcycle and state of the art sports bike for the road in those days. When I say he owned it, what I really mean is that a finance company owned most of it, and doubtless racing was one of the 'do-nots' in the terms. For his racing debut Colin purchased, cheaply, for cash a Yamaha RD250 or 350 LC. Even in my day (I raced motorcycles in 1991 and 1992) these hot little, liquid cooled two strokes enabled a lot of people to go racing relatively cheaply. Colin tested his new acquisition, it blew a piston. Colin purchased a piston and fitted it, tested again, the new piston blew.

By now Colin had entered his first race meeting at Castle Combe, same place I had my first car race. In club level car racing you're very lucky if you can get more than one race in a day, motorcycle race clubs structure the day differently and a bike may be eligible in a number of categories, even if not totally competitive in all of them. The result is that it's often possible to enjoy four races on the same day, great value, for competitors and spectators alike as grids are usually very healthy as a result.

Colin was entered in four races, two of which were for large capacity bikes. He'd intended running the LC in all the races but, having rebuilt the engine more fully now, still wasn't sure if he'd sorted the problem of the short lived pistons, or not. He decided to enter the Kawasaki GPZ900R in the two large capacity or 'open' races and the LC in the two remaining races. This was a brave thing to do, if he wrote the bike off, his pride and joy, he'd still have to go on making the repayments, probably for another two years. The only race preparation the Kawasaki received was the temporary removal of lights, indicators and stands and the addition of numbers.

On the day of the race meeting it panned out that Colin's first race would be on the Kawasaki. Despite this being his debut and despite the risk, Colin finished second, first race, pride and joy, unpaid for road bike and he finished second! The one bike that beat him was a fully prepared race bike. This had to be a sign of great things to come. I was fully engrossed in my car racing then, but made a note that one day I would like to try racing bikes. I followed Colin's career, best newcomer at the Isle of Man one year, then killed there several years later. Other riders I've known through Yamaha have been killed in the sport, one also at the island, I was quite friendly with Steve Hislop as well, who tragically died in a helicopter crash, but Colin's death hit me hardest.

Having won the Yamaha advertising account now seemed the ideal time to switch from car racing to bikes. I started making enquiries and doing my homework, which led to a meeting with Martin and Karen Sweet who ran Slipstream Motorcycles at Hildenborough near Tonbridge. They prepared race bikes for a number of customers and turned up, at not a few race meetings, with help and encouragement. Martin's preparation was meticulous, his engine building skills were legendary, and I have no idea what I'd have done if he'd been a Honda or Kawasaki dealer, but he wasn't, or rather they weren't. Martin and Karen were a team and they were Yamaha dealers, so no political problems there then!

I purchased a one year old FZR600 from Slipstream, which had already seen a year of action on the track. It had been ridden as hard as can be then, but I'd never had a race car so new, and Martin would prepare it for me on a regular basis. The only expense that was greater in bike racing than in Formula

Ford car racing was tyres. Although a bike only has two, to a cars four, a set of Formula Ford tyres can be made to last a season. Three meetings of four races and qualifying are plenty for soft sticky motorcycle tyres if you really are pushing them, and they're expensive.

About to go out and race my Yamaha FZR600 Supersport. Also in the picture my dear friends Bob and Angie. The object in my right hand is a dipstick for the fuel, so professional! Got to keep the weight down you know, can't over fill it!

They won't wear out in that time, but they do become less grippy, and frankly that's no good. I pushed one set one meeting too far and ended up with my bike in the gravel needing an engine rebuild. A false economy! I suppose it's fair to say that most accidents cost more too, in that it's possible to spin a race car without hitting anything and get away scot free. When you lose control of a race bike it usually hurts and usually damages something! Anyhow, leathers are a similar price to car racing overalls, helmets the same and gloves and boots roughly equivalent. Soon I was fully equipped and ready to go. This time I decided to test first and one of Martin's other customers, an experienced club racer named

Graham Marchant was going to be riding at the test at Brands. He said he'd show me the line for bikes and I duly followed him around for a few laps.

In action, although judging from my relaxed posture it's probably the slowing down lap!

Of course I already knew where the circuit went from car racing and adapting to a slightly different line was no problem, things felt good and right immediately. A few years previously I'd purchased a Laverda Jota 1000cc road bike. When it was launched in the seventies the Jota was hailed as the first true superbike. It was capable of 140mph, it was also loud, tall, heavy and brutish. The Yamaha was very different, being light, powerful and very well balanced, with far less unsprung weight too, not to mention wider and grippier tyres. It's a bit like comparing an old Le Mans Bentley with a birdcage Maserati, the one being a monster in need of taming, the other light and delicate but quick too. Interesting that the muscle bike was the Italian in this case.

Bike racing seemed to come relatively easily to me and I've often thought that years of riding the unforgiving Laverda which needs a strong hand and has to be set up for each corner properly, if it's to be hurried through, must have helped.

The Yamaha seemed so easy to ride fast, if I'd been brought up on bikes like this though I'd not have known any difference. The Yamaha's brakes were a revelation, you could brake so late.

From Bob's enthusiastic welcome back you'd think I'd won, but third was OK at a circuit I didn't yet know fully.

In 1991 I went to four race meetings to feel my way in. This meant that I would still be eligible for the Kent Racing Combine Novice Championship in 1992. As with car racing you obtained signatures from officials at race meetings to upgrade your licence; I would still be on a novice licence at the start of 1992. When I purchased the bike I had no delusions about winning championships. In fact, in 1991 the novice championship was open to bikes of up to 750cc and was won, by another of Martin's customers, on a 750 Suzuki. If I was serious about winning it I'd have gone for a 750, whereas my ambitions amounted to racing affordably and reasonably well. Industry insiders at the time, of which I was becoming one, would also admit that most 750s were built to a standard, most 600s to a price. Therefore the more powerful 750s also had alloy frames, 600s used steel, and there were differences too in the quality of suspension and braking components and so on.

In motorcycle racing the bikes have no rear view mirrors, it is the job of the guy behind to get by cleanly, or at least to get fully alongside so as to be visible. In one of my early races someone touched my rear wheel with their front wheel. Dan, the rider concerned was a journalist for Fast Bikes magazine. As a result of the contact he fell. He was riding a 250 two stroke, less powerful than my FZR600, but we were at Lydden, the shortest and twistiest circuit of any I raced on. If there's any place where the 250 might have an advantage this is it. When the magazine came out Dan talked about me drifting wide as I applied the power of the 600. The implications were that I had an advantage and that I had been at fault not him, not possibly him. I kept the article on a makeshift dart board at work. Imagine my joy when years later that same guy became a client, after he was one of two new marketing guys employed at Yamaha!

I kept in touch socially with one other competitor from my car racing adventures, Chris Nowobilski. By now Chris was trying to put a sponsorship deal together with a guy called Richard, who I also came to meet, along with his beautiful sister Suzy. I hoped that Chris would get his sponsorship, but all I wanted was to get to know Suzy. I did, and she would be my girlfriend throughout my bike racing career. Suzy was the true English rose, dark wavy hair, fair complexion and soft wonderful curves. She had a good career organising conferences and interests of her own, such as aromatherapy. This was a woman with many qualities.

CHAPTER 19

A Fresh Start In Sevenoaks

When Margaret and I were kids Dad made home movies and took the trouble to give them titles and edit them. He called them Sevenoaks Productions and made up a logo with acorns. The reason for the Sevenoaks bit was our surname. He reckoned he'd read about it somewhere. Apparently it had been Snooks until only a very few generations ago when one of our forbears decided to drop the 's' on the end. Snooks had apparently evolved from Snoakes and Snoakes is just an abbreviation of Sevenoaks. So when I went to work there I was just going home really, and in fact it almost felt like that, strangely.

Once I'd been forced back into Newton & Godin, by the sale of BBB, they changed the name, but it was still the same firm to all intents and purposes, I started job hunting in earnest. What I found was MA&P in Sevenoaks, I was told it stood for Marketing, Advertising and Promotion, if that was a measure of their creative brilliance then it didn't bode well. However, it could have stood for Mainwaring, Anstruther and Ponsonby, the sort of pompousness one has come to expect of advertising agencies, so I kept an open mind. The really good thing about MA&P though, apart from location of course, was that they did work for Toyota. This was something I could potentially enjoy.

I went and met their MD Phil Watson, despite the by now unfashionable pony tail he seemed pretty ok. Perhaps I just wanted him to be a good guy because I wanted the job, wanted out of N&G, into Sevenoaks and most of all back into a car account. I got the job and things started very well. To begin with I found myself working with a really great group of people. The Creative Director Dave McLeod was actually very good and easy to work with, not one to take things personally, or get hurt or difficult if you criticized something, more someone anxious to get it right, make things work, satisfy the client. How refreshing, and he had a good team around him who were all equally upbeat.

When things were really busy Dave would call on the services of an excellent freelance artist, equally adept at visuals or finished illustrations for artwork called Martin Wellard. The creative and production departments were on the ground floor, of a charming little building, with an alleyway leading right out on to the High Street. Account handling and management was on the first floor. The two existing account handlers who I would work closely with were Malcolm Compton-Bishop and Clive Winstone. The agency also used the services of Clive's brother Reg Winstone a freelance copywriter.

Reading between the lines I think the other Malcolm was a little bothered by my arrival, but I wasn't there to oust him and before long we got on ok. The Winstone brothers were both petrol heads like myself and I liked them immensely. The one had a passion for Citroen, well strange things happen, the other later got an old Lamborghini to restore, now you're talking! It looked like this was going to be a happy time and indeed for a while it was.

When I worked on SEAT I had forged good relationships with my client, when I worked on Fiat promotions at Westex I forged good relationships with the relevant national and regional managers, at BBB I'd forged a good relationship with the more productive of the two Neils and an acceptable one with the other, but when I'd worked on Fiat advertising at N&G it just hadn't worked. I got on well with the parts and service guy but the Marketing Manager and Director I couldn't get along with, not that they knew how I felt, naturally I was as friendly and professional as possible, but I just wasn't getting through. Possibly it was down to personality, possibly because I was associated with N&G which was really yesterday's agency, maybe it was because of poor work coming out of N&G. Whatever the reason I found the marketing guys at Fiat hard work. And since I found N&G management hard work too it had been a rock and a hard place scenario.

Now I was to meet a new client, Toyota, for my new agency MA&P. What a delight, from the ladies on reception right through to the Directors we came into contact with, all were great to work for. No arrogance, or self importance, agency personnel were made to feel a part of the team, you could speak your mind and they got the best out of us. That clinched it, the N&G experience had been the odd one out.

I also worked on a second account, The Met Office of all things. Up to this point I didn't really appreciate that weather forecasts were sold. Naively I thought it was just a public service, but no, they sell forecasts to all sorts of people. Local authorities need to know when to grit, big building projects need to know it's safe to deploy tons of concrete and that there will not be a frost to ruin it, shipping lines and as I know now, yachtsman need forecasts and in this modern world where money is king all can be made to pay. The Met Office has competitors too. The raw data comes from the same satellites, the trick is in the computer programmes that predict what will happen next. I'd always assumed also that the BBC and ITV both used the Met Office, but it wasn't so. A fascinating account, but ultimately not as interesting to me as either Toyota or Yamaha.

When I made the move to MA&P, Yamaha stayed put at BBB as was, now merged into N&G. I didn't try to prise them away, but I did keep in touch socially.

For a while peace reigned, I enjoyed my work, made new friends and I also discovered Sevenoaks, where at lunchtime there were nice, pubs, bars and restaurants, decent shops and friendly people. At weekends I raced my bike with increasing success and when there was no racing, simply spent time with Suzy.

My sister had, with a friend, founded a choir, their standards were very high. Suzy and I, together with Mum and her second husband went to Paris to hear Margaret perform her first solo at La Madeleine in Paris. Life was, finally, good again.

CHAPTER 20

Champion At Last

AT THE END of 1991, either the club or the racing authorities decided to limit novices to 600cc, so even if I'd been racing a 750 in 1991, I'd not have been able to race it in 1992! Really this was a great stroke of luck for me, suddenly my bike was competitive. The Honda 600 was also very good, there was an FZR400 which was a full on race bike with alloy frame and all the trick bits, but on a power circuit its advantage would be nullified. Some of the two fifty two strokes were very good too, as powerful as a four hundred four stroke and terribly light, but all in all if I'd been choosing a bike to suit the new rules the FZR600 would have been my choice.

Even with this stroke of good fortune I had no expectation of being a winner, most of the other riders were younger than me and jokes were told about novices who unzipped their heads and left their brains in their helmet bags while racing! At this time I was dating the stunning Suzy, again a relationship that must have been doomed since my mother worshipped her! With hindsight I think she may be the only girlfriend who ever truly loved me. What a fool I was to let her go. Anyway, she had tickets for a very posh charity ball and made me promise that whatever else came up I would not let her down for this one weekend. When the championship race dates were announced the first race meeting clashed with the charity ball.

I decided to put Suzy first. I entered all the race meetings for the year except the first, well I wasn't going to be champion so it wouldn't make any difference in reality. I enjoyed the ball, but it did make a difference. In car racing grid positions were determined by practice times, in Kent Racing Combine motorcycle racing the first two or three rows on the grid went to the championship leaders with points already in the bag. At the first race meeting, where no one had points already, grid positions were decided by a kind of lottery, put your hand in a sack and pull out a ping pong ball with a number on it.

My first championship race then was the second round. All the quick guys, and one gal, were securely at the front of the grid, I was half way down it. Despite this I carved my way up to fifth by the finish. Immensely satisfying and a points scoring position, would probably see me on row three for round three. So it proved to be and suddenly I was finishing in the top three on a regular basis. Not long afterwards I was finding myself on the front row and pretty soon leading races. The number I led and didn't win is beyond count! This was an amazing feeling though, after years at the poor mans end of the car racing grid I was now on equal terms for money and equipment and I was at the sharp end!

I started testing at the few circuits I didn't already know, such as Cadwell Park in Lincolnshire. At Pembrey in Wales there were no suitable test days available, so I entered a race meeting there organised by another club, just to make sure I knew the circuit before my championship went there. My attitude became more professional too. I took a much closer interest in the preparation of the bike, experimented by buying different brands of tyre and thought constantly about anything I could do to make myself better. I had spare wheels with wet weather tyres and my friends and I rehearsed changing them – quickly, every spanner needed was colour coded. My attitude to races which didn't count towards the championship changed too, no point hurting myself or damaging the bike in races that didn't count, especially say in a non championship race the morning before a points scoring race in the afternoon, an accident there would be a disaster.

Pembrey was about half way through the season and by then I'd clawed my way up to about third in the championship, still playing catch up from missing the first race. Suzy was worth it, no one ever supported me more. My volunteer car racing mechanics Howard and Ken made the switch to bike racing with me too and now they had the added pleasure of being in a competitive team! Well, actually, along with Suzy, being the team! We had some T-shirts printed with a picture of me racing and the legend Cool Hand Snook. Suzy and the lads had them and any friends or relatives who turned up to support had to wear them too. One of the non championship races at Pembrey was wet. There was racing on Saturday and Sunday, which meant two points-scoring races for me, very important. I went well in the wet, especially with my wet tyres, but I couldn't risk an accident in one of the support races so to speak, potentially I could leave Pembrey in second place in the championship.

In the wet, non-championship race I backed right off and was actually lapped by the leading duo, a couple I would normally be dicing with. They made a joke of it and asked if I'd be playing in the next race. Probably they thought I didn't like the circuit and was no threat today. In both the championship races I was back up in the top three although not a winner. I was up to second in the championship and I thought ruefully, I could be leading it if I had points from the first race. Still there was time.

My worst accident bike racing was at Lydden. It was another meeting that didn't count for my championship, so no harm done there. I led for a lap or two and then someone came up the inside of me very fast entering the left hander before the hill to the hairpin. I thought they just had to run wide, so I braked hard and switched sides, then put the power back on. Unfortunately the other party didn't run wide and was still on the brakes, we touched and I went down. The rider in third place had nowhere to go. A professional video was being made of this race and the commentator blames me for the accident, but in my view it was a pure racing accident the result of dicing closely in a corner, these things happen and both riders had their own strategy.

I can remember seeing the tarmac come up towards my face, and, I think I can remember my visor going away, but then

I'm unconscious. The video shows the front wheel of the third placed Kawasaki hitting my head and bouncing up, he then leaves, stage right, on to the grass. In slow motion it appears that my head is bounced between my feet and then back out. (I've tried to achieve this position out of curiosity, but I can't get anywhere near it.) Meantime I've finished up on my back, but what of my bike? Well, it's in the air right now, but won't be for long as it lands across my chest. Even if I was conscious I wouldn't be throwing that off in a hurry and so I'm left lying there in the centre of the track, red hot fuel-filled bike on top of me, whilst the whole field streams by and eventually an ambulance joins the circuit behind them. The ambulance has to travel two thirds of the circuit to reach me, once the other competitors have gone past, so probably several minutes have elapsed with me lying there unconscious.

About to go out for my last ever race, as I thought at the time. In the wet at my favourite circuit, Brands Hatch. With my girlfriend, helpers, friends, employers, clients, sister and terminally ill mother all watching, a race I could and should have won was about to end in tears.

I believe, from memory there was a rule that if you've been unconscious you have to take two or three weeks off. By the time the marshals lifted my bike off my chest I was starting to come round and so, as the weight came off, I sat up. For all they knew I'd been conscious throughout, just pinned down. I was able to stand and walk into the ambulance. The recovery crew took my bike and I went to the medical centre, well hut really. They sat me down and watched me. After about half an hour someone said to me "how are you feeling?" "Fine" I said "well, off you go then". I walked back to my spot in the paddock. Martin Sweet was there and some of my friends including Graham Snook. The bike hadn't been badly damaged, as a result of coming to rest on me! The only casualty was the steering damper which Martin had already removed, and I had a spare, so the bike was fine. My helmet was a mess. I borrowed one, got the bike scrutineered and raced again that afternoon. My best result was fourth, not my usual standard, but pretty ok under the circumstances.

Only one championship race went badly really. It was at Snetterton, a circuit I really love and where I had previously finished second after a fabulous dual with Eddie Hamilton. At the last championship race at Snetterton I should have been on the front row, but a marshal made a mistake I suppose and I was put in the middle of the grid. I didn't want to bump myself up and be disqualified and anyway was very confident in my ability to get back into the top three from there. Snetterton has a long straight where the power of the 600 would give me an advantage over the smaller-engined bikes even if the 400 four strokes and 250 two strokes were lighter. Further I just love the circuit, a tight chicane but also a long sweeping corner I really enjoy and the bomb hole, real fun another corner that just suited me. Unfortunately there were either several, or one large accident and the race was shortened and called a result early, by which time I'd only clawed my way up to about eighth.

At the end of the year I was over twenty points clear of my nearest rival. It sounds good when you consider that each place you moved up in a race only netted one extra point. My championship win though was the result of consistency, I had a lot of top three finishes but never actually won a race. Some of my second places were oh so close, side by side even, just a thousandth of a second in it, but no actual victories. Eddie Hamilton was named most promising newcomer, which I agreed with wholeheartedly.

My final race was to be at Brands Hatch, another circuit I really like. There was a championship race which I didn't need to win, since I couldn't be caught on points and at the end of the day I really could throw caution to the winds in the final race of the afternoon which was not a championship round anyway. A retirement from racing party was planned for the evening. Suzy, Howard and Ken would obviously be there, I was also expecting a couple of my fellow racers, notably Eddie Hamilton and a guy already mentioned called Graham Snook. He was no relation but the commentators always just assumed we were brothers and so we'd become friends. In addition my mother was coming. This was a big thing. She was seriously ill with cancer at the time, in fact dying. She came to the race meeting too where I foolishly promised her I would not crash in this my last ever race. Martin and Karen Sweet from Slipstream were coming to the party as well, and my, at the time, relatively new boss from the agency MA&P.

In the championship race I got into the lead but the short circuit at Brands is tight and twisty. I was swopping the lead with a young guy on a light and nimble 250. On the last lap I made a fairly risky move to get past about three back markers at once, get them between me and that damn 250 I thought. I nearly outbraked myself at Druids, my nemesis in my Formula Ford days, but I got past them. I didn't want to crash out of the lead on the last lap and I thought I had a little space now so I backed off just a whisker, and that was enough to lose the lead. We crossed the line side by side but he was just ahead. I was heartbroken. There was one race left now in my entire career and no reason to hold back at all.

In this final race I was in third place from the off and as we went into Druids at the top of the hill, the two leaders collided and both went down. So now dear reader you're thinking it has all come right at last and I will cruise to an easy win in my final race. Well by all the laws of natural justice I would certainly have been in the lead of a weakened field, but no.

One of the fallen riders, who normally slide conveniently out of the way, was right in front of my front wheel. Instincts take over and no one wants to run someone over. I braked so hard that my rear wheel became airborne, motorcyclists call it a stoppie, done on purpose it's a stunt. I've done two accidental stoppies in my life, once when a fox ran in front of me and this one. When the back wheel had landed and the fallen rider had scrambled out of the way I was able to continue, by which time most of the field, who had had more time to see what was happening and react to it, had filed past. Instead of leading I was almost last. The red mist came down, I was angry and was making up places right, left and centre.

I recognised a bike in front of me, I knew the rider slightly, he was about my own age, but it was the first time I'd ever been behind him! I lined him up and was slipstreaming him along the start finish straight, the fastest part of the circuit, 120 mph right past the grandstand occupied by my mother. In front of him there was a pile up going into Paddock Hill Bend, he immediately backed off, or worse may have braked. I was so close to him there was no way out, I tried to slow down and go round him all in one but the bike was down in an instant. It was wet, my riderless bike took out the guy in front and I slid off the circuit and half way down Paddock Hill. He slid to the other side. Strange how these things work.

My mother and sister were mortified, but my sister standing up in the grandstand could just see me get to my feet, so she knew I was up and reassured Mum. So much for promises. The wet race was stopped at this point and we all went home. In fact just before going home I sought out the rider I'd unhorsed to apologise. He saw me coming over to chat and said "you'll never guess what happened to me, some ****** took me out from behind". "I know" I said "it was me". "You?" "Surely you were miles in front!" Clearly he'd not recognised me when he filed past at Druids as I tried to preserve the life of the fallen rider, nor recognised my bike when it skittled him. Still we parted on good terms. So career over, championships one, race wins none, something which haunts me still.

I didn't want to admit it, with my retirement party pending and I had to put on a show for Mum, but I was in pain from this accident. The party went well and I numbed the pain with copious quantities of strong liquor, which I realised later could have been very dangerous. By morning about 20 percent of my body was black, blue or yellow, or a curious mixture of all three, the bleeding seemed to centre around my kidney. I didn't see a doctor and made a full recovery. Some of the guys at work insisted on taking polaroids as mementos, but by then they'd missed the best of it!

CHAPTER 21

Difficulties in Docklands

JUST WHEN EVERYTHING is going great, someone has to go and spoil it all. MA&P was a terrific little provincial agency, with loyal clients and a great staff. As well as working on Toyota and The Met. Office, I had also introduced a new client. Neil Cowell, the second Neil, one of my clients from BBB, when he'd been at Arjo Wiggins, was now Managing Director of Samuel Jones Paper. He expressed an interest in working together again and asked how my new agency was shaping up. I assured him there was a good team at MA&P, introduced him to the agency and Samuel Jones Paper duly joined the agency roster.

Then MD Phil Watson decided that everything would change. Time for a quantum leap forward, MA&P would launch a prestige London agency. Big name clients like Toyota would be handled from London, smaller clients from MA&P, which would also take new premises, overlooking the famous green and the seven new oaks and one remaining original one in Sevenoaks. Never mind that it was further for the staff to get to banks and facilities at lunch time, or that the parking situation was far worse.

In London things were much worse still. Phil committed the company to premises in East India Dock, one of those huge shiny granite blocks off to your right as you emerge from the northbound Blackwall Tunnel. At the time the buildings were mostly empty, so it was more eerie than prestige. Inside the development it was possible to buy vastly overpriced sandwiches for lunch, for anything else it was out through a back gate into the third world, or Poplar if you prefer. I've not returned recently but after applying for and enjoying a job in Sevenoaks, lunchtime in Poplar was a shock. Of course I now had a commute up to docklands from Tunbridge Wells, rather than the more pleasant little drive to Sevenoaks.

Naturally I had to go to the new agency, because I worked on 'prestige' accounts. I don't know how the guys who were left behind in Sevenoaks felt about being classed as good enough only for the second string agency, relieved I should think! The other Malcolm and I were the two account handlers chosen for the honour of heading up the new agency, but it would have been difficult potentially for Phil to make either of us MD, without putting the other's nose out of joint. Phil himself wasn't going to leave the rural idyll of Sevenoaks of course, so he brought in someone else as MD, one Ian Burgess.

I hadn't really known him much when I was there, but Ian Burgess came from N&G, the agency that would keep butting into my life. I believe he was an Account Director there, whether he'd ever been on the board I don't know, but a senior position at N&G was no recommendation in my book. I wondered how he'd got the new job, at such a senior level, at such a crucial time, and as an unknown entity. Had he promised to bring in new business, or had he bought shares? My time at N&G had been one of strife and dispute with the management there, what prejudices might he have about me?

Clearly the two agencies needed to find new business, overheads must have virtually doubled even if there were government incentives to go to docklands, and even if the new premises in Sevenoaks were cheaper than the old ones. There was still the extra travelling costs, new print and identity and I'm sure Mr Burgess didn't come cheap either. So now there were two agencies, each with their own costs and each with half the number of clients the single agency had before. You don't have to be a genius to see where this is going.

As regards the new identity, Phil asked us all to suggest names for the new agency, possibly something that would link it with docklands, possibly nautical, or maybe to do with spices or whatever used to pass through East India Dock, when it was still a great port. I suggested Tradewind Advertising, I doubt you need me to explain the connection. Phil chose to name the agency Hawksbill, after a breed of turtle.

Well I did my bit, I finally brought Yamaha into the fold. Now Yamaha isn't a huge account, in terms of billings, but it is a great name and alongside Toyota on the roster I thought it was very good for credibility. Mr Burgess, who had brought no new business, as compared with my two new accounts in about a year, decided to take me out to lunch to celebrate. He chose an eat all you like for £3.50 curry house in Poplar. I could see we were going to get on.

Not long afterwards my relationship with the new boss was so bad that he suggested I leave. In fact I was counting on this, determined to stay there until they had to pay me to go. When we parted Ian Burgess said to me "and you can take Yamaha with you, I'm going to win Triumph." He may have had good reason to be optimistic, his father in-law, or another relative through his wife was apparently a top Triumph dealer.

I took my small payoff and launched my own advertising agency at last, called as you might expect, Tradewind Advertising, after one year Tradewind Advertising Ltd. Yamaha came to me, Neil left Samuel Jones Paper and they abandoned MA&P too. Ian failed to win Triumph and steered Hawksbill to its final destiny. It aptly, and promptly, turned turtle. MA&P helmed by Phil Watson in Sevenoaks hit the rocks too. All the staff lost their jobs, unlike me most lost money too. Martin Wellard the freelance artist was owed money and many others too.

Limited liability is both a curse and a blessing. Many a company would never be born without it, but many other companies and freelance workers are hurt, when companies hit the rocks, are protected from their debts and start up again within the week. Serial offenders, should be seriously punished for the harm they do to their employees and local suppliers. I know one in particular, he and his wife are now running a business as a partnership after having had several failures as limited companies. However MA&P and Hawksbill were gone for good.

I felt particularly sorry for Dave McLeod the Creative Director, he'd done what he did best and done it well, whilst leaving others to do what they did best, on the face of it a sound strategy, but the others let him down. How Phil and Ian could take such a fantastic little company and destroy it so quickly, hurting so many good people in the process is a mystery to me.

Sometime later, Phil Watson asked Martin Wellard to do some work for him, Martin gave him short shrift and that's the last I ever heard of Mr. Watson. Ian Burgess I would bump into one more time, hopefully for the last time. Some years later I attended an industry awards dinner organised by Motorcycle News. I had nominated and entered Yamaha for a raft of awards, most of which they won. I've no idea why Ian Burgess was there and care less. He, however, greeted me as if I were an old friend. Ha.

CHAPTER 22

Entrepreneur

IT'S NOT AN easy thing running your own business and fortunately for me I learnt some very important lessons at quite a young age, lessons that would stand me in good stead after the turtle died. When Bob Acraman left me in charge of the parachute club at the tender age of twenty one and went off to Africa I suddenly found myself taking the money, checking it, banking it and undertaking a whole variety of tasks I'd never really given much thought to before. I grew up quickly at that point, I think, and of course later I had a couple of full years in charge. Even so I was only twenty five when I left. After Westex Fiat Promotions, Paul Webster set up PPS with David and myself as partners. I learned a lot from that too and realised that being a junior partner wasn't going to work for me, I couldn't put my time, money and effort into something and really have no control over the outcome. Luckily I was able to retrieve my investment, with a profit. Pretty soon I would lose all that money in a business venture called MS Fabrics. Yes I'm ashamed to say the MS stood for Malcolm Snook in the same way RSA stood for Robert Sydney Acraman and RLA stood for Roland Long Advertising.

Even before I left PPS for RLA I was reasonably flush with cash. I was commuting from Andover where I had a friend called Mary. Not a girlfriend, just a friend, so no complications or mixed agenda there. Mary was a single Mum, seemingly working hard to bring up her daughter. She worked for a firm that made curtains and blinds and soft furnishings. I was amazed at what they could charge just for made to measure curtains, not to mention a fully co-ordinated make over so to speak. It looked like a good business. Then, apparently the lady who owned it, and employed a couple of other girls as well as Mary, fell in love with some fella from up north.

Newcastle upon Tyne I believe, and she was taking off, the girls would all be out of jobs.

There was a workshop with several industrial machines and a top of the line domestic Husqvarna, that did all sorts of fancy things, and a huge cutting table. Mary, I thought, was quite knowledgeable and presentable and eloquent enough to see clients and front the business. I talked to her about taking it over, I'd give her a minority shareholding as an incentive, she'd be a partner in the business, but day to day she'd be the boss, I'd be at work in London. We decided we could afford to offer a job to one other girl only, given the order book and she would have to be self employed, so we minimised the risks and jumped in.

My idea that being a partner would motivate Mary proved erroneous. Before long I was getting calls from friends in Andover, they were seeing Mary out shopping when she should be at work. It wasn't long before Mary was not paying for fabrics we'd ordered and bouncing cheques. I took as close an interest as I could given I had a full time job, and I put a bit more money in and tried to mentor her. All to no avail. I wasn't going to work hard all day in London to subsidise Mary, so I closed it down, kept the accounts the required number of years and now it's just a short passage in the history of my life. There was no way to sell it as a going concern so I lost a bit of money. Not a fortune, the table and the industrial machines got sold, I kept the Husqvarna as a memento, though I've no idea how to use it.

So I learned two more valuable lessons without too much pain. Don't get involved in a business you know nothing about, and don't trust anyone unless you've known them a very long time. There are guys I know through parachuting, and David O'Brien also, who I'd trust with my life, but they're too valuable as friends to go into business with them. Which is another consideration. So its no to almost all partners and no to businesses I'm not knowledgeable about. And I suppose there was a third thing I thought; that I would need to be there every day with my hand on the tiller, if I was to become an entrepreneur in future.

After the disaster in docklands it seemed to me it was time to take control of my own destiny at last and do things my way. No sooner had I got my pay off than I was on the phone to Yamaha. Not only did I need them, but I had an open invitation from Mr Burgess to poach them anyway. Not that it was really poaching. When I spoke to Jeff Turner at Yamaha he kindly said that they'd only gone to MA&P/Hawksbill in order to work with me again so if I was working for myself obviously they'd be with me. "Oh and by the way" he said "I've got a full page ad in MCN I need turning around in a hurry". I collected the brief; at this point I didn't have premises, a name, stationery, not even a computer, but I did have friends.

I told Alan Miller, the only original partner still at OWM&M, what I needed, having decided on the creative, i.e. the words and picture I would use and he produced the visual. I got it approved, he produced the artwork and I despatched it. There we were, within about forty eight hours my first advertisement was published. I decided on the name Tradewind Advertising, not just because Phil Watson had rejected it, it was my idea and I liked it. It got away from the initials thing and although I would never go back to work in docklands, I thought a mission statement, as loved by a particular type of client, could spring from it along the lines of being a following wind for business, the usual advertising agency rubbish – if required. And it was sufficiently memorable, but gave no clue as to whether this was a new agency or a long established one, perfect. In fact people who I'm sure had never heard of the company before thought they had. Strange the effect a name can have.

I then sat down at the coffee table in my lounge in Tunbridge Wells and started making lists and plans, things to do, things to buy, people to talk to. I wanted to create a proper little agency, not be a one man band working from home, but equally I did not wish to risk my home and everything I'd built up. I wasn't going to get into long term leases I couldn't get out of, it would all have to be done with low overheads, smoke and mirrors. I could be price competitive then too. All the answers would come from the network of people I'd come to know in Tunbridge Wells, Tonbridge and Sevenoaks, everything and everyone I would need was there.

I bought my first AppleMac and a printer and started learning how to use it! I bought myself a car. I'd been driving a company Toyota Celica; too down market now and I'd create a bad impression in one sense, too upmarket and I'd look flash, but Yamaha knew about my racing history and they wouldn't expect to see me in something too staid. On this basis, I bought a few years old Mazda RX7, the one that looks a bit like a Porsche 944. When I sold it a few years later for something more practical, my new wife then being with child, she told me she'd only married me for that car. Charming, how strange people are sometimes!

I spoke to a lot of people including a friend called Andrew who worked for a reprographics company, they made films for printing. I moved into their premises, for a modest rent, and promised to give them my film work. Now I had an office and an address, and I could get up and go to work as usual. The psychological value of that, and of being around colleagues is not to be underestimated, as was really brought home to me when years later I did downsize and worked from the house. Andrew's boss was Ray, thanks Ray and Andrew and thank you for introducing me to Margaret Shrapnell. Margaret would do all my bookkeeping and do it very well, making the auditing work of my excellent accountant John Duncan pretty simple. In the last year or so that I was in business Margaret tragically died. That bereavement came close to being as painful as of a close relative of my own. Margaret was a rare sort of person, cheerful and bright, hardworking and with only good things to say about others, ever, in my experience. She was the sort of person, who if she said she would do something, unfailingly did it, no forgetting, no excuses but more than that,

Margaret would see a need or recognise some way in which she could help you and she'd just do it. I'm not just saying this because she's no longer with us, Margaret Shrapnell was an angel on earth. She wasn't famous, but her funeral was packed, with people who, I'm sure, felt the same as I.

Now I had an office, a car, a computer, a name and I could create my own stationery on the computer, although rather better printed letterheads etc were on their way. I had an accountant, a book keeper and most important a big name client. However, as loyal as I thought Yamaha would be, one client is never enough, so I started looking for more. I wrote to everyone I knew, literally, to tell them I was open for business on my own account. For a couple of years everything would go right. I was no longer racing and all my time and effort went into the business.

I contacted Martin Wellard, the artist who I'd first met when he did freelance work for MA&P in Sevenoaks. He's a brilliant visualiser who will make ideas come to life and do it quickly too. He's also very capable at highly finished illustrations and paintings for actual artwork to be scanned in a finished advertisement. Back then his ability was a great asset. The AppleMac computer is a superb tool, but it's changed the face of advertising and not entirely for the better. Now people with no background in the industry can knock something up, they may save cost, but often at the expense of efficacy, and great talents like Martin are stocking shelves at Sainsburys. Martin was renting desk space from a lady called Louise French at the time, her design business was called French and Galbally. Their glory days were long since over and Patrick Galbally had left the scene well before. They had done very well out of mail order fashion catalogues, which had been lucrative and must have been fun too. Louise was stuck with a long lease but the offices were in Tunbridge Wells rather than on the outskirts and they were rather nice.

Martin asked if I'd be prepared to move in with them, pay rent to Louise and give her work too, since she could produce finished artwork, and knew a thing or six about production as well. He was worried that if her business failed he'd have nowhere to work from other than home. He clearly also liked and respected her and thought she'd be an asset to me, so I'd be helping myself as well as them. I'd never met her, but Ray wanted to make changes to the building he was in and it would help him if I moved out temporarily anyway. So I moved in with Martin and Louise, and it worked out splendidly. We made a great team. Martin billed me as a sole trader, Louise as French and Galbally, they both obtained work from other clients, but for a while at least I, or Tradewind Advertising, was the biggest source of work coming into the building. I had a very presentable place to bring clients and a team of qualified, talented people to present as well. The arrangement became permanent. Ray and Andrew continued to get film work but I stayed in the new premises.

My first account win was Sempol Surfaces in the West Midlands. Yet again it was Neil Cowell, who I'd first worked with at Arjo Wiggins, then when he was at Samuel Jones Paper he'd followed me to MA&P, and now that I was going it alone he'd become MD of a firm that manufactured specialist floors and walls. They installed them at factories, sports centres, even prisons. It was a product that was hard, seamless, and impact, chemical and graffiti resistant. It wasn't a car account, but it was quite interesting and I learned about a whole new industry. Compared with the Japanese, who are incredibly honourable, Sempol were slow payers, but at least with Neil there I was pretty certain I would always be paid in the end, which is an important consideration for a small business. For the first couple of years, almost everything I touched turned to gold and everything I went after I seemed to win.

I decided that if I was choosing what business to go after I should choose things I enjoyed, and preferably things I knew something about. Skiing I thought would be fun, so I went to the ski shows in London and Birmingham and started making contacts. A pitch for Nevica and Killy ski clothes, all one company in fact, was about the only pitch I made that came to naught, but I did meet a chap running an organisation called Ski 93. This was really the ski resorts of New Hampshire which being based around highway 93 had formed a sort of alliance to promote themselves internationally. I did a little work for them and then they introduced me to The New Hampshire Department of Travel and Tourism. In effect this was the government of New Hampshire and they seemed keen to work with me, particularly on brochure fulfilment and handling enquiries.

Sending out brochures involves warehousing and postage costs, if the client didn't pay their bills I could be seriously out of pocket, bankrupted even, and recovering bad debts internationally and taking on governments, well that would be tough. Reluctantly, and expecting to be turned down, I explained my reasons and said I would need to be paid in advance. I would receive their dollar bank draft, it would be converted into sterling, I would show them the receipts and then account for all costs, including my charges, in pounds. When the float got low I would send an invoice for a top up. They agreed and years later when I wound the business down they were one of the last two clients I kept. The people were charming, professional and easy to work with and though modest, the cash flow was very positive!

Through a business networking organisation I met the MD of a consulting firm, he was a ski enthusiast too and we hit it off. Marlborough Consulting joined the agency roster and we created a new corporate identity and literature for them. A couple of years later they would change their name and we'd get to do it all again, great business. I met an importer of motorcycle bits and pieces through the work I was doing with Yamaha. His name was Michael Brandon and at the time his biggest brands were ABUS locks from Germany and Nippondenso spark plugs from Japan. Michael remains a friend to this day. Although his business is in Scotland he'd actually grown up a stones throw from where I did. Michael added other brands to his portfolio such as Taurus electronic immobilisers and Bikers clothing. As he did so, these brands were added to the agency roster as well.

For a short while we handled another importer of motorcycle bits and bobs, but the relationship was never as close as the one with Michael. In fact the other chap, who was a charming gentleman on the face of things, was the only client ever to sack us , giving as his reason, the fact, as he put it, that he didn't like the work. He'd approved it and he was running it, but apparently he'd decided he didn't like it. Years later he was still running one of our advertisements, you can read what you like into that.

Through a journalistic contact I got a lead about a company called Boyer-Bransden Electronics. This company manufactures electronic ignitions and is run by Ernie and Kathy Bransden. Again these two lovely people have become very dear friends, even though we no longer have a business relationship.

I was fortunate that Ernie agreed to that first meeting, he resisted it on the phone. The gentleman who had previously handled advertising for him had sadly died, and Ernie was content really to just let things carry on as they were. He said, "just send me a brochure". I told him we didn't have one and that we were to be judged by the work we did for others, I asked for half an hour of his time to show him and he eventually agreed. When I met him we had so much in common. We were both petrol heads and his brother had worked for Lola Race Cars at the time of the Lola T70 Le Mans racer and the Formula 5000s. The half an hour meeting lasted well into the afternoon and Boyer Bransden Electronics joined the agency roster too. Later I would introduce Ernie to Michael, and Ernie would come to offer advanced platinum Nippondenso spark plugs to go with his electronic ignitions, thus adding turnover for him and adding value, whilst at the same time helping my other client Michel Brandon.

Ernie Bransden's own story is a fascinating one too. Back at college as a youngster he'd studied electronics. Electronic ignition was in its infancy. The Lucas Rita system was the state of the art and was being used by the works Triumph Motorcycle Race Team. Ernie told his tutor that he had ideas about electronic ignition, that he would take a look at the Lucas system and do his thesis on the subject. His teacher suggested he didn't look at other people's ideas, but develop his own. This is what he did, and he produced his first analogue electronic ignition. He fitted it to a Ford Anglia and raced it. Word of his ignition came to the ears of a company called Boyer of Bromley, they raced Triumph Motorcycles, but were not the works team. They had some difficulties with effective ignition and were looking at any option to remain competitive. They asked to try Ernie's system, and of course it worked, well, very well in fact. The powers that be at Boyer invited Ernie to go into business above the shop, figuratively and literally, at the dealership in Bromley. The Bransden MKI ignition became the Boyer-Bransden MKI ignition, was manufactured at Boyer's and went on sale to the motorcycling public.

Life is not a fairy story and I believe there were some difficulties when Ernie wanted to take control of his own business and to go it alone. Nonetheless, he was allowed to use the name, both companies survive to this day and any ill feeling is long in the past. Ernie went on to produce power boxes for race bikes that didn't want to carry the weight of a battery and more recently after the MKIII analogue ignition he's gone on to produce digital ignition systems. There is also a very basic system for cars with coil and points ignition which relieves sparking at the points, but Ernie has never really pursued the car market and these days all cars and motorcycles have electronic ignition as standard. It amazes me, even though he had our advertising of course, that Ernie continues to grow his business, however, there is a vast pool of classic bikes in the world. Mostly British. Once upon a time there were about three hundred and fifty motorcycle producers in the UK, even Wilkinson the shaving people produced motorcycles once.

The purist may not want electronic ignition on a classic, but if it helps to keep it running, so that it can be used on today's roads then to my mind it's a great thing. I like to see motorcycles being used, not in museums and the lower their emissions the better it is too. Ernie's electronic ignitions certainly make them more practical and often if you look at classic bikes being advertised in the Motorcycle News classifieds you'll see the word Boyer, to indicate it already has Ernie's ignition fitted. A real world endorsement if ever there was one.

Our next client win was a small health foods and supplements company who had won the UK franchise or importership for Anne-Marie Borlind cosmetics from Germany. The famous actress Cameron Diaz was their model around that time. Anne-Marie Borlind cosmetics eschewed animal testing and used natural ingredients, so their message was essentially a green one.

Therefore, a year or two after start up, and given the various brands imported by Michael Brandon and the other chap the agency roster looked something like this: YAMAHA, ABUS, Nippondenso, Sempol Surfaces, Marlborough Consulting, Ski 93, The Government of New Hampshire, Bikers (Clothing), Taurus Immobilisers, Anne-Marie Borlind Cosmetics and there was a small brand of motorcycle intercoms and a small local magazine publisher we produced exhibition materials for, but I'll come to them later.

It looked very impressive, but in fact most of the turnover was split between Yamaha, Michael Brandon and Sempol. Further, new leads were becoming harder to find. There was a local design company I'd come to know. A partnership between two guys who were entrepreneurs, in some ways a bit like me, but although very competent designers, they didn't have an advertising background and I started doing some writing for them and coming up with creative concepts based around the disciplines I'd learned at RLA. Their main client was Hornby, the model trains people who also had Scalextric, oh what a dream job for a couple of boys. However, one day they said they were to make a pitch to a company from Belgium who manufactured beds and they wanted some ideas that would win them the business. I duly came up with a raft of ideas, which they of course visualised.

The senior partner of the design company asked to buy a day of my time and to have me go to the presentation with him at the Belgian Embassy in London and effectively for me to make the presentation. I was happy to oblige, I've always felt comfortable making presentations when I believed in the work and since these were entirely my own ideas, which I'd already sold to my client it would be a fun day out, selling them to their client. The day before the presentation my client was called to an important meeting at Hornby. He felt he had to go. Hornby was as vital to him as Yamaha was to me, not just a bird in the hand, but his single biggest client and most prestigious brand.

Agency's need prestigious brands for credibility. He asked me if I was prepared to go to the Belgian Embassy and make the presentation alone. I was happy to do it. His next request was more difficult. He didn't want to tell his potential new client that he'd ducked out of the presentation to go and see another client. He wanted me to tell them he'd been taken ill, but wanted the presentation to go ahead. I hate lying, I really do and the older I get the more anti I am. However, I understood his reasons, I'm not sure I'd have done the same were it my potential client and my business, but the truth would make the new business seem a lower priority, not a good impression. The lie would make it seem they wanted the business no matter what, a rather more positive spin. So I understood his reasons.

I went to the Embassy. The presentation was around lunchtime or just after. It went incredibly well. One knows when ones ideas are being well received instinctively, and I'd had a lot of experience in presenting ideas, good and bad! I left feeling we couldn't lose, they'd loved the work. My client would have a new client and undoubtedly I'd be called on again.

Further I love the creative side of advertising. I left on a real high. My office was in Tunbridge Wells of course and being on public transport I would not be back in time to do anything much with the day. Therefore, since the sun was shining, I decided to spend the rest of the day enjoying London. Have a bite to eat, go to one of the parks, stroll around the shops, or maybe a museum. I couldn't phone my client to tell him how things went until much later because he'd be in his meeting with Hornby.

I enjoyed the next few hours and on my way home I phoned my client from my mobile phone to tell him the good news. I was sure we would win the business and I told him exactly what I'd said regarding his health, since he had to tell the same story!

The following day was one of the most surreal of my life. I went to see my client at his office elsewhere in Tunbridge Wells, to return the presentation and to find out how things had gone when he'd telephoned the Belgians. The first shock was on walking in, when I saw my client talking to a ghost from my past. It was Andy, the print rep from Basingstoke, who'd put his mate up to seducing my first fiancee Cindy, all those years before when I was a skydiver. He didn't recognise me, but I sure as hell recognised him, and surprisingly all the hurt and anger came flooding back. I held it in check, bit my tongue and put my clenched fists in my pocket. I'd been truly in love with Cindy, probably my first true love and that family had hurt me deeply, but it was ancient history.

When Andy had left, my client hit me with shock number two. He hadn't got the business, and the reason defied belief. After making the presentation I'd spent three hours or more in town. How many millions of people are there in London? When I'd called in from my mobile phone all that time later and told my client about the meeting and the explanation for his absence, which was of course a fabrication, one of the Belgians who'd been at the presentation was stood somewhere behind me, within earshot! What are the odds on that! They told him that he would have had the business, and they loved the ideas, but wouldn't do business with a liar. Well what can you say!

My client was honourable enough to pay me, but the Belgian Beds business which could so easily have been won, was gone for good. I decided I needed a new, new business approach. I could go to potential clients and say here we are we're a new young agency with great ideas, give us a chance, but anyone could say that. We could target companies and produce speculative presentations to show them, but it's an expensive and time consuming route. They could steal our ideas, or pass them on to the incumbent agency. And, although advertising is the most incestuous business on the planet, with accounts moving around often, it's still a bit of an upheaval changing agency, it's not undertaken just because a small agency like mine comes knocking.

I decided that what I needed was a promotional idea that could be sold to, or at least presented to a number of potential clients. One speculative presentation that could be used over and over. Further, if we could sell a single promotion to a business it's not as threatening as trying to take over the whole account. However, once a business relationship is established then expanding it is less difficult, possibly until you have the whole cake. Well, that was the idea anyway. I spent much of my spare time thinking about the problems and the opportunities. I thought about it on the way to meetings, in the bath, in the evenings, even on the loo. What I came up with wasn't quite within the parameters I'd originally set for myself. The idea, I felt, was far bigger than say Air Miles, which I believe set it's creator up for life.

A rather smaller entrepreneurial idea that occurred to me during this era was to produce a training aid for skiers. Actually having a manufactured product you could hold in your hands appealed to me. The idea that I had was a bit of a gimmick really, but if I could have got it to work and had been able to get it made and packaged at a low enough cost I'd have gone for it. If I'd sold thousands of them cheaply enough it might have made a bob or two! I'd learned to ski on a school trip at around fifteen or sixteen and I loved it. I thought I'd try and go every year, but between the John Ridgway School of Adventure, the Arctic Expedition and then the parachute club it was put on the back burner until I was around thirty.

The idea was to attach fitments to the skis in front of the boots and behind to which, elasticated straps, which also pivoted could be added, making a sort of parallelogram arrangement. It was supposed to help skiers trying to break the snow plough or wedge habit go parallel, without actually preventing them from spreading the tails if they really needed to. I had four stainless steel clamps made by an old friend on the industrial estate at Thruxton. They could be fitted to, and removed from the skis with no drilling, damage or marks left and looked rather flash. For the elastic component of the prototype I used those black rubber hangers for car exhausts, moulded with a loop at each end. They're available in a variety of lengths and would pivot nicely on the clamps I'd had designed to accommodate them.

I took the whole lot on holiday with me. I could go up on the chair lift with just the clamp parts attached and then put on the rubber parts at the top. I tried out different lengths, but basically they didn't give enough, they controlled the ski's too powerfully. I might have got it to work if I'd been able to experiment with different materials, but I didn't have a budget for that. I'd costed manufacturing in the UK too, and although it would have been possible to make something similar to the prototype and blister pack it for quite a good price I thought it would probably be too expensive for a short lived training aid, unless I got it made in China or somewhere, which I didn't really want to do. Besides which, I didn't really have a budget for travel or patents, and I had my new business scheme for the agency to pursue, so along with many other things it's now gathering dust in my garage.

I had some fun with it though. I didn't really want to give

the idea away, whilst I was still experimenting with it, just in case it worked, so I looked for quiet runs to try it on and only attached the rubber connectors when no one was around. The rest of the time I just skied with the clamps in place. I was in America, so no language barrier and the Americans are always friendly and talkative. As a result I was constantly being asked about the stainless steel 'knobs' on my skis. What do you think they are I'd ask. They became everything from balance weights to vibration dampers, seems skiers love gimmicks, perhaps I was on to something after all!

CHAPTER 23

Whirlwind Romance and Marriage

Having the job of purchasing advertising space in motorcycle media, for Yamaha and others, I found myself invited to a motorcycle magazine launch party, at a Rock and Roll Club, at a place called Johnson's Café, just up the road from the Brands Hatch racing circuit. The venue had been a genuine Rocker's haunt in the fifties and sixties, the magazine launch was for a Harley Davidson inspired magazine and I had a great evening. There were some very interesting characters there to say the least, some of them members of the Hells Angels. Membership of the 'Rockers' Club was inexpensive, so I joined and decided to go back from time to time on regular club nights. I'd done a bit of jiving with Cindy at the parachute club, but we were self taught and could only really dance with one another, besides, that was years before. I decided I should learn some Rock and Roll dancing, or basic jive, rather than just prop the bar up.

Within my social circle was a lady called Keely, who also had the desire to learn, but her boyfriend didn't. There was a six week basic course, one evening a week at The Medway School of Dancing in Tonbridge. Keely and I decided to enrol. We did the six evenings and learned some basics, then decided to do the intermediate course, which was on the same evening, just a little later. So we were in the ballroom after the next lot of beginners, the ballroom being on the top floor of the three story building. Our instructor was Graham, who demonstrated with a lady called Eileen, who was an enthusiastic volunteer it seemed and didn't actually teach as such.

One week I was running a little late and ran up the stairs taking them two or three at a time and not adequately watching where I was going, when I charged headfirst into a six foot tall, stunning blonde coming down. Our relative heights and the stairs being as they were, meant that my head smacked straight into her breasts. Then I looked up and thought wow. Despite the embarrassment I decided that next week I would turn up early and watch the last few minutes of the beginners class! I did, but Heidi as her name turned out to be had a regular partner, I had no idea if they were a couple or not, after all people might take Keely and I for a couple, but we weren't.

Nonetheless, the opportunity to flirt or get to know her didn't really arise for two or three weeks. Then, that one week, I watched Heidi and her partner carry on practising something for a few minutes after their lesson ended. At that moment Eileen came over to me and said "that girl you're staring at is my daughter". I thought she was telling me off for being a letch! And fair enough, so what could I say? What I did say was "well you have a very beautiful daughter Eileen". "Yes" she said "and that chap she's dancing with is not her boyfriend, why don't you go and talk to her?" That was unexpected. However, "I can't just go and barge in, boyfriend or not they're dancing together" I said and of course our lesson was about to start. Eileen said something to Heidi when she finished practising, Heidi and her partner left and our lesson got underway.

As our lesson ended Heidi reappeared, at Eileen's suggestion I can only assume. Strange since parental approval is usually the kiss of death to a romance! Finally I got to talk to her and I asked her on a date. Since we were both learning to jive I said I would take her to a genuine Rock and Roll Club, a real biker's haunt. The Rocker's Club had by now been turfed out of Johnson's, but was thriving at that time in Dartford. I'd taken one previous girl there on a date, but it was a disaster, she wasn't into Rock and Roll, or bikes, more a champagne and caviar kind of girl, what had I been thinking? Heidi however was far more down to earth, loved the authenticity, the atmosphere, motorcycles and of course dancing, at which activity she was quite gifted and very natural.

When we left at closing time we sat and talked in the car for ages. She told me about her previous divorce and how her previous husband had declared himself bankrupt and she'd had to pay many debts. She appeared to be a very sweet and honourable lady, who'd been through a hard time. Now, as well as fancying her like crazy, my heart went out to her and I felt sort of protective towards her too. We started seeing each other seven nights a week. She told me she'd had to break one or two hearts to do this, as she'd been playing the field quite extensively!

Not long after we started seeing one another Heidi had a holiday in Greece, to visit a childhood friend, we decided it would be good if I went out there a few days after her. We were already planning to get engaged. When I got to the airport at the other end Heidi was not there to meet me. Everyone else who'd been on the flight went on their way and before long the airport was like a ghost town. I began to doubt my sanity, the girl said she loved me and wanted to marry me, where was she? Had she changed her mind, or had she had an accident? I waited for several hours and then she and her friend drove up. They'd hit a kerb, punctured the tyre and buckled a wheel. It had taken them a long time to sort out the spare and get it changed, but everything was alright now, big hugs all round and we were off. We got engaged and planned to marry almost immediately, after about three months only! This was pretty out of character for me, but the way I looked at it was this. When I'd married Juliet I'd tried to be terribly sensible about it. We'd lived together for over a year to see how it worked out and we'd discussed how we would live and made agreements about my motor racing and about money. Agreements which meant nothing to Juliet once I'd signed the register. So why not go with my heart, I felt like I'd not done since Angela and that had been the real thing I was sure. So was this then, I was certain of it.

I also had a previous commitment which I had to honour. This was a visit from a lady called Grace who I'd met ski-ing in California the previous winter. I told her all about Heidi, but Grace and I weren't lovers and the holiday would be fine.

When she got to England she got more than she bargained for. Heidi had lost her nerve about a whirlwind wedding and had not only called it off, but had also dumped me. Heidi had some things at my house so I decided to take them back to her parents. On the way I saw Heidi in her car, flashed my lights, pulled into a lay-by near Sevenoaks and gave her things back. It was an emotional meeting though, so clearly the game wasn't over.

Grace duly arrived and I took her to Paris by motorcycle. Grace was a student but also a country and western singer, experienced on stage, comfortable in front of an audience, with an awesome voice and great ability, never a note off key, range and great musical interpretation and emotion in her singing. We ended up in a karaoke bar in Paris, she did one number and that was it, the clientele would not let her sit down again for the whole night.

Heidi meantime had decided she'd made a mistake and wanted to get back together, even to reschedule the wedding. I still felt the same about her, so we started to make the arrangements. We had originally considered not telling friends and family until afterwards, you know, just grab a couple of witnesses off the street, that sort of thing. Now it came to it, we decided our nearest and dearest would be hurt if we did things that way, so we told parents, siblings and a couple of close friends each.

Eileen, my future mother-in-law, who'd effectively made the initial introduction, was very against the idea of us getting married. Not a good omen. My own family were delighted I was settling down again and I'm sure my mother, who'd been battling cancer for years, hoped for a grandchild she would live to see. My family may have had reservations about the speed with which everything had happened, but as they'd always done, they declined to interfere in this area of my life.

I took poor Grace to see Stonehenge and Salisbury on the motorbike as a last treat, and sadly had a minor accident on the way home. Poor girl went back to the USA with a fractured collar bone. My best man at this wedding was an ex girlfriend, Melanie, well I've never been conventional. Having broken my own motorbike in the accident with Grace, I borrowed another. Heidi and I got married at Tunbridge Wells registry office in the morning. Had lunch with our very small group of guests at an eatery in Tunbridge Wells, and then rode off to spent the afternoon at Chessington World of Adventures for our honeymoon. Heidi then promptly went off on holiday. With her brother!

When she came back, we settled into married life, without too much difficulty. The plan was to have a couple of years enjoying being a couple, then start a family. Heidi was on the pill and had been, for some long time. I was surprised then, when within a month of being married Heidi announced she was pregnant.

I said in my introduction that I wanted to tell the stories of other interesting people, I've met on my travels through life and at this point I have to mention Melanie, my 'best man' and her husband Trevor. Melanie is the daughter of a very rich man. A billionaire in fact. He was brought up in the heart of the English countryside and not in a wealthy family. It appears that as a child he swore to one day own the manor house in his village, which today he does, as well as a ranch in Colorado, a place in Singapore and I believe in Texas and in the Pacific somewhere. The details are unimportant.

To Melanie, growing up, her father was her hero. He had married a wonderful lady, half Irish and half Indian, who today is my daughter's Godmother and someone I love and respect immensely. Melanie's mother was incredibly beautiful as a young lady and worked as an air hostess with Air India. She too was from quite a poor background. Melanie's father had left England for India and made his fortune selling aircraft. They fell in love, were married, despite many difficulties, stayed together for many years and had a large family. Melanie's feeling is that as they got richer and business clients became more exalted, her father felt he needed a more sophisticated partner. Whether this is the explanation, or not, Melanie was devastated, having been brought up in Singapore, when as an adolescent she was packed off to school in England and her parents split up. She had very little further contact with the father she had adored, for many years.

When I went out with her, she read a constant stream of self help books and would admit that she wasn't very 'together'. After a while we became more like brother and sister, she became my lodger and more or less my best friend on a day to day basis, as my spiritually close male friends all lived far away. Around the time I met Heidi, Melanie met Trevor, an American businessman who was a director of a market research company making consumer surveys. In fact Trevor's company became another Tradewind Advertising client, briefly.

Melanie met Trevor on a blind date that changed everything. Eventually they married in Melanie's father's wonderful house and I think it's true to say that Trevor has helped Melanie build a bridge back to her father. He's helped make Melanie happy, strong and stable, far more than I accomplished although much of the credit must also go to Mel of course. Over and above all this they've both proven extremely strong, and good for one another, through quite incredible and unexpected hardship.

A few years ago now I heard about the shooting of an American businessman in Surrey, on the television news. I just knew it had to be Trevor and although the house was cordoned off, when I saw the pictures of the street I knew for sure it was Mel and Trev. Basically, a couple of druggies had knocked at the door, claiming their dog had been knocked down on the road outside and they needed to use the phone, but as Trevor opened the door they burst in and shot him in the arm, shattering the bone. They then demanded his credit cards and the pin numbers. Then to cover their tracks, and so as not to be identified, they executed him, by shooting him in the head at point blank range.

Miraculously, Trevor survived though. His recovery was a long painful process, with many operations, more to repair his shattered arm than on his head wound bizarrely. Melanie, once an emotional wreck has coped brilliantly and helped Trevor as much as he's been totally remarkable. I remember Juliet wanting to move from our house after we were burgled. Trevor and Melanie decided to stay put, despite what happened to him, because they didn't want to be defeated by criminals. They're still living in the same house today, although despite extra security, last time I telephoned they had no computer, due to a burglary!

I thank God that Melanie was out with her mother and her baby when the attack happened as I'm sure they would all have been shot and Trevor's survival was a miracle; they may not all have been granted one, or possibly their absence was the other miracle. The culprits were finally caught after executing another couple in the North of England, almost certainly using the same modus operandi, neither of them survived. Trevor's survival enabled him to identify the culprits and ensure a conviction, today he assists a House of Commons committee, representing victims of serious crime. Two more fantastic human beings I'm privileged to know.

CHAPTER 24

The Goose That Lays The Golden Egg Is An Illusive Bird

My big, new business idea was inspired by experience. Toyota had launched their own credit card as had many other product and service suppliers. In fact new credit card and credit based offers seemed to be announced daily. Promotions based on low cost loans, even interest free credit and deferred payments were common place. It seemed to me that everyone was marketing to people who had to struggle to buy the product, but no one was addressing those people who wanted to save first and buy second, let alone those who could comfortably afford to buy whatever they wanted, where was the sense in that! I'm not knocking the credit promotions, many work well, and interest free credit will appeal to people with money too, but promotions aimed specifically at savers and those with disposable resources just didn't seem to be happening.

And this against a backdrop of media coverage about consumer borrowing being a potential time bomb. In addition I couldn't help remembering watching Colin Barker at BBB, a man with some money, spending large chunks of time worrying about his shares, buying and selling and annoying his colleagues until the partnership fell apart. It seemed to me that people with money had a strong interest even a compulsion to protect it and get a return on it. However at times of low interest rates, how do you get security, a good return and instant access to the portion of your wealth that you want to spend, or at least be able to spend.

One of the big success stories since the war has been the growth of Building Societies, lending money to help people buy their own homes, returning a good rate of interest for those saving, be it for a home deposit or something else. They also provided security, their money was in bricks and mortar effectively, if you had two hundred, two thousand, or twenty thousand pounds in your old fashioned passbook it was safe, solid and growing, it was accessible and the figures were there on the page to see.

Gradually the Building Societies eroded their own position, the rates they gave to investors fell as they became slow to follow base rate changes, or didn't move at all, whilst the rate they charged borrowers changed promptly. The gap between what they gave with one hand and took with the other widened. Then many of them became banks, now they were no longer there just for the benefit of their members, now they had a profit motive and shareholders.

The real power, I realised, lay not so much with the financial institutions, as with the companies who made the products the people wanted. The products that improve our standard of living, particularly the high price items, people have to save for, or borrow for, if they're not rich enough to purchase these things comfortably. However, expensive as they are, we're still talking about items which a significant minority are able to afford comfortably, especially in countries like Britain, the USA and many western European countries. Not to mention Australia, New Zealand, Canada and others too.

Yet all the marketing efforts seemed directed at the borrowers, but not at the other two groups, the wealthy and those who prefer to save first and buy second. If companies with high ticket products got together their power would be very significant. I'm talking about the kinds of products people often save for, and which the wealthy can buy easily, sometimes in the plural! Things such as cars, holidays, home improvements, motorcycles, boats, caravans, expensive cameras, home cinema or flat screen TVs, weddings, jewellery and so on.

The promotion was given the name SAVERS and I put together a presentation to show people. It pointed out all of the above and suggested that people be offered the chance to save with this bullet proof group of companies, say a car company like VW, which could of course offer Audi, SEAT and Skoda, even Bentley, so something for every pocket and taste, allied to a Lunn Poly or Thomas Cook, Yamaha, a conservatory or home improvement company, Beneteau yachts which owns another brand too and a Sony or powerful electrical retail group. Cars and holidays were my priority. I felt instinctively they were the two main things people saved for. And, importantly, most wealthy families had multiple cars, changed them frequently and took a lot of holidays.

Customers could save with the SAVERS scheme, or they could put a large amount in from day one. If you change your car every year, and your wife's car, and your children's cars and you take several holidays a year then you're going to get through many thousands of pounds, euros or dollars and you don't want to mess around selling shares every time. However, it would be nice to get a decent return on your money while it's sitting around, and of course it has to be secure.

The companies running SAVERS could offer a much higher rate of interest than the banks, or even mutual societies, because their profit comes from the sale of product. Financial institutions don't make anything, that's why the real power lies with the manufacturers. Now we have to make our proposition to the consumer, who has to see the benefit and be assured there is no catch. The proposition is this; save with us, or invest with us and we will give you extra interest, with complete accessibility, and total security, provided that when you take money out, it's to buy one of our portfolio of products. However, if you take money out for an emergency or simply want to buy something else, in other words, for example, you want to buy a car from another manufacturer, then we'll give you the same rate of interest you would have got from a normal building society. The customer cannot lose, and neither can the companies behind the scheme, because they've had the use of that money whilst it was invested, very positive cash flow, and they now get the profit that the building society would have made, even if they fail to make the sale. It may not be as much as the profit on the sale of a car, but it's not to be sniffed at.

However, in reality, the scheme will encourage people to stay with you and buy your products. Your competitors may discount, but being offered something at a reduced price is quite different psychology from giving back money you appear to have already earned in your savings account. If they wanted the SAVERS companies could also offer discounts anyway, unlike other product and service suppliers they should be making extra money from banking. There's more to it than that though, the marketing possibilities are almost bottomless. Suppose you ask customers to nominate the product or products they are saving for, or have an interest in buying in the near to middle future. There's no commitment on their part, beyond buying something, anything, from your portfolio or losing the extra interest only on that sum of money alone.

Let's say then that someone nominates a Golf GTI motor car, at Christmas you can write to them and offer a tie or rally jacket. No one wants to have the jacket but not the car, not if they can possibly have the car too, so you're gradually locking them in.

That's just a small example, there are many. Suppose a Golf GTI costs £10,000, a new model is out next year and you have a lot of the old model to shift. It would be possible to write to, or telephone customers with less than £10,000 in their account and say, "we see you have nominated that you're saving for a Golf GTI, which costs £10,000, how would you like to have it now, for the £9,000 in your account?" The possibilities for building loyalty go on. If someone has genuinely saved for your product you can make them a small gift as a congratulatory gesture to build loyalty. If someone takes all the money out of their account to buy your product you could put £100 or £50 back in the account, to keep them in the scheme and make them feel good.

These then are the basic tenets of the idea. So what happened? I thought then and I think now that it's a great marketing idea and one that's been missed, however, I wanted to run it by someone with experience in a senior marketing position in a major company. I contacted my old client Paul Evans, the former Marketing Director at SEAT UK. We met at a hotel on the M4. I explained my logic about how companies marketed to borrowers, but not to the savers or the wealthy to anything like the same degree. I went on to explain how these powerful companies could take business from the banks, improve their cash flow, which also provides money to lend of course, and put the flesh on the promotion as far as I'd developed it.

Paul agreed with everything I said and what's more he wanted in! Now here was a man who's CV would open doors to people in high ranking positions, people I would find it difficult to reach. Even if I reached them, they probably wouldn't sign the confidentiality agreement I'd had prepared, and then if they wanted to they could go ahead and cut me out. Paul would be a persuasive ally. I started writing to everyone I though might be a useful member of the SAVERS group of collaborating companies. I even got Richard Branson's home address from a pilot friend going back to my parachute club days. Meanwhile Paul was making approaches too.

We made a presentation to a Marketing Director of a major DIY chain who was the first to open the door to us. He agreed with me that cars and holidays were the priorities, but said if we got that and the club looked like forming they'd want to join. A very encouraging first presentation. Richard Branson was not alone in declining to sign a confidentiality agreement. Of course the letter may well have been passed straight to a member of staff or even have been filtered at home. The reply was something to the effect that they wouldn't sign in case they'd already had the idea themselves and didn't want to be locked out of using it. Of course they'd sign afterwards if it really was a new and novel idea! I didn't pursue that avenue.

Paul got us in to see a senior manager at VW, but it wasn't board level. If he did kick the basic idea upstairs he'd never have tried to sell it with the passion we would have done. There's another factor too, this is a project that would entail an enormous amount of work and some employed people in secure jobs don't necessarily want to increase their workload, especially when they can stay with the herd and not be criticized.

Paul did get us in to see the board of the Inchcape Group's car leasing division and they seemed very interested, but I wasn't sure they were really the right partner, ideally I wanted a manufacturer to get behind it. I made the presentation but didn't push as hard as perhaps I should have, but that's with hindsight and even so I feel this is something for major manufacturers to embrace. I told a contact at Toyota about it but didn't get to the board, I told Yamaha about it and they expressed interest, if and when I got the car and holiday companies in place. It felt like the car company was the key, get a major car manufacturer and that would be a powerful ally to open the door to Lunn Poly, Thomas Cook or Virgin. Get cars and holidays and the others would surely follow.

Then Paul worked his magic and got us in front of the board of MG Rover. They liked it, they had queries and questions, things they wanted researched, but basically they were very interested. And then it was all over with Rover. BMW were making a takeover bid, everyone's attention and energy was redirected, refocused. We hadn't been home and dry as had seemed to be the case with the SEAT race team deal years before, but I was still crestfallen. Eventually, I gave up trying to open doors, get confidentiality agreements signed and so on. The presentation went in my garage to gather dust and mildew. The process was hurting my head far more than the brick wall.

Not so long afterwards Paul came to me and said he had a business proposal and since I'd shared mine with him, he was returning the compliment. What Paul wanted to do was to become the UK importer of a German lubricants brand called Liqui Moly. My interest was immediate, apart from the business opportunity, I'd seen the Liqui Moly logo on Formula One cars on occasion and on World Championship Sportscars. As a petrol head I was bound to be excited.

We made a fact finding visit to Germany. Paul had already made the approach and was in the running. We found out all about their products and got to see around their research and development facility, amongst other things, which was a great privilege. Bizarrely, some years later I would see around Castrol's research and development facility as a journalist. Liqui Moly started life by producing an oil additive based on molybdenum, in suspension in oil. It's a very good product as the electrically charged particles repel each other and so don't settle out in the can and molybdenum is about the best solid lubricant known to man.

By the time Paul and I visited, Liqui Moly made a whole range of products including a molybdenum product which was liquid, no particles at all, although I no longer remember the details or benefits over the original product. They were also producers of synthetic oils and other things. A great range of products for car nuts!

Back home I was buzzing creatively and started coming up with advertisement concepts to add some glamour to Paul's presentation, which was largely to do with the business side of things and why he was the right guy to manage the UK for them. The man we had to convince was very interesting. His name, which I no longer remember was quite difficult anyway, and he turned out to be of Yugoslav origin. He was Liqui Moly's international development director, or something of the sort and the UK had been a thorn in his side I think. He was close to retirement. Although his family had come from Yugoslavia originally, they had emigrated to the USA years before and he had gone out to Germany with US intelligence, as part of the post war de-Nazification programme. He'd married a German lady and stayed. A fascinating man who I liked instantly.

We, or really Paul, with some help from me, won the business. Paul wanted and expected me to be his junior partner. So did I. Although it went against the lessons I thought I'd learned in previous business partnerships I would have made an exception for Paul. After all he would have come in on the Savers business under me. The problem was I couldn't endorse his business plan. So investing and probably putting my house up as security when I didn't believe in the business plan and couldn't change anything, Paul and his wife having the majority of shares and say so, was clearly a non starter. It caused a lot of ill feeling when I told Paul how I felt. We have talked since and I hope that feeling has passed, but I'm not entirely sure how he feels.

Paul's plan might have been fine for a Lonrho company with plenty of resources, a company which could invest now to make a profit a year or two down the line. In other words, the sort of company that Paul was used to working for. Paul wanted for us to invest in a large prestigious looking warehouse with offices. He wanted several salaried sales reps to cover the country, all would need cars. He, his wife and I would all have cars too and there would be computers, probably a receptionist come secretary, not to mention all the other start up requirements, stationery and so on, or the stocks to fill this warehouse.

I felt it was too much too soon. We would have to buy enough stock to keep Liqui Moly happy obviously but I was for the lowest possible overheads, selling hard ourselves, mail order and creative ways to sell direct without getting margins hammered by retail outlets or powerful chains. I had a lot of ideas, but I felt Paul would do things his way and I'd be a passenger, a working one, but not one with the power to make decisions. I told Paul, and maybe I shouldn't have, that his plan was a recipe for disaster in my eyes. I wanted him to prove me wrong, I wanted to see him fly, and for me to kick myself for being a lily-livered ass. However, with much regret I had to go my own way and struggle on with my little advertising agency. I decided too many near misses had to be telling me something, maybe they'd be a chapter in my book one day.

Sadly Paul's Liqui Moly adventure did fail and I believe he lost his farm in Wiltshire as a result. I didn't want to enquire too closely in case he thought it was a case of I told you so. I really do wish it had flown, he's a great guy and it's a great product.

CHAPTER 25

Fatherhood, Bereavement, Divorce

My second marriage was not as short lived as the first, but it certainly wasn't long lasting. To begin with it was very exciting and having given up racing, and with my own business thriving, I bought a replica of the Le Mans winning Ford GT40. Similar to the one built by John Schofield all those years before. This was a present to myself to compensate for giving up racing. Heidi was very supportive, and we had a wonderful trip to Le Mans in the new car. It had been built by GTD Developments in Poole for the ex Formula 1 driver Dr Jonathon Palmer to use as a demonstrator and track day car. Accordingly it had been set up by him.

I found it handled superbly, understeer when the tyres were cold but really neutral and predictable once everything was up to temperature. I'm led to believe there was some acrimony between the good doctor and the company, that he thought it was his to keep, but in fact they later took it back and sold it. Whatever the truth of that matter, I found it through a gentleman named Brian Pepper who was a real GT40 enthusiast and kept a list of cars for sale, as well as building replicas for sale himself, and helping owners maintain them. Brian was a member of the British Racing Drivers Club. Membership is restricted and it shows he had enjoyed some considerable success as a racing driver in earlier years. He showed me several cars and I bought the ex Jonathon Palmer car. I immediately spent quite a bit of money on it, with Brian, as the previous owner had let it go a bit.

When Heidi and I collected the car it looked stunning, with a new red paint job, new wheel spinners and other cosmetic touches. When we went to Le Mans there was a parade through the town organised by one of the owners' clubs and I was very embarrassed when a young French child asked for my autograph!

Sadly Brian Pepper passed away not long afterwards. Back home in Tunbridge Wells, I was soon introduced to a local engineer, Frank Catt, who helped me improve the car in any number of ways. Amongst very many other things, he fitted new cylinder heads and a new inlet manifold for me, plus, given the enhanced performance, new much more powerful brake callipers. He fitted a quick release steering wheel which helped security, as I could remove it when I left the car. He also designed hidden door locks, and built two aluminium luggage boxes which were mounted either side of the gearbox, as in original MKI road going GT40s. Like Brian before him, Frank became a firm friend into the bargain and today his hobby is a full time job and he's a very sought after engineer.

Heidi and I continued our rock and roll dancing activities, we were both employed, and although Heidi was still somewhat in debt to her father, there was no pressure and life was sweet. Too sweet to last perhaps. When Heidi announced she was pregnant, I was very surprised and taken aback. It did not mean I didn't want the baby. It was simply something other than we'd discussed, I thought we were taking precautions. So I was surprised, it showed on my face and from that moment she felt I didn't want the baby.

I got rid of the Mazda RX7 and got a Jaguar saloon, so we'd have a car with a boot and proper back seats for the child seat, and all those things you have to transport when you have a kid around. I got rid of that a couple of years later, for an early Mustang convertible. It had the same basic engine as the GT40 and I bought the parts for Frank to build a really superb engine. The idea was to put the all singing, all dancing, balanced, hot engine in the GT40, the GT40 engine in the Mustang and keep the Mustang engine, rebuild that and have it as a spare for either car. Our daughter Francesca loved the light blue Mustang, she still talks about the car with the horsey and wants me to buy it back. Not possible of course. The Mustang and the parts for the hot engine were a financial casualty of the divorce when it came. Later the GT40 was sold towards buying the yacht that is now my home.

So, shortly after getting married Heidi and I found ourselves going to prenatal classes together and I tried to assure her that I was very happy to have a child on the way, which I was. When Francesca arrived, it was early in the morning, after a long night. Longer for Heidi than for me certainly, but not without stress for me too. I was in the delivery room with Heidi, she had agreed to have gas and other forms of pain control if necessary. In the next room was a lady insisting on a completely natural birth with no drugs, gas or whatever. She was screaming her head off and all the available staff were in there much of the time. Heidi and I were left alone for long periods. Now amongst the hospital gizmos, was a device that showed the baby's heartbeat and whilst Heidi and I were in there it stopped, or went flat. I honestly thought our baby was dying. I didn't want to panic Heidi, so I told her I needed a pee, and as soon as I was out of the room I was running around the hospital corridors like a mad thing trying to find someone to help, as I thought every second was crucial.

When I did get someone to come it was a false alarm, the sensor had moved and was no longer detecting the baby's heartbeat, but the heartbeat was still there, thank goodness. Eventually Francesca was assisted out with one of those sucker things they put on the baby's head. I may have done first aid at the parachute club, but I'm really terribly squeamish and I found that quite disturbing. Not least because babies look so fragile. The mark it left on her head scared me a bit too, but it soon went.

I decided when I started this book I'd be totally honest and that I'd tell the whole story, so far as I could, without hurting those close to me. I know memory plays tricks, so I'm trying to omit anything where my memory seems even faintly unclear. In addition there are some things I don't feel I have a right to tell, since the information really came to me in confidence. However, the next truth I find unpalatable, yet feel I should confess since it was part of the experience. There was a moment, just a split second in the delivery room, when I was disappointed I didn't have a son. And then I fell headlong in love with my girl. A love that has grown unfailingly. I can't imagine having a boy now. Francesca was an angel. I know, rose coloured spectacles and all that, but she really was. She hardly ever cried, she slept through the night, she ate everything given to her, she smiled, gurgled and the other thing from the other end, but it's not a big price to pay considering, and yes I did change nappies.

After she was born I telephoned Heidi's family and mine, and a little later I went home. After getting some rest I got some work done. I went to the hospital every day they were in there. Heidi subsequently told me she felt I didn't spend enough time with them. At the time I didn't appreciate that she felt that way and I wanted to keep the business going, I didn't have much in the way of staff to fall back on, and now I had a new responsibility. Sadly the cracks in my relationship with Heidi were widening.

I bought a video camera to record Francesca growing up. By the time Francesca was two I was even more besotted with her. People talk about 'the terrible twos' but in fact Francesca was now becoming a person I could communicate with and play games with and she was totally enchanting.

Around the time Francesca was eighteen months, my mother dying of cancer was moved into a hospice. One day Heidi and I took her beloved granddaughter to see her. She was weak and found it hard to speak but I didn't feel she was quite at death's door. Just before we left the hospice, near Southend Essex, to drive home to Tunbridge Wells mum held Francesca briefly and whispered "goodbye my precious". They were her last words. On arriving home we had a phone call to say mum had died.

My relationship with mum was sometimes tempestuous, we were too alike, adventurous, rarely satisfied, stubborn and strong willed. My relationship with her second husband wasn't close either, firstly because of the break up of my parent's marriage, and at the end because I felt he was looking elsewhere even before mum died. There was another lady at mum's funeral whose relationship with Eric was probably a very close one. That information, probably wisely, was kept from me until after the funeral. I've already stated how much I loved my parents and how much they did for me, so we'll leave the subject there.

Heidi was a tower of strength and a great help to me throughout the period my mother spent in the hospice and through the funeral. Not long afterwards our relationship would deteriorate. Heidi left her job, under difficult circumstances, I'm convinced she tried to do a good deed, well two in fact. The first involved going over her boss's head to help a disabled customer, quite right too. However, I'm sure her immediate boss became an implacable enemy from then on, so that when she tried to help out a colleague, who in all probability had made an honest mistake, he took the opportunity to try and implicate her too. Heidi resigned. For obvious reasons those are just the bare bones, but it's all I feel I should tell. I felt Heidi did the right thing at every stage, but naturally the stress put a strain on us both, emotionally and financially.

I was working very hard at my still small business and doing any and every job I could get. As well as producing advertising and literature for Yamaha I helped them run-in their press fleet bikes each year, run-in the race school bikes and I was running promotions at race meetings. At every round of the British Superbike Championship, the UK rounds of the World Superbike Championship and the British Motorcycle Grand Prix I'd be there with a stage show or other promotion.

Motorcycle manufacturers have a lot of bikes in their range and every winter when the new models came in there would be a new press fleet. Journalists will of course push the bikes to the limit, so they have to be fully run-in, checked and serviced before they're sent out. That's many thousands of miles of winter riding. I'm sure I have arthritis, or something, in my fingers as a result. I did as much of the running in as I could in the evenings and at weekends, so the job would not detract from my time in the office.

Still at it! Helping to run an advanced riding course at the Nurburgring for Yamaha when I worked on their promotions.

There were about sixteen race meetings I had to attend in the year, of course they're all in the summer, so most of my summer weekends I'd be away. I enjoyed those jobs immensely, but I also felt I had to do them, we needed every penny and we needed Yamaha's goodwill. Letting someone else in the door would not be good business. I came up with something called the Yamaha Spirit programme. The name came from me, the way it worked largely, but not entirely, from them. We had circuit ride-arounds at lunchtime and free or half price entry for Yamaha riders at many races. If you're a race nut choosing between a Yamaha or other sports bike it's quite an incentive.

At the international meetings we would have a stage show. I would interview top riders such as Noriyuki Haga, Colin Edwards and even my all time motorcycle racing hero Wayne Rainey. I also ran quizzes with members of the public up on stage with me and other competitions with a sort of electronic race circuit which had a buzzer if the loop touched the wire, a little physical test of skill. The prizes were worth having and our shows were popular. On many occasions I had to entertain the audience, ad lib, if riders were late showing up for interviews and autograph sessions. It was challenging but good fun, and I met loads of motorcyclists, some of whom are still friends.

For these jobs I employed promotions girls, to meet and greet and to assist on stage. I think Heidi may have suspected something was going on. It wasn't. Nor was this the reason for our split. The girls were very fanciable, but I didn't try any extra curricular activities, we had a laugh together, but they were simply employed to do a job.

One of the highlights of the later period working on Yamaha was helping to organise and run an advanced riding course, at the Nurburgring in Germany. I learned the course by following a local 'Ring Meister' an instructor who'd ridden the notoriously long and difficult circuit for years. Well I say learned it, you don't learn that circuit in a hurry. He kindly said he was very impressed at the way I pushed him, it's much easier following though, especially following someone who knows the lines and braking points intimately, and has brake lights on his bike!

We were both on Yamaha R1s, very fast motorcycles indeed. On the long straight I saw 177mph on the digital speedo. Speed is a strange drug. At 300mph in an airliner there is no sensation of speed, at 180mph tracking in freefall in a cloudless sky there's a slight sensation of speed and yet at anything over 150mph on a motorcycle, or in a fast car, the sensation of speed is incredible. Maybe not if you're an F1 driver who's become accustomed to it, sadly for me I cannot say. I know from the rev counter, rev counters being more accurate than speedos, that I've done 160mph in the GT40. 177mph on the speedo of the R1 is probably a bit optimistic, but 160mph certainly and maybe closer to 170mph, the fastest I've ever gone on land.

Heidi's next job was a disaster, because one of the partners in the firm tried it on. When she went on a business seminar she even felt she had to lie to him about which hotel she was staying at, and sure enough he turned up at the other hotel uninvited. She left the company. With so many outside pressures Heidi and I were rowing too much. One of our fights, not physical I must stress, took place upstairs, whilst Francesca, just two and a half years old was downstairs. Francesca heard us and came upstairs to try and mediate. When I think about it now I weep, just two years old. I told her to go away, quite aggressively, not that I was angry with her. I can't even remember what the row with Heidi was about now. Francesca's little face crumpled, the tears gushed out and she fled. I tried to console her. I've never felt so guilty in all my life. I will take that feeling of guilt, shame and pain to my grave. I'm not at all sure Francesca even remembers it, possibly she thinks she does, because I still apologise to her for it.

At her business seminar, Heidi had made some valuable contacts, the firm she subsequently joined as a result, has, since our divorce, been taken over by a very famous and prestigious City of London stockbroker and Heidi is a highly paid professional. During the last year of our marriage things didn't look so rosy. Back then most of our disputes were over money, home improvements and the like.

The straw that broke the camel's back was probably over double glazing. Tragic really. My relationship with Heidi has had its ups and downs since the divorce too. However, we both love Francesca deeply and usually find compromises. One weekend I was working at Oulton Park race circuit in Cheshire. It was a long drive home and late when I got there. Not surprising then that there were no lights on. However, Heidi's car was no longer out front and as soon as I put a light on I could see pictures were missing from walls, some items of furniture had gone and so on.

Heidi told me it was a trial separation. It was in fact a day or two before Francesca's third birthday. Heidi and I had been together about four years only. Within a few weeks of Heidi's leaving, a divorce petition arrived in the post. Solicitors became involved and for a while things became very nasty. It seems to me that our legal system could use some overhauling, since it seems to require allegations of unreasonable behaviour, at the least, to actually obtain a divorce without waiting. Why can't two adults go to the court and state that they have irreconcilable differences and need to divorce in order to move on?

My new solicitor told me I could defend the divorce if I wanted. I didn't think Heidi and I could resolve our differences and in time she would be able to divorce me anyway. On balance it seemed best to get it over with.

Of course I'd still need a solicitor, there was the matter of custody and financial arrangements. Although recommended by my accountant, the new solicitor was not helpful and I dismissed her before the second hearing. I saw a newspaper article recently about the collapse of the pressure group 'Fathers For Justice'. Some members were getting too extreme in the view of the founder and he didn't want things to go too far it seemed. Eminently sensible. I could understand the desperation of some of the men, when I read their stories however. Fathers still need justice was the conclusion of the newspaper article. I concur.

Knowing what little I do, I felt I could never win custody of Francesca. Nor indeed would it have been the best solution for Francesca herself, if I chose to try. In addition to the bias in favour of mothers, as I and many others perceive it, Heidi had parental support, she could go to work and grandma or grandpa would take and collect Francesca from school and so on. I couldn't compete with that, nor would I argue with the logic, my mother was dead, dad elderly and miles away. Heidi and her family, together, could provide the best solution, under the circumstances, for Francesca. And so I lost my daughter. Not completely of course, but largely. I've missed seeing her grow, lost the opportunity to talk with her, influence her, help her with her homework, on a day to day basis, all the things my parents did for me.

Before matters were finalised Heidi decided, on medical advice, that Francesca needed her tonsils removed and a grommet in her ear. I had my tonsils removed as a child and have always doubted the wisdom. Too many colds, sore throats and sneezes as an adult. I queried the need, Heidi was not pleased. I threatened legal action to stop the operation if I wasn't given medical information, or the chance to talk to the doctors. It didn't help the relationship between Heidi and I, but I did it out of concern for Francesca, not to offend Heidi's feelings. Ultimately, the operation went ahead, on the day of Jill Dando's tragic murder. Heidi and I sat together in the ward listening to the news on the TV playing there, whilst trying to amuse and reassure Francesca.

In the end it could have been a lot worse and I know of many men who've lost all, or nearly everything. I can't help but believe that government's sole interest is that the state should not pay, justice can be sacrificed in that noble cause. After all, we have wars to pay for and men who go to work can afford it, let's take the easy route. Personally it hasn't been like that for me. I'm very far from being the worst affected. Financially at least Heidi and I have come to amicable agreements between ourselves. Why then does the Child Support Agency go after men who are already paying, or where ex husband and wife have an amicable agreement? It hasn't happened to me thank goodness, but it does go on.

In my case Heidi got a lump sum and I got a period of grace to get my finances in order, before I started paying child maintenance. I was supposed to have Francesca every other weekend, every Boxing Day and a weeks holiday at Easter to take her ski-ing. Heidi would give her a summer holiday. Things rarely worked out like that. In the first place Francesca was enrolled at the Medway School of Dancing for a large part of every Saturday. Ironically the place where Heidi and I first met. So, my every other weekend became every other Sunday. I love dancing and I didn't want to be a hypocrite, or deny Francesca a great opportunity, so I didn't rock the boat. Of course with holidays, family commitments, or special treats not every alternate Sunday came my way either.

Today I look at my daughter and I see a gentle soul, generous and able to share with other kids. Not perfect, no one is, but even allowing for my natural bias, I'm sure she's on the side of the angels. I cannot take the credit, well, in part I hope. I have to accept she has Heidi's genes as well as mine though, and that although I wanted more input Heidi has brought her up, and done very, very well.

CHAPTER 26

Swing Dancer

THE LINDY HOP is a dance. When I was dancing Rock and Roll with Heidi, I'd never heard of it. Heidi and I had made friends with a lady in Tonbridge, who we'd met at our dance lessons, and we sometimes took her with us to the Rocker's Club. After Heidi and I split, Marji continued going to Rock and Roll with a new friend of hers called Mike. One evening I was to accompany Marji and Mike to a Rock and Roll do at Twickenham, quite a long drive from Tonbridge. Mike was usually a very reliable guy but he didn't show up and the time wore on. Sadly Mike's mother had been taken into hospital and Mike had been too worried to think of phoning. Eventually Marji suggested it was too late to go to Twickenham but the two of us would still have time to go to a thing called Jitterbugs just up the road in Sevenoaks.

Sounded fine to me. At Jitterbugs a lovely lady called Julie Oram was teaching the Lindy Hop. I'd never heard of it and I found it difficult. I also found that I loved the music. I'd never really listened to jazz or swing before. I'd been brought up with classical music and jumped straight to rock and pop as an adolescent. This whole new genre of music I found delightful.

Marji and Mike continued their Rock and Roll journey, I jumped ship and became a swing dance addict. Not only did I love the music, but I was relishing the challenge. Despite my sports teacher's disdain I'd really always found physical things relatively easy: ski-ing, horse riding, sailing, learning to drive, practising badminton with my mother who was excellent at the game and of course I'd taken to skydiving like a duck to water, and won a motorcycle racing championship. Yet here was a physical activity, requiring co-ordination which I found really hard, despite knowing the basics of Rock and Roll dancing already. Even in recent years I've seen new dancers, Jamie I hate you, of course not really, who've come along and seemingly become terrific dancers really quickly and easily.

I went to Jitterbugs in Sevenoaks every week, but my progress wasn't fast enough for my liking, and anyway I was enjoying it so much that once a week every Friday really wasn't enough for me. I said to Julie "is there anywhere else I can do this?" She was mortified "why, don't you like my teaching?" she looked terribly wounded. "No silly, I want to do more, are there other places, other nights?" "Oh" she said "well if you're really keen you could come up to my club in Leicester Square on Wednesday nights." That worked rather well, it wasn't cheap but the train went straight into Charing Cross and I could walk to Leicester Square. So every Wednesday I was making my way up to town on virtually empty trains, as all the commuters were returning to Sevenoaks, Tonbridge and The Wells on packed ones.

Jitterbugs, held in those days in the Notre Dame Hall, Leicester Place just off Leicester Square, was fabulous and it probably had the best sprung dance floor in London. Sadly for dance, and ironically, given the revival of interest in dance recently, with Strictly Come Dancing and the like on television, the venue was subsequently purchased and converted into a theatre. As if London is short of theatres. The first production there was the life story of Boy George. A few years ago however it was a thriving Lindy Hop Club every Wednesday, very often with other dances on other nights. In London I met many, many new dancers and discovered another club I could go to on Monday nights at the Grosvenor Rooms, later the Improv Club in Tottenham Court Road where a chap called Martin Ellis was teaching. He'd only just started teaching then and appeared a little nervous, but he was a fabulous dancer and I loved the moves, steps and links he was teaching, so now I was dancing Lindy three nights a week and because of my much wider social circle I was learning about new venues and special events all the time, so that very often I danced Lindy four or five nights a week.

All dressed up in a World War Two GI uniform like the ones I later sold. On this occasion I was to perform as a dancer at an event being held to honour American veterans from the daylight bombing raids that left the UK to bomb Germany in the later stages of the war. The losses were as horrific as it must have been to be below. The event moved me greatly and again contributed to my belief that human beings have to grow out of this lunacy called war.

The investment of time and money started to pay off. I got better, slowly but surely, and was getting the confidence to dance with girls who really knew what they were doing, it was wonderful. So what is Lindy Hop I hear you ask. Well I've read a few books now, watched videos and spoken to many, many dancers and although sometimes the information is slightly contradictory, well it is history now I suppose, this is the basic story as I understand it.

In the nineteen twenties there was the Charleston craze, whilst before that ballroom dancing was the thing. Ballroom dancing is, like Lindy, partner dancing. You get to hold the girl, I like that. Also in the nineteen twenties there was a degree of racial segregation in the USA which meant that ballrooms like the Savoy in Harlem were mostly frequented by black dancers, ballrooms like the Roseland mostly frequented by whites. Although the Savoy was the first ballroom not to be officially segregated, so white dancers could, and did, go there. The big bands sometimes had black and white musicians, less so in the early days when most were one or the other, even much later on some had a predominance of one or the other.

In the Savoy ballroom in Harlem, as early as nineteen twenty six, (the Savoy opened its doors for the first time in March nineteen twenty six), black musicians were experimenting and leading the way, swing music was emerging. The Charleston dance craze was declining. Later, the new musical style would be copied by Benny Goodman. Some historians credit the start of the swing age to a later tour by Benny Goodman, nineteen thirty five in fact, which to my mind is somewhat after the fact! He'd listened to the musicians in Harlem and his band were swing pioneers, as far as white folks were concerned. A great band they were too, I'm a big fan, but they were not the first innovators of the genre. Benny Goodman was playing swing on his late night radio slot in New York, during the thirties, and when he went on tour he struggled, well he struggled in New York and all stations west until he got to California where they were queued around the block. The reason being that his late night New York radio programme was being picked up at peak time all those miles west, different time zone of course, and the people loved it. And so, officially the swing age was born. However, back to nineteen twenty six in Harlem. Black dancers there were experimenting with new moves to fit the new music, and they'd adapted Charleston moves to fit their new style too.

The new dance didn't really have a name. It's been suggested to me that they called it the breakaway, because in ballroom you kept the lady close, but in the new dance you swung her out. Others say breakaway is rather the original name for a move which today we call a swing out and that the dance was simply called The Hop. So to 1927. There were dance marathons then, remember the movie 'They Shoot Horse's Don't They'. I'm told it was at a dance marathon, but whatever the event was, a newspaper journalist asked a black dancer by the name of Shorty George Snowden "hey, what's that new dance you're doing?" Presumably no one outside the Savoy had seen it much. Well George, who has a dance step named after him, the 'Shorty George' unsurprisingly, was a bit of a wit. Furthermore, that week or maybe even that day a young man called Charles Lindbergh had made the first solo aeroplane flight across the Atlantic, non stop. America was in love with its new hero and a newspaper headline had read 'Lucky Lindy Hops The Atlantic'. "We call it the Lindy Hop" quipped George and so a new dance craze was born.

The dance had its apogee in the forties and went through the dark days of the war, surviving into the fifties when smaller, less costly rock and roll bands put the big bands out of business. Well mostly, it was still possible to find some swing even in the ironically named swinging sixties, and jazz of course goes on through every storm and changing fashion. Fair enough, music has to progress, Rock and Roll, Bill Haley and Elvis they were the immediate future in the fifties. Swing and swing dance had ruled the roost for twenty five years a remarkable thing when you look at popular music today. In that time swing produced a great variety of great music, and the dancers innovated so many steps and styles that you could learn the dance for a lifetime and still not know it all. I've met a ninety one year old dancer, more of whom in a minute, who says he cannot lay claim even to knowing all the different Lindy Charleston variations.

So why was I learning Lindy Hop at a club called Jitterbugs. Jitterbug is a dance too, right? In fact Jitterbug and Lindy Hop are the same dance! Now history gets written by many different people often with slightly different ideas. At this point in the story there's a chicken and egg situation. Frankie Manning is a ninety one, at the time of writing, year old swing dancer and teacher. Yes he's teaching at ninety one, two hip replacements, but he's still teaching an energetic dance like the Jitterbug!

Well he and I would prefer to call it the Lindy Hop. What is fact is that Frankie danced at the Savoy ballroom in his youth. Only the best dancers danced in an area there known as the Cat's Corner, dancing has always had a competitive side to it. From the Cat's Corner a dance group known as Whitey's Lindy Hoppers were recruited, by Herbert White. These guys and gals were professionals, Hep Cats and Gators in the slang of the time. Frankie danced in all sorts of exciting places, The Cotton Club, the famous Roxy Theatre and in the movie Hellzapoppin' amongst others. He knew Bille Holiday personally and danced on the same bill, but the crucial engagement was on Broadway, in 1939, where Whitey's Lindy Hoppers were hired to dance in the musical Swingin' the Dream. Loosely based on Shakespeare's Mid Summer Night's Dream, it was a big show, with big stars such as the Benny Goodman Quintet and Louis Armstrong, Fletcher Henderson played piano. In the show Whitey's Lindy Hoppers danced the Lindy Hop, but they appeared on stage dressed as grasshoppers and bugs, jumping out of the trees and bushes.

The scene was called the Jitterbug scene. Now, did they

call it the Jitterbug scene because people were already calling the dance the Jitterbug, or did the dance become the Jitterbug because of the show. Certainly the name Jitterbug came into common parlance after the show, despite the fact that the show itself was not a success and closed early. One dancer suggested to me that white dancers may not have wanted to call it the Lindy Hop because that was a black dance, so Jitterbug fitted the bill. However, I don't know if there's any evidence for that. Certainly society was more racist then, so appalling when you meet a man like Frankie who's such a wonderful gentle man, with so much to give, so much in fact that he has given, and with a rich, deep, infectious laugh that reminds me of my own grandfather in fact.

Some will have it that Jitterbug is a different dance, that whites danced more upright, more jerkily and that makes it a different dance. To me it's semantics and just to muddy the water further Jitter Sauce was slang for booze and a Jitterbug someone who drank too much of it. There are reports that Benny Goodman made a comment after a 1938 concert, which had the kids dancing in the aisles (So Bill Haley that wasn't new either!) that they looked like a bunch of Jitterbugs, this of course pre-dates Swingin' The Dream, but did it catch on? So now you know as much as I do! Romantically speaking I like Frankie's story about Swingin' The Dream.

Frankie Manning also tells a story of how he and his colleagues were removed from the rear of an auditorium where they had already performed. They were waiting to hear Billie Holiday sing, but the management, who were quite happy to have black performers were not prepared to have them in the audience. After the show Billie Holiday asked them why they weren't there as expected. They explained and she refused to perform there again unless there was a table for her friends and colleagues. The management backed down, good on her.

I was thrilled to discover that one of Whitey's top Lindy Hoppers in the nineteen thirties was a guy named Snooky, less thrilled when I discovered that Whitey and his henchmen had worked Snooky over after he agreed to dance for someone else. Harlem was a tough place.

Jitterbug as it had become known, came to Europe in the war. Hitler had banned swing, the strongest possible recommendation in my book! However, after the war, during the occupation, Germans were exposed to it as well. It's my pet theory that the British, French and Germans, took the dance and did different things with it. Swing died out and Rock and Roll took its place, Jitterbug became Jive. Interestingly if you mention Jitterbug to most people they think of the girl being thrown between the gentleman's legs, over his shoulder or back, all the really athletic stuff.

Those moves are called aerials and jivers do them too. Who was the very first person to do aerials? So far as we know it was Frankie Manning again, who practised them at home on the roof of their apartment block with his partner Freida Washington, who was a near neighbour. They practised until they got the timing perfectly on the beat for everything they did. Then they introduced them competitively in the place where it all started, the Savoy Ballroom. Sadly the Savoy is no longer with us, now there's a housing estate where music and dance history was made. However, Frankie campaigned for and had a plaque put up, to at least commemorate a place that was, in many ways, the heart and soul of musical Harlem. Certainly it was the largest and most beautiful ballroom in Harlem and some would say in the world.

The French developed a style of jive they called C'est Le Rock, the Germans developed something they call Boogie Woogie, although the Americans have a dance called Boogie Woogie too. In Britain we kept it very energetic, so indeed did the Germans with their Boogie Woogie, but the style is quite different, look at fifties film footage if you get the chance, or go to authentic Rocker's clubs like Rockola, still going on Canvey Island to see authentic British style Rock and Roll jive.

An entrepreneur in England brought back the French style to Britain and created a franchise called Ceroc, which is a registered trade mark. The name being taken from C'est Le Rock, (It's The Rock). The French style is less energetic than the British and it's more adaptable to different sorts of music. Personally I'm not that enamoured, but then I've only ever been a very few times. My problem is that I see dance as an extension of the music, as a way to interpret the music. I love swing music and it inspires me. The dance should be like a clarinet, cornet or saxophone solo weaving its theme around the theme of the music but in harmony with it. Well that's the aim as I see it, I'm not claiming it's something I always achieve!

So the French style allows you to jive to all sorts of music, even music that is neither swing nor Rock and Roll. That doesn't mean it's always appropriate to jive to every piece of music. It just doesn't always suit or harmonise with the music. Then there's the way you do it. Ceroc, registered trademark, teaches routines, some of which are almost choreography but most of which, fair's fair can be lead. Many swing dance teachers do the same and novice dancers can only dance what they know, I understand that too. I've been there, but many Ceroc, registered trade mark, dancers that I see at other venues, just repeat their repertoire of set moves over and over regardless of what they're dancing to. At the least keep moves small and subtle, when the music is gentle and make them big and extrovert when the music is upbeat, fast tempo and big in character. Then move on and try to be selective, interpret the music in the moves you choose and the way in which you move.

What I must say in favour of the Ceroc, registered trademark, organisation is that they've brought a whole load of people into dancing and have popularised it to the benefit of all dancers. Many Ceroc, registered trademark, dancers do go on to try other things, especially it would seem the Lindy Hop, so no complaints there. And I think a lot of people have met lovers and partners at Ceroc, registered trademark, events. So that's a service too, in its own way.

Lindy Hop is one of a family of swing dances from the

era, there's Balboa, Collegiate and Carolina Shag, the Shim Sham, Big Apple, Black Bottom and others, but Lindy Hop is probably the number one, the most innovative and best loved. However, Balboa and Shag are being taught these days, there's even an annual London Balboa Festival. Whilst Jitterbugs still thrives albeit at a new venue, Stern Hall, near Marble Arch and Simon Selman's London Swing Dance Society has the wonderful, famous old jazz club, the 100 Club on Monday nights. Martin Ellis who started out teaching at The Improv is one of London's top dancers and teachers and the organiser of a fabulous annual Savoy Ball in London. Robert and Claire Austin, teach Hollywood style Lindy Hop as pioneered by a famous dancer called Dean Collins. He started on the East coast and migrated to Hollywood where he took the Savoy style swing out moves and re invented them, making them look more whippy. Some dancers are very particular about which style they do. I love both and it's hard to judge which is the most dramatic. You can only realistically compare when you watch superb exponents of Savoy style like Julie Oram or Hollywood style experts like Robert and Claire.

The swing dance revival is not just happening in the UK. True there are very active swing dance scenes in London, Edinburgh, Gloucester, Leeds, Northampton, Leicester, and Bristol that I know of, but it's also happening in Los Angeles, New York, San Francisco, Barcelona, Stockholm, Gothenburg, Paris, Montpellier, Munich, Melbourne, St Petersburg, Moscow, and too many places to list. I even went to Budapest, with no idea that there was any swing dancing there, but I found it. So how, after virtually disappearing did Lindy Hop make a comeback? It's a fascinating story and many people are involved, but largely some young Americans and some young Swedes can take the credit.

About seventeen years ago a group of young Swedes who'd been watching old black and white movies, featuring dancers like Whitey's Lindy Hoppers and The Nicholas Brothers started trying to copy the dance routines. They were teaching themselves, slowing the movies down, even examining them frame by frame. Then one of them thought, why don't we go to America and see if we can track down one of the original dancers, maybe they're still alive and we could learn from them. Strangely some young Americans, Steven Mitchell and Erin Stevens, had the same idea around the same time. Frankie Manning, who'd gone to work for the US Mail after the dancing and performing dried up, was about to become a dance teacher. We'll stick with the Swede's story however, because they went on to create another phenomenon.

You can just imagine three blonde haired, blue eyed Vikings tracking down an old black dancer in New York, "go on, you talk to him, no you" and when they did, what was he to think, were they Feds, IRS? However, it all worked out rather well. Sadly the first dancer they found and learned from, Al Minns, is no longer alive, but he did lead them to re-discover Frankie Manning, who's largely responsible for Lindy Hop's amazing world wide popularity again. The Swedes formed a dance group called The Rhythm Hot Shots, there was also a group calling itself the Swedish Swing Dance Society. They collaborated and started a dance camp in a village north of Stockholm, on the coast, it's called Herrang. It's such a tiny place most Swedes had never heard of it until 2005. Unless they were dancers!

Herrang has a lovely marina and a small beach. It also has a beautiful lake with deer wandering past and rowing boats on the water. It's quite a large village, once there was a mine and an associated factory, when the iron ore ran out both closed. So there are many homes, but more than a few are unoccupied as people moved away in search of employment. There is one shop, a village school and a Folkets Hus, in English a Folks House or Peoples House. Once every Swedish town and village had one. Often it housed a library and had a dance floor, it was a social amenity for the community. Sometimes it would have a Danse Banaan attached, an outdoor dance barn. The one at Herrang has all these amenities a dance floor upstairs and one outdoors by the lake. Over the main road is the school which has a gymnasium and a canteen.

The small group of Swedish swing dance enthusiasts used the Folkets Hus to learn and to teach in. The number of interested parties grew. Word got out and it grew some more. Today there is an annual swing dance, dance camp. Visitors can learn Lindy Hop, Tap Dance, German style Boogie Woogie and there are always a few Blues Dance lessons and often some Balboa and Shag. Dance camps happen all over the world. Mostly they start on Friday afternoon and finish on Sunday evening, people drifting away early if they have work on Monday. A few dance camps last a week, yes a whole week of dancing – exhausting. Herrang lasts for a month, the entire month of July. There are five dance floors, two at the Folkets Hus plus the school gymnasium and two marquees. I think they will need more soon!

I've never suggested it to Lennart Westerlund, the prime, but by no means only mover and shaker, but I dream about the old factory being made into a recreation of the Savoy Ballroom. I've never mentioned it because I've never been inside the factory, it's almost certainly unsuitable and anyway a project like that would cost millions. However, Herrang is a place you can dream, it's almost a surreal experience. Certainly it's a sleep depriving one. It gets dusky around 11pm, by 1am the sun is back up. You can have dance lessons all day and dance socially all night and people do. Some of them for the whole month. You can go for one week, two, three or the whole four. Herrang attracts the best dancers and teachers from all over the globe, not just Europe and the USA but I've met people from India, Australia, South America, in fact almost everywhere.

Famous jazz musicians turn up there, Hollywood choreographers, I even met Fayard Nicholas one of the Nicholas Brothers dance act, a great dancer and a big, big star of the old black and white movies. It's quite something to meet people like this, in an unheard of village in the forests of Sweden! In 2004 a well known Swedish film and television producer decided he'd like to make a documentary programme about the Herrang phenomenon, to be called Swing Invasion, since it brings in hundred's even thousands of dancers from around the world. They rent different levels of accommodation in the marina, in empty houses, in the school, above the shop, they share with local families, they camp, they caravan, they come in boats. The broadcasters weren't that interested, so Svante Grundberg went ahead and filmed in 2004 at his own expense. The resulting documentary was so stunning that it sold instantly to a national Swedish TV channel and went out at peak time, nationally during the 2005 event.

Every week at the camp there is a cabaret night, a blues night, a fancy dress night, in fact there's something special every night and the energy and enthusiasm that goes into sets, costumes, surprise guest appearances and other surprises is quite incredible. Visitors never know what will happen next. It's totally remarkable.

The first time I went to Herrang I stayed for three weeks. I came back so drained I felt my dancing had gone backwards, but other people said they could see the improvement. On my fourth and most recent visit I stayed for the whole four weeks. Today I'm not the best swing dancer by far, but after a slow start I'm happy with what I've achieved. I've even taught a beginners course in Tunbridge Wells, I've given private lessons at Dance Works and Pineapple, danced in a movie and confidentially I gave lessons in Lindy Hop, at studios in Hammersmith, to the movie choreographer for a day, a few weeks before filming! She avoided me like the plague when she found I was one of the dancers on set in the film, how embarrassing for her, but I didn't tell anyone except the lady from Jitterbugs who I was dancing with. The choreographer had told me prior to her lesson she could learn a dance that evolved over a quarter of a century in one day. Such arrogance. I saw her demonstrating to one couple and winced at her style.

CHAPTER 27

No Limits

I FIRST MET Robin Bradley when he was selling media space for a magazine called Motorcycle International. I was buying space for Yamaha at the time. He seemed like a decent kind of guy and it seemed a shame that his media space selling business went to the wall. Robin then started his own magazine. It was called European Dealer News and it wasn't at all a bad idea. It was all to do with the Harley Davidson market, or more accurately the American V-Twin market. The American motorcycle scene is an interesting arena all on its own. In America, Europe and in Britain there are sports bikes, classics, tourers, off road and other classes of motorcycle. In the UK sports bikes have always been very popular. The bike heading the sales charts in the UK is more often than not a sports bike. In France, Paris Dakar style bikes are very popular despite all the other classes being present and in the US, likewise all types are present, but, over there Harley are top dog. Years ago they put their main competitor Indian out of business and although there is a re-born Indian brand, just as Britain has a re-born Triumph brand, the new Indians are numerically small fry, alongside the Harleys.

There are very few Harleys on the road however, that are as they were when they left the factory. Harley owners love to customise their bikes and Harley sell thousands of accessories to help them, but they're not the only ones. Some customisers merely play with the appearance of the bike, others change engine components, even engines and gearboxes. It's possible to build something that looks like a Harley Davidson without a single Milwaukee made bolt in it. And many companies do, American Ironhorse, West Coast Choppers, Choppers Inc, to name just a few of the many. Companies such as S&S, famous for carburettors, now make complete high performance engines, as do Rev Tech and others. By the time you've looked at everything else, through gearboxes, frames, suspension, lighting, braking, wheels, exhausts, luggage, controls and everything else you may find on a motorcycle, not to mention helmets and apparel, you find you've got a vast, varied and fascinating industry all based on and making a living around the American V-twin motorcycle. There are some incredibly talented engineers at work too.

In Europe, other styles of motorcycle may be more popular, but Harley Davidson sales this side of the pond are not inconsequential and there are many European firms involved in customising and building custom bikes too, especially in Germany, but also in Britain, France, Italy and others.

Robin's idea was to send his European Dealer News to all the Harley dealers and customising firms and so on, involved in any part of this business in Europe. The magazine would be free to them and it would open up a new market for all the American parts manufacturers to advertise their wares. It wasn't an unqualified success but it did fly, even though it pretty soon became clear that Robin had missed an obvious trick. Before very long, Americans were asking him why his magazine was Europe only, America is a huge market and a vast country, they wanted to advertise on their home turf too. Robin confessed to me he'd just assumed they'd be catered for at home, never checked! Not only that but European manufacturers of parts and accessories wanted to advertise their wares to American bike builders and distributors. It should have been a two way street from day one.

European Dealer News became American Motorcycle Dealer and AMD was sent to people in the trade in Europe and America. In the early days of Robin's publishing business, when his now wife Sonja was his German sales rep I gave him some help and he helped me acquire some parts for the old Harley Davidson Shovelhead I was restoring. Later when Tradewind Advertising was up and running I produced an exhibition stand for him. He took an age to pay me and had to do it in instalments. The writing was on the wall, but I still saw Robin as a friend.

Later still Robin and I had a conversation where he asked me if I'd like to write for the magazine. Now Tradewind Advertising was ultimately closed down, by me, in order that I could pursue my interests in dancing, acting and sailing. It paid all its invoices in full, always, but by the time Robin asked me if I'd like to be his Editorial Director Tradewind had lost some key business.

Neil Cowell at Sempol had sadly lost his wife Jenny. When he remarried he took his new wife off to Australia and on his return promptly announced there was more to life than work and retired. The new MD felt we were too far away geographically and that he wanted to work with someone local. We'd never put a foot wrong but it was goodbye to that client. The group of business consultants we'd been working for split up and went their separate ways, nothing to do with us but bye bye to another client. At Yamaha our main contact moved from motorcycles to another branch of the company. Such was his contribution that two people were employed to replace him, both with their own contacts that they wished to use. They were to discover our expertise was useful too and we did get work from them, but it was reduced. Michael Brandon had a son at university, when he joined Dad's firm he started producing the work we'd previously been creating. You just can't odds those things, and so we still had Yamaha, but in part only, New Hampshire and Boyer-Bransden, were still there, not huge pieces of business themselves, but everything else was really small potatoes.

And so my choices were to go back to a vigorous campaign for new business on behalf of Tradewind, or move in with Robin and get work straight away, work I would enjoy, writing about motorcycles and components, meeting engineers and designers, research and development guys. I would travel to international shows, visit firms at their premises, take photographs. There was no contest really, but I didn't want to go back to being employed, least of all by someone who'd been a friend. So the arrangement was that I would take a desk in Robin's premises and move my phone lines in there, one for Tradewind Advertising and one exclusively for New Hampshire. I would bill Robin's company, No Limits something or other as Tradewind Advertising. I say something or other, because Robin's own publishing business had now gone to the wall once or more already, been sold to another publisher and bought back again. Stable it was not. So No Limits Publishing and No Limits Media were two of the names the company went by at different times.

Martin and Louise continued much as before in the old premises. Louise found someone else to rent the space I'd vacated thankfully and I continued giving them as much work as I could. In fact Louise handled what was left of the Yamaha business nigh on single-handed. I dealt with Boyer and New Hampshire from Robin's offices. Thank goodness I didn't let it all go.

Robin told me that his current Editor was not up to the job in his opinion. Nonetheless, I was employed as Editorial Director, Karen retained her title as Editor. She must have been justifiably suspicious of me when I arrived, but I found her capable, knowledgeable, enthusiastic and hard working, as well as a decent and jolly work colleague, and all that given the difficulties of my being foist on her as a superior in the company. She was superb, what the hell was Robin talking about?

He had a really strong team in fact. By now Sonja, his previous German sales representative was his partner and German sales were handled by Michael a very Christian and moral man with a strong work ethic, Paul handled UK sales and was effusively enthusiastic, Roger handled accounts and worked hard to protect Robin from himself, Carlotta, the daughter of a charming English lady and an aristocratic Italian handled Italy, but there were too many staff to list here, Robin was rushing things again. He launched an industry-wide British motorcycle trade magazine called British Dealer News.

I worked hard at making it a success and wrote much of it personally. When Robin's overspending got the company into difficulties again it was at least a saleable asset that delayed the next bankruptcy a little.

My first business trip was to a V-twin Expo in Cincinnati, I really enjoyed it and found some swing dancing on the first evening. The second trip was to a larger motor cycle exhibition in Indianapolis. This was all industry, not just V-Twin. I remember the trip well, because it's one of the few times in my life when I've really lost my temper. Karen came on that trip as well as other members of staff and the company had a stand. Karen and I spent most of our time, on our feet, going around interviewing, photographing and making editorial contacts, it was satisfying but exhausting work.

At one point I said to Karen, "come on lets go and get a coffee". We're used to good service in America, but this took the biscuit. Karen sat at a table I went to the counter. "Two coffees please", he took the money. "Help yourself from the flask", there was an enormous vacuum flask with a spout and a push button in the top, but no cups. "Can I have a couple of cups then please", "we've run out", "well I'll use Coca Cola cups then", "can't do that, they're not for hot liquids", "well I'll have my money back then", "can't do that". By now he was serving the next customer. One of the canteen staff left. Had he gone to get cups? It appeared he had, but he came back without any and still they wouldn't return my money. Time was dragging on. Karen, who's table was around the corner out of sight, came to see what was going on. I explained to her in a loud voice, so that other customers, who were by now no longer ordering coffee anyway, and the staff could hear. The staff were not the least embarrassed, or interested and then I snapped. "Well, if you're not going to give me anything to put it in I I'll take my coffee in this." I pulled the huge flask off the counter, balanced it on my shoulder and marched off with it. They just carried on serving as if nothing had happened.

I marched back to our stand with the flask, Karen trotting

along beside me giggling. I put the flask in our magazine store and acquired some cups from someone or somewhere. We all had coffee for the rest of the day and when the show emptied I put the metre high flask back where I knew the canteen staff would find it. Not that they were in the least concerned I don't suppose.

On another occasion I went to France to see a motorcycle dyno manufacturer. These are huge contraptions, where the bike is ridden up on to it, the rear wheel of the motorcycle drives a roller and the machine measures the power produced at the wheel. This one also had diagnostic functions, with probes inserted in the bike's exhausts. Fascinating. I met a fabulous engineer and engine builder in Nevada and a guy building a motorcycle world land speed record contender, intended to substantially exceed 300mph on two wheels. One of the most bizarre experiences was in Virginia City Nevada.

I've always had a strong interest in Greek and Roman history and to some extent Egyptian. I own a few small artefacts too, an oil lamp, some coins, a household god or lares. And I've visited numerous museums, and read as much as I get time to. Virginia City is an old gold rush town, in Nevada in the western United States, its history is relatively modern. I strolled up the wooden boardwalk, looking at the Victorian era buildings and then I saw it. A sign saying Egyptian and Roman antiquities for sale. There was an arrow pointing up a side street. I couldn't resist looking, in the shop I saw Egyptian scarabs and statuettes, Roman coins, pottery, jewellery and glass. It looked genuine too. I asked the man behind the counter how come he was selling such antiquities in Virginia City. He told me he'd been collecting them for years, was a student of Egyptian and Roman history, and it had been his passion for donkey's years, he'd been to any number of fairs and antique shops in Europe. The house was full of this stuff, but his long suffering wife had finally had enough. Some of it at least had to go, so they put it in their tourist gift shop! He was totally genuine I'm sure, and knew his stuff. I didn't have a lot of cash on me, but

I bought a Roman bracelet. Just so I could tell people I found it in Virginia City Nevada.

During the time I worked for Robin I had many great adventures, but at the back of one's mind the whole time was will I get paid! Eventually Robin's bubble burst again, he was officially bankrupt once more. Well, that's to say that the limited company was, not Robin. And, all those really decent and talented people he'd employed were now unemployed. My prospects didn't look too good either, I still had some Tradewind business but not much and Robin's now dead, but protected by limited liability, company owed us over two thousand pounds.

Robin and Sonja asked two people, myself, and Ben the designer who produced the artwork for the magazine, to help them get back on their feet. I'd write the magazine, Ben would produce it, they'd go back to selling. They also said that "as soon as money starts coming in we'll pay you what we owe you from the last company". There was nothing else on the immediate horizon and the magazine was good and viable, with the right overheads and a small team, it really had potential, always had. Ben and I both agreed. Today I've lost count of Robin's business failures, it's telling that they had to re-start in business as a partnership, no longer with limited liability status, but still they carry on. In their wake a trail of bad debts and innocent people hurt, both employees, my goodness they've got through a few of them, and suppliers. I was distressed to learn that Alan Miller at OWM&M was also a victim of one of Robin's earlier bad debts. Alan being the man who produced the first ever piece of Tradewind artwork for me, and a thoroughly decent chap.

Often they've had to pay printers up front or nothing would be printed, and advertisers have suffered too, print runs haven't always been very impressive. I feel a little guilty about helping them come back, but you have to hand it to them, they're survivors, they'd have found a way. It's their victims I feel sorry for. I am one in a small way myself of course. Robin and Sonja went back into business as a partnership, they were barred from being company directors, at that moment anyway Robin told me. So a limited liability company was no longer an option for them. I checked at Companies House, via the internet and their names are not on the list at the time of writing, so maybe they're free to take risks with other people's money once more. I don't know, if so it's a strange system the UK operates. We started to make some money, but instead of paying me back, the money they'd promised but had no legal obligation to pay from the old company, they started employing people again!

The first was Steve. Today he's a very close friend. We shared an office, and shared jokes and good times. We frequently went to lunch together and saw one another outside work. Not straight away though. For one thing I was not at all happy that Steve had been employed. I felt his wages were being paid out of the money promised to me from the old debt. After all I'd honoured my commitment to Robin. I fully appreciated that this was not Steve's fault but what was I to say to him. I wanted to tell him the sort of people he was working for, but it would probably come across badly, he'd find out soon enough anyway, but most of all I didn't want to burst his bubble. Steve had relocated from Luton, with his beautiful, young Polish wife and their adorable baby girl. They had high hopes and I could certainly put myself in his shoes from past experience. So I said nothing, nothing at all. I'm sure Steve was none too impressed with his new colleague, in fact I know he wasn't and he told Ewa so!

It couldn't last though, Steve and I share many interests and a similar sense of humour and so before long we became really good buddies. We enjoyed working together and got the job done. However, my relationship with Robin was strained and sliding, with Sonja it was even worse. Robin complained that I spent too much time chatting to Steve and he didn't like me going off to dance in the evenings when he worked late. My attitude has always been to get the job done and enjoy life too, so bearing in mind that I was employed by Tradewind Advertising Ltd. not Dealer-World.com as the new company was known, that I'd helped bail Robin out, that he'd broken his word to me, and that I had enough editorial written in the computer for the next two issues, I decided to do as Robin asked! It was farcical, for a couple of weeks I worked like a demon, now we had enough stuff written for about five issues! Probably more, and of course I invoiced Robin for the number of words or articles written. Suddenly he was presented with some large invoices. Well he'd asked for it. Now he didn't want me to be so productive! Suddenly he was reluctant to hand over press releases!

Anyway, he would never pay me what he owed me I was certain of that, he'd taken enough others for money, what he owed me didn't mater a fig I'm sure – to him. He carried on employing people and trying yet again to create his business empire. It's still going this time, but there is more incentive, if they go down again there's no limited liability protection, this time Robin and Sonja's house and all their assets will be on the line, although you can be sure people like them spirit things away at need.

As Robin employed more staff and my relationship with him deteriorated he started trying to manoeuvre me out. He didn't have the courage to come right out with it. I'd probably have slugged him, but he did say that as I was technically an outside supplier and since he needed space for new people, would I work from home? That was nearly enough for me to take a swing at him as it was, but frankly the atmosphere was so awful, who would want to stay if there was another way. I knew that once I left the work would dry up, he had plenty of editorial in stock from me anyway. And he's had quite a few writers since!

I moved my phone lines home and started trying to rebuild Tradewind Advertising again. Then Margaret, my wonderful book-keeper, died. My equally terrific accountant showed me how to do it myself, but really my desire had gone out.

Tradewind I thought was dead on its feet, our client losses having been for the most unlikely and unavoidable of reasons, my marriage had failed, access to my daughter was difficult. Were it not for the fact that my father had died also I'd have struggled to make the child maintenance payments. Whilst my ex wife who'd been in debt when I married her and in poorly paid employment, or out of work for much of our marriage, had a high flying city career now.

Dad's passing and the inheritance he left me, kept me afloat, but God knows I'd rather have him than the money. If it hadn't been for the lesson I learned, attempting suicide all those years before I might well have given way to despair. Working from home was also a mistake, one I'd avoided when I first went into business, it's good to get up in the morning and have somewhere to go, it's good to have colleagues and social interaction. This is true even at the best of times, but when things are as bad as they were then, it's a life saver. I needed a new direction.

CHAPTER 28

A Racing Comeback At Daytona

THERE'S ONE EVENT during my time working for Robin that's worthy of a chapter to itself, before we move on. The year 2002, ten years after I retired from motorcycle racing, all racing in fact. Robin's magazine is effectively a Harley-Davidson trade magazine. There had been a Harley-Davidson Sportster race series, and Harley dabbled with a Superbike for a while, but in reality, racing isn't a big thing for Harley Davidson. Therefore the opportunity to race, as a journalist covering the American V-Twin trade market, seemed the most unlikely thing in the world. The world however is a strange place.

Years before, the Harley Davidson company, looking to expand its market and product range had purchased an Italian motorcycle producer, Aermacchi. They later disposed of it, but for a number of years the world was treated to the Aermacchi Harley Davidson. Italian motorcycles have always been as different as can be from American ones, even my own large, heavy Laverda 1000cc triple, the famous Jota is totally different from a big heavy Harley, the latter being a laid back cruiser, the Italian built with just one thought in mind, to go fast.

Aermacchi had produced 250 and 350 cc lightweights known as Sprints. Their single cylinder faced forwards, with the transmission behind. What weight there was, was carried low, these bikes handled, stopped and cornered. The factory raced them too, so today they are eligible for historic racing in the USA and elsewhere. As with many vintage race bikes there aren't too many originals around, so race clubs accept properly specified, accurate replicas as well. Enter enthusiast John Basore. He was involved as a sales representative in the Harley parts market and he was a classic racing devotee. He realised that the standard road going Aermacchi Sprint had essentially the same frame, engine and transmission as the race bike. Therefore, old road going Aermacchi Harley Davidsons would provide a very good and affordable platform to build a GP race replica. It didn't matter how tired the engine was, as it would be rebuilt to race specification anyway.

Getting ready to race at De Land, Florida as a guest rider. My sixth place equalled the bike's best ever result up until then. Not bad, ten years after I retired from racing and on a bike I'd not ridden before, with back to front gears on the wrong side, (compared with the bike I used to race) and at a circuit I'd never seen before. Sadly things wouldn't go so well at Daytona.

On this basis John had put together a package, he would sell complete replicas, or customers could buy the race bits necessary to build their own replica, and simply go buy an old road bike and do the work themselves. A cheap way to enter the otherwise expensive and exclusive world of historic motorcycle racing. John had a couple of bikes prepared and one regular rider in the USA, what he really needed was publicity. Robin pointed out to John that Dealer-World.com had a journalist who had won a race championship in the UK. By this time I was listed as a contributor in the magazine, no longer the heady title Editorial Director, since Robin who had no intention of repaying the money from his last failure now had not just Steve, but a staff of twelve, including we 'contributors' in addition to himself and Sonja.

John was very keen that I should race the bike at two meetings to be held only about a week apart. The first was at Deland Florida, an old airfield race circuit, the second at Daytona, around the famous banking. I sent details of my past experience off to America and John arranged the necessary licence for me. Various advertisers in the magazine came forward with sponsorship in the form of a helmet, gloves, boots, and Vanson Leathers agreed to produce a set of full race leathers, made to measure, in my own design. When they arrived the colour scheme was wrong, but they were superb looking, thick leathers, with body armour and the magazine's name across the back.

Some motorcyclists see scuffed, repaired leathers as having street cred, but I had two sets of crashed and repaired leathers from my previous race career. Since the Vanson leathers were mine to keep I vowed to keep them immaculate! Four practice sessions and just two races, surely I could manage to stay in the saddle that long.

A few days before I was due to fly to Florida a fiftieth birthday party was arranged for my very good friend David O'Brien, who I'd worked with at Westex and PPS. The party was to be held at a grand house in Derbyshire, the home of another friend of both David's and mine, who had been a FIAT regional advertising manager and my competition for the job at RLA, Martin Shead. Two very dear friends, it was inconceivable that I should miss it. My father had been in hospital with prostate and other cancers, but had nonetheless been pronounced potentially curable and after a stay as an in patient was now back at home fending for himself and seemingly on the mend.

I decided to look in on Dad on my way to Derbyshire. When I got there he was in pain, with what he said was indigestion. He didn't have stomach cancer so I figured it was indigestion and went to find a chemist and get something for it. I didn't like to leave him in pain but it seemed like it was probably just something some Milk of Magnesia would deal with. Nonetheless, I suggested to my sister that she look in on him the following day. With some misgiving I continued to the party, where I had a bed and breakfast booked nearby.

The following morning my sister rang to say she'd seen Dad and he'd been much worse, she'd dialled 999, he'd been rushed into Whipps Cross Hospital and wasn't expected to live out the day. I was supposed to be lunching with Dave and partner, and Martin and family. I jumped into the car, called by the house to quickly explain, and then drive from near Ashbourne to Whipps Cross hospital in East London, as fast as I legally and safely could. They were doing everything they could for Dad but said it was inconceivable that he would live. Due to the cancer treatment the wall of his stomach had become very thin, it had ruptured and he'd got blood poisoning as a result. For all that, they gave him drugs to fight infection as well as to control pain, so someone somewhere must have thought there was a chance. Dad did not die, that day, nor the next or the one after. In fact after several days he seemed decidedly stronger.

On that basis and feeling that Dad, whilst not out of the woods, certainly wasn't about to die and wouldn't want me to miss this great opportunity, to race internationally at one of the world's great circuits I decided to go to Florida, but it wouldn't be a case of a quick race and return, there were two races, Deland first then Daytona, and Robin wanted me to cover Bike Week, photograph it, interview people and write a whole series of articles.

As the aircraft flew over the state of Florida I identified the Daytona Raceway, unmistakable from the air, I thought I identified the old World War Two airfield at Deland as well. After disembarking and getting out of the airport, I turned my phone on and changed the settings to pick up a signal in the USA. No sooner had it fired up than there was a call from my sister, Dad had contracted pneumonia in the hospital. I felt like turning right around, but now I'd taken the flight, the equipment from the sponsors and Dad might pull round even now. In my heart all sorts of emotions were tugging at me, my mind was a whirl of self doubt and guilt.

I'd already beaten myself up emotionally for not having taken dad's indigestion seriously enough and going off to a party of all things. Now I was fulfilling the sort of ambition I'd dreamed about, a chance to race and be paid, to have someone else run the team and just concentrate on one thing, racing. Yet how could I concentrate on that while dad was in all probability dying at home. I knew dad would want me to grab the opportunity, my parents had never held me back in anything, quite the reverse they'd always pushed me, not always quite as I'd wanted to be pushed, but hey no one's perfect. And how was I repaying Dad, by not being there when he needed me.

I was in a dark place, but Margaret was there with Dad, I had spent every available moment with him before I left, I'd read one and a half Harry Potter books to him to keep him amused, and I'd left with a clear conscience, he had seemed so much stronger. Finally these thoughts and the fact that I knew dad would want me to grab this opportunity and make the most of it won out. If I was going to do it, I'd better try and get my head around the job and do it right.

I hired a car at the airport and drove to the home of the owner of a company that advertised in the magazine, I was to be a guest in his house and to meet John Basore there. When I'd raced my Yamaha it had been prepared by, and I'd been mentored by Martin Sweet of Slipstream Motorcycles, then in Hildenborough near Tonbridge. They had lost their Yamaha franchise, but an East German motorcycle manufacturer had asked Martin to develop and run their works racers. Martin and Karen were in Florida with their team to race too, what a wonderful piece of luck, I found I had friends there.

The first race was at Deland. I was to race a bike I'd never raced before, never even sat on before, a bike with the gear change on the right, my Laverda has the gear change on the right, but the bike I'd always raced, had the gear change on the left, in the heat of battle would I forget and stomp on the footbrake instead of the gear change? That wasn't the only difference, this machine had drum brakes not discs and on every bike I'd ever ridden first gear was down the others up, on the Aermacchi, first gear was up, the others down! Being a race bike in the old style it wouldn't tick over either, it was essential to keep it spinning or it would stall. There was of course no electric starter, or even a kick start, this bike had to be bump started and being a single it very often wasn't that obliging, one had to time it perfectly or the back wheel would just skid.

When John Basore, witnessed the pom's difficulty in starting it, followed by swiftly stalling it, he must have wondered, what the hell have we got here. He kept whatever thoughts he had to himself, but he can't have expected a top ten finish. I was told that John's bikes had always run top ten, but that sixth was also their best result to date and they'd got a seventh last time out with my bike at the Mid Ohio race meeting the previous year. That was what information I had to measure myself and my performance against. However, in addition to never having seen the bike before I'd never seen the circuit before, at ground level anyway! In order to go fast I would have to learn the circuit on two levels, where does it go next and then what's the best line, where's the last possible braking point, when can I get back into the throttle. It was a tall order on a bike so different from anything I'd been on before and in a strange land so to speak.

I applied myself to the task in the two practice sessions and in the first I was further hampered by a slipping clutch. It wasn't the end of the world though I was still learning where the circuit went at that point, and John had it fixed for the second session when I wanted to push a little. I found the bike underpowered, compared with what I was used to and the brakes not as strong. Naturally, this was historic racing! The bike's heyday had been in the early sixties, when it had won at

Daytona and had won a World Championship. It's first outing had been as early as nineteen sixty one, so it was almost fifties technology, much different from my experience. However, the bike was light and chuckable, too chuckable at Daytona, but what I mean is that it handled well and once I got used to the strange gearbox and brakes I was able to throw it into corners with confidence, and more importantly, carry corner speed, since acceleration wasn't stunning.

Quietly I was very confident I'd show John Basore that the pom was more competitive than he could possibly have hoped! Come the race, things got off to a bad start. The bike was not running cleanly for the whole of the first lap and I was well down the field, when it suddenly cleared its throat and ran as it should have. My feeling is that whilst waiting on the grid for the off I didn't rev it hard enough and that the spark plug had become partially fouled. After one lap of hard use it must have burned off any deposit and away we went. Most galling but not unexpected given his experience, and the fact that he'd had a trouble free first lap, my team mate on equal machinery was ahead. One never likes to be beaten by someone on equal equipment in the same team, even if they are familiar with both bike and circuit. It's not logical, it's emotional. I wanted to beat Craig. Even if he was the current 350 champion from the previous year (on a different bike) with a big No1 on his fairing! I did beat him, but only because he retired. An adjuster on his gearbox, or gear change, had backed off as I recall, with the vibration. However, I was now the only representative of John Basore's team in the race and my bike was running well. When Craig retired he was running sixth and I was up to ninth, but I was still moving up, oh the joy of overtaking people in competition again.

I was of course eighth once Craig retired and I made two more successful overtaking manoeuvres, which I made stick and pulled clear. I was now in the best position the bike had ever finished, better than last time out and if I could make one more place I'd have set a record for the team. Realistically I had already achieved more than I could ever have hoped for in the circumstances. The rider in fifth was some way ahead and it was getting towards the closing stages of the race. Maybe he felt comfortable and not under any threat, but I was getting closer all the time and my blood was up. At turn three I made a move, up the outside I think, which would put me on the inside for turn 4 which is immediately after three. Memory plays tricks and a lot happened in that race, but whichever side I went, it was too brave. I'm not sure now whether I expected too much of the old style drum brake at the front, by now very, very hot with the hard work I'd subjected it to getting past other people, or whether the front end just couldn't hold the tarmac, but things got a bit hairy as we say! I got out of the brake and reapplied it, stayed on, but ran wide, I'd been in fifth, with my nose ahead for just a split second, but I couldn't make it stick. Further, the other fellow was wide awake to the threat now and that was how it finished. I never got another chance. And, I decided, on the last lap, the tyres were definitely not as good as they had been, the rubber was going off.

After Deland and before Daytona I expressed my doubts about the tyres to John Basore, who said something about new tyres from Avon not having arrived. I don't know how many races the tyres on the bike had done, but I'm pretty sure they were left over from the preceding season. A man in John's position, with all his contacts, could certainly have bought new tyres from somewhere if he wanted to, but he took a look at them and pronounced them fine. The problem with racing rubber, is that it can look fine and have masses of tread left, but if it's heated up and cooled down, through too many cycles and been stored into the bargain, it can start to go hard and lose its stickyness. Whatever my thoughts on the subject, I was racing at someone else's expense and if they said no to new tyres, that was that.

In the first practice session at Daytona I compounded my problems by making a mistake that was entirely my own fault, no excuses. The night before there had been one hell of a storm, with driving rain. When we went out to practice the circuit was dry in some places, wet in others and of course I had to learn a new circuit in these worst of all conditions. Even an all wet circuit is better in some ways, at least you know where you are and the grip, or lack of it, is consistent. I got some very good results in the wet at home.

If you've not been there you may have heard about Daytona as on oval circuit, which indeed it is for some types of racing, but there is also a twisty infield section, with two hairpins which look a little similar. On the second lap only I'd got through most of the difficult bit when I realised too late that it was still wet on the apex of the sharp left hander back on to the main oval. Down I went and I couldn't blame the tyres this time, I'd simply been going too fast when I got on the wet stuff. My immaculate new leathers were scuffed, right through in one place. Damage to the bike was fortunately light and mostly cosmetic. Boy was I embarrassed though.

John put the bike back to rights and Vanson leathers are probably unique, in having a repair truck at many US race meetings where they will repair their customers leathers for free. So pretty soon my leathers were legal again too, not as pretty as before, but safe. And it turned out, that at Daytona there were three practice sessions not two, so I had two more practice sessions to learn the circuit after all. In one of those I had to come in with a misfire, which was down to an electrical connector, that had vibrated loose. Nonetheless, I clocked up a good number of laps, the bike ran well once the misfire was cured and I felt I knew the circuit reasonably well.

I was not as confident as I had been at Deland though. The bike felt as though it were on a knife edge everywhere. Daytona Speedway is like a big bowl and being on the coast the soil is sandy and there's a beach nearby. Strong winds like the one we'd just had will scatter sand everywhere, maybe the tyres were shot, maybe there was a fine layer of sand like ball bearings under the tyres, maybe both, whatever, the bike lacked grip, grip for cornering and grip for braking. It did not feel good through the seat of ones pants!

Nonetheless, this would be my last bike race, ever in all probability. I just had to do well. I was determined and I thought about my strategy. In particular I'd keep the engine spinning on the grid, no fouled plug, no slow first lap. I was on row three of the grid, one place in from the inside, so two riders outside me. I have strong feelings about the first corner, it's always a bit of a lottery, but on the whole I much prefer the outside. For sure, a rider falling inside of you will slide outwards so you cannot eliminate risk, but the outside is always less crowded, everyone still seems to take to the apex like a magnet. It's a traffic jam with great potential for a collision.

I made a great start and made up places, but I couldn't get to the outside, there was always someone to my right and the run from start line to turn one at Daytona is short. I went into that first corner with a rider outside of me who was turning in for the apex, despite my presence on his left, oh for goodness sake. I would have been happy to let him go and continue my race but I couldn't lose enough speed, the front tyre wouldn't hold. I was down and so was he and this time it hurt. In the melee I'm not sure if it was the rider who turned in on me who was hit and hospitalised, or another faller, but my race was certainly over and I was sore, physically and emotionally. After the race I trudged back to face the music. The bike looked worse after this accident than after the earlier one, but again it was mostly cosmetic and not very expensive John assured me. I can't help wondering if he left those tyres on for the next guy or not! At least I was there to make a race of it, not just to make up the numbers and in racing accidents happen, people get hurt, it's in the nature of the beast.

Next morning I woke up stiff and sore, then my sister phoned. Dad had died. There was no point my rushing back she said, the funeral could be after my scheduled return. And so I decided to finish the job for Robin, to cover Bike Week take photographs and get as many test rides and interviews done as possible. It was a measure of the man, that when I got home I found he had not paid me. I'm not talking about the old debt, clearly he was not going to honour that verbal, but not written agreement, not when he was employing people and downgrading me to contributor. No he hadn't paid me for the preceding month or the trip! I wondered what he'd told his new editor about me as well and remembered the way he'd spoken about Karen to me once. Certainly the new 'Managing Editor' Celia did not treat me to any respect or give me the benefit of the doubt that I'd given Karen. Neither was she anything like as familiar with motorcycles or the market as I, so she could have had help from me, had she wanted it, but no, Robin had doubtless done a good hatchet job. Celia learned what she'd gotten into, after not too long a time however. Staff turnover is a good indicator of a company's health I think, Celia soon joined the long list of the departed.

Eventually Robin caught up with the current debt, but I was not unhappy at being shouldered out by a so called friend. Without what happened at home, Daytona would have been a wonderful experience, racing accidents or no, but working for Robin and wondering if one would get paid at the end of it was no fun. I carried on contributing for a while, since it was better to be writing articles with a chance of getting paid, than wasting time when there was no other work on the horizon. An attitude that annoyed my girlfriend intensely. The situation couldn't last, and eventually, I pulled myself together and took myself in a new direction, after a period of feeling completely rudderless, a new experience in itself. Hadn't I always been the one who had a goal or an ambition to pursue?

I spoke at Dad's funeral through a miasma of tears. I spoke about his goodness and the way he, servant like, was always ready to help people. Then I tried to deal with the guilt I felt for having left him, twice as I saw it, when he needed me. I know it is not how he would see it, but still it gnaws at me sometimes.

CHAPTER 29

The Siegfried Line

I MET CARON at dancing and a wonderful dancer she was. I first saw her at my spiritual, swing dance home, Jitterbugs, but she and I both frequented the 100 Club as well. She was not my first regular dance partner, that was Diane, who was also my girlfriend for almost two years. Diane and I went to Herrang together and of all my trips to Herrang it was the best. I had someone to learn and practice with, someone to share the experience with. Diane made wonderful costumes for the fancy dress and we produced a sketch together for the cabaret.

It was a comedy sketch based on 'Men Are From Mars Women Are From Venus'. I thought the book a little simplistic and so I wrote the cabaret sketch and I took the mickey ruthlessly. This was my second trip to Herrang. On my first trip I had not taken too much notice of the details about fancy dress and the cabaret which were published in the advance publicity. When I'd arrived there and realised just how much effort other people put in I felt a little ashamed. I had also come to the conclusion that, pro rata, the stiff upper lip Brits were under represented in the cabaret too. After that first trip I resolved I would have to do something in the cabaret on any future trips.

What could I do though, I didn't want to perform dance in front of such a highly qualified audience, my singing wasn't up to it either. Which only really left comedy. The sketch was in three very short acts, there was driving to a party, getting lost and the ensuing row, act two was about how people change once the initial attraction is over and in act three the husband died whilst running errands for his wife, she meanwhile sat facing the audience doing her makeup, as he expired. It was a bit sexist, but in its defence it made 'em laugh, so it fulfilled its purpose. At the end of the day it was just a bit of farce such as I'd acted in years before at Thruxton Players.

I played the narrator and two wonderfully gifted friends played the husband and wife, whilst Diane took a minor role as the stooge. A remarkably generous act on her part. Since then I've written two more short pieces and performed them at Herrang. The next was another farce based around a talk show with a very peculiar guest, it had a large cast, all British, including dance teacher Martin Ellis, the female lead was a beautiful young dancer named Mithi, who turned out to have a natural flair for comedy. She quite rightly stole the show. The final sketch, on my last trip to Herrang was called Lindy Hop Heaven, which again involved someone dying on stage, but it was me this time! I'd always intended my sketches to involve the Brits but for the final one I couldn't find any British volunteers extrovert enough to join in; some of the Swedes from West Coast Jitterbugs in Gothenburg happily took up the challenge.

My parting from Diane, was my fault once more, ridiculous really, given that we had just one row in two years. However, after my experiences with Juliet and Heidi I'd resolved never to do confrontation again and so I told Diane it was over. In hindsight, that was one relationship that truly was a victim of my 'baggage'.

Anyhow, the upshot was I was off dancing on my todd when I came across Caron. I didn't really intend a romantic relationship with Caron. However, I loved dancing with her. She was easy to lead and I loved her style. They say a good male dancer knows how to show his partner off, not difficult with Caron. Her extrovert, but balanced and musically appropriate movements combined with the fact that she radiates joy from her face when she dances meant that eyes were naturally drawn to her.

As a result I started dancing more and more with her, and as I did so we became more and more attuned with one another. Caron had a boyfriend Joe. He was not into dancing and liked to go to the gym, so Caron's dancing with me was fine, they could both do their own thing and then come together later. I was happy to go round to Caron's house as there was no conflict of interest. It started to become routine, that I would drive to Caron's house on the outskirts of London from mine in Tunbridge Wells and she'd drive us both up to town, since she'd have made the same journey without me anyway. Sometimes she'd give a lift to other dancing friends as well.

If there was any difficulty for me at all, it was that people on the dance scene were probably starting to assume that Caron and I were a couple. At this rate I'd never get another girlfriend, but I was having fun. The understanding between Caron and I, on the dance floor, became more and more pronounced. I think she could sense what effect the music was having on me and knew what I'd lead even before I led it. It wasn't long before we started dancing in the odd competition or two together. We even won one and came runner up several times. Although it has to be said they were very minor competitions. Then Simon Selman, who runs the London Swing Dance Society and frequently has to arrange performances, asked us if we'd perform for him, occasionally we'd do a little teaching too.

Caron ran the café at Pineapple Dance Studios in Covent Garden and so we started to offer private lessons there as well. When Caron went dancing, she generally wore a period dress, or top and skirt. If they weren't genuine period clothes, which tend to be fragile, then she'd choose something modern, that nonetheless looked somewhat forties. She'd do her hair in forties style too quite often and frequently wore a snood. I on the other hand was notorious for not making the effort. Jeans and t-shirt, that was me, the t-shirt varied, but it was always jeans and t-shirt and my beloved Gandolfi dance shoes.

Now that Caron and I were performing, competing and even teaching occasionally, I thought it was about time I did something to rectify the situation. I didn't need to dress up to teach, but I was sure it would help in competition and it was almost de rigueur for performing. I started researching where

I could get vintage clothes, both civilian and World War Two uniforms. Strangely it's relatively easy to get uniforms, aside from genuine vintage, one can make up something pretty authentic using plain battledress and sewing on appropriate badges, whilst in some branches of what were the allied services uniforms have changed so little that modern ones will suffice.

Civilian clothes are more of a problem. Post war, America was wealthy and vintage clothes are not so hard to come by there, whilst in Britain, still struggling to get back on its feet and still with rationing, men's de-mob suits were often worn until quite threadbare. Civilian clothes were quite a challenge. It's also a fact that people were smaller then, the poor in particular did not eat as well as we do today, particularly whilst growing up, so finding vintage clothes to fit can be problematical. Nonetheless, I soon had quite a good collection, both military and civilian and one dealer asked Caron and I to perform at re-enactment events up north, which was great fun. I even bought my first vintage watch to complete the look.

I'd never really been interested in watches and years ago, when my friend David bought a Rolex Daytona, for a month's salary I thought he was barmy. When I bought my forties watch to go with my vintage clothes for dancing I had the choice between a more or less unknown Swiss brand for £40 or an old Omega for £120, both worked. I took the cheap one, it was only for looks, but when I got home I regretted it, if I'd bought the Omega I could wear a nice watch whenever I wanted, not just for dancing and £120 wasn't so very much. About a week later I caved in and phoned the dealer. "Have you still got that Omega?" I asked, "yes, as a matter of fact I'm wearing it now." "Oh, you've decided not to sell it then?" "No of course not I'm a watch dealer, if you want it you can have it." I gave him a credit card number and the watch duly arrived. A new interest was developing for me.

Caron and I had taken our dancing together to almost semi professional levels. Employing 1930's slang, we called ourselves Hep Cat and Gator and produced full colour business cards, with pictures of ourselves in dance poses and wearing vintage clothes. Although the size of a standard business card, these had three folds, so you could stand them on a table like a letter M and accordingly they had eight faces. They contained a lot of information, a bit about swing dance, something about the music, our contact details and question and answer panel. Their purpose was to bring in private students.

With travel costs, renting studios, producing cards and so on we never made a profit, so at least there was no tax implication, but it was fun. Meanwhile Tradewind Advertising was down to three small clients, even if one of them was a big name, and working from home was no fun either. What if Caron and I could make a profit from dancing. That would give me a new direction and bring the spark back.

We thought about running a club night, but it would really need to be in London to have the necessary catchment. However, we didn't want to tread on the feet of our friends and the people who'd taught us. Simon, taught on Mondays and Tuesdays, Martin on Tuesdays, Thursdays and Fridays I think, Julie on Wednesdays, I can't remember which evenings Robert and Claire taught back then, but the week was crowded and at some stage Dan and Christie started Balboa lessons on Fridays too. Weekends were out as people have other things to do, so if we were to make some money from dancing we'd have to think outside the box and find another way.

When we performed, or just dressed up, it was not uncommon for people to ask where we got our clothes. Instead of giving away all our research, why didn't we sell vintage clothes to dancers! That was the idea we'd been looking for. We started to plan a strategy. Since the dances we loved included the Charleston, as well as Lindy Hop, Shag, Balboa and Shim Sham we'd sell vintage clothes from 1920 to 1959, that way we could incorporate all the aforementioned and the Rock and Rollers too.

We knew we'd have to shift a lot of product to make even half a living, but half would be enough, since I still had some income from Tradewind and Caron still had the café. As well as clothes we could sell accessories, shoes, gloves, handbags, hats, sweetheart brooches, watches, even gas mask boxes for those who wanted to go the whole hog. Sweetheart brooches are an interesting subject in their own right. In the war many girls wore a sweetheart brooch to show which branch of the services their husband, or sweetheart, was in. Some were professionally made jewellery, others, more working class shall we say. Kids would put those big old pennies on the railway line. A passing train would flatten a penny, very effectively, obliterating the head and tail design. From this flat piece of metal a Spitfire, or an anchor or another symbol could be fashioned and a safety pin could be soldered on the reverse.

Caron and I bought all the genuine sweetheart brooches we could, but since Caron had studied jewellery making and had a small workshop in her garage we made replicas of a Spitfire brooch like the one described above and a navy brooch, from sterling silver, to sell as replicas, with a source of supply which need never dry up. They were fastened to an attractive card detailing the history.

We literally scoured the country looking for enough vintage clothes to open our business, and we spent a fortune. Although our stock of genuine vintage garments was growing we realised it would be very work intensive to keep replenishing it. We also worried about whether dancers would pay the prices necessary, given that vintage clothes are quite fragile, especially if you dance energetically in them and sweat a little. Glow obviously for the ladies. Then there was the problem of sizes, we could get plenty of small, a few medium, but large was rare indeed. In addition women were easier to cater for than men, especially if the men didn't want military outfits. Women tended to have as many dresses as they could afford and quite a few survive. Men's suits in particular were a problem, shirts and ties less so, even classic looking shoes and hats are still available, but a forties suit is very distinctive, quite stunning actually and good ones are in short supply.

We decided that in order to sell enough product at a profit we would have to offer alternatives to the real thing. Accordingly, we decided to offer four lines under the Siegfried Line umbrella. Line number one was called Genuine Originals these were genuine vintage clothes, dated as accurately as we could by style, fabric, method of stitching and so on. We bought copious books on the subject and sorting, dating and labelling with old style labels became a huge task. Unlike many other retailers, we had all our vintage clothes dry cleaned and where necessary professionally repaired before offering them for sale. These were for dancers and re-enactors who prized authenticity, were prepared to pay for it and who would take care, we hoped, of these historical items, which we saw ourselves as rescuing.

Line two was called Siegfried Line Pre-Owned Reproductions. This was the Siegfried line budget range, largely culled from charity shops and jumble sales. As we all know, fashion goes around and around. Caron had a great eye for clothes which looked like twenties, thirties, forties or fifties but weren't. I developed the skill too and of course we studied those books. We bought appropriate garments and cleaned them and they were priced cheaply, so people could look the part on a budget and not worry too much if they got sweaty, or if a thread was pulled while dancing.

Line three was called Siegfried Line New Reproductions. These we had manufactured for us, as off the peg items. They were robust, period style clothes taken from originals we'd bought, or from vintage patterns. In some cases we even had patterns made from old photographs. Modern fabrics and overlocked stitching, where necessary, meant they could be danced in with gay abandon and with little risk of damage, whilst looking very authentic.

Line four was Siegfried Line Made to Measure. This service was for the customer who knew what he or she wanted, but was unable to find it, whether through us or elsewhere. This would be particularly useful for large guys wanting a nineteen forties suit, but we could also offer Zoot Suits and Rock and Roll drape coats. Virtually anything really. It's hard to paint a picture for you of just how much work and effort Caron and I put in. After scouring the country for genuine items of clothing, we scoured it again for the new lines and for tailors and seamstresses, who could make what we needed at competitive prices. Neither of us wanted to send the business to the far east, but we examined this area too, in order to see to it that we'd be competitive if anyone copied us.

We sourced a company that could produce a web site for us, it had to be a website that could take orders and payments too. We had meetings with the bank and arranged a mobile phone technology machine to take credit card payments when we took our stall to dances. We produced vintage style labels, bought clothes rails and hundreds of hangers and then we produced our literature and jewellery. We went to any number of fabric suppliers, to find vintage stock, or fabrics that looked period. Many forties pinstripes had a third stripe with a colour running discreetly through. We even found that.

Eventually we had ladies clothing produced in Nottingham and we found a wonderful pair of tailors near Manchester. They were brothers, and not youngsters. Their father had been a tailor before them. They would make some off the peg men's clothes and also our made to measure menswear. We could offer made to measure period suits purely because of their expertise; at sensible prices because of a computer programme they employed. Programme in the customer's sizes, the width of the fabric and various other details, such as the design! And the machine would print a single use paper pattern, showing every panel, and there are many in a man's suit, which is then laid over the fabric for cutting out. It was a fabulous system that absolutely minimised waste and speeded the made to measure process. We made a forties suit straight away in my size, being pretty average and therefore saleable, but also for me to model, together with a fabulous Zoot Suit and a couple of colourful Rock and Roll drape coats.

Don't know what a Zoot Suit is? They were primarily a west coast USA phenomenon and largely worn by swingin' Hispanics. They used a vast amount of fabric, possibly as a protest at World War Two sumptuary laws. The jackets were incredibly long, trousers were extremely high waisted and baggy, being drawn in at the ankles, or cuffs as the Americans say. They used a lot of fabric. The whole ensemble would be finished off with a wild colourful silk tie, a broad rimmed hat, often with an extrovert feather, fancy shoes and a long, shiny swingin' key chain. Fantastic, why should the gals have all the extrovert clothes?

There was a riot one day near the San Diego Naval Base, some Hispanics had become embroiled in a fight with some sailors. The cops took the sailors side and the Hispanics came out in force. That's one version anyway. It went down in history as The Zoot Suit Riot!

In addition to all this we had our accessories, which, in addition to the hats, gloves, shoes, watches and so on mentioned previously, now also included hair accessories, handkerchiefs, military insignia, cuff links, shirt studs, detachable collars, ties, tie pins, braces, medals and ribbons, 'I've done my service' badges, fingernail polishing stones as used in wartime, stockings and hosiery mending kits. We'd even sell vintage money to have in your purse or wallet, period newspapers, cigarette boxes and cases, lighters, hip flasks, scarves. We used vintage cigarette cases and the little tins handkerchiefs were once supplied in as our own business card holders. If it was part of a period ensemble we had it.

It had taken the best part of a year to get organised, uncountable hours of hard work and incredible expenditure on stock, travel, meetings, food and accommodation, print, display equipment and cases, website, credit card reader, reference books, and fabrics. We were both exhausted, but now we had a launch event to organise and our personal relationship with one another was at a low ebb.

During most of the period where we were getting everything ready Caron and I split the expenditure straight down the middle. Towards the end when we had our opening stock, but still had some business essentials to buy and the launch event to pay for, Caron felt she simply couldn't invest any more. We couldn't stop now, so I paid for the things we needed and it was agreed that this extra investment would come back to me from the initial takings, until we were all square again. So that sorted that out.

Another development had been the departure of Joe, Caron's boyfriend. I had always wanted to keep my relationship with Caron to friends and business partners only, even that relationship was having an effect on my life. I hadn't found a girlfriend and I put it down to a number of factors, primarily the amount of time I was spending with Caron on our 'sideline' businesses, the fact that I danced much less with other girls and the likelihood that everyone else saw me as part of a couple anyway.

Caron knew how I felt, and when Joe left she seemed much more interested, in dancing with other men. Which made it easier for me to dance with other girls of course. So, life could have looked up, now I felt more able to dance with and get to know other girls without offending Caron. As it turned out, neither Caron nor I immediately found new partners and on one of our business trips to look for suppliers our relationship went in a direction it probably shouldn't have.

Having mixed our private and professional relationships at a time when we were both under great financial pressure things eventually started to go downhill. So it was against a background of personal stress, with both of us stretched as thin as piano wire financially and personally, that we came to prepare for our launch event. We set a date, hired the Conway Hall in Red Lion Square, we hired a van, we arranged a DJ and a sound system, we found friends to act as bar staff and receptionist, we stocked a free bar, mostly soft drinks as dancers tend not to drink alcohol thank goodness, we printed flyers and bought a guest book for people to sign. Another small fortune.

Our choice of dates was limited, largely by the availability of the hall and after all the work and expenditure we'd put into it, this one night, to sell and to make a return, but more importantly to start to obtain a reputation for quality merchandise, and for variety, together with making the website known, was incredibly important. If it went well it would probably erase all the stress between Caron and I and we'd finally be in business. The event would be free entry, since we needed the largest possible attendance with as many dancers from as many clubs as was humanly possible. Anyhow, our business was not selling dance nights it was selling clothes.

Whatever night of the week we settled upon, we would clash with someone running a club night. In the event, due to the availability of the hall alone, we clashed with one of Martin Ellis's regular nights, which at that time he shared with Dan and Christie Guest. It was better for us that the availability of the hall made the decision, we didn't want to choose who we'd clash with, and we had a plan to make it OK by them anyway. Bear in mind that we'd decided to go into selling clothing for dancers, in the first place, rather than start our own club night so that we wouldn't be going into competition with our friends. We went to see Martin, we didn't want him to suffer and we wanted to make sure that he knew it was a one off event only, and to see if he would consider combining his club night with our event as a one off thing, so that he would get something out of it too.

Martin was very unhappy that we were putting on a free event that clashed with one of his club nights, but what could we do? We explained what it was all about to Dan and Christie, who listened, understood and subsequently came to our launch. Today my relationship with Martin is fine. I've always admired his dancing and the things he teaches. Over the years he's grown as a teacher too, grown in confidence and stature. To my mind he's a fabulous DJ as well, but then that simply comes down to personal preferences, however I do like his taste in music.

It's ironic that he also organises the Savoy Ball, the dressiest swing ball in London once a year! We put out our fliers at every other club from Rockola on Canvey Island to those in West London, we had it listed on internet 'what's on' lists, we spoke to everyone we possibly could, we e-mailed people on the scene and our friends did likewise.

In many ways the launch was an outstanding success. Sadly there were also two problems, one stressful at the time, but not a great disaster in the scheme of things, the other made a difficulty that lasted some time, with the result, that, the launch event rather than being the beginning of the beginning, came to be the beginning of the end.

On the plus side the hall was packed from start to finish, we sold about £1500 worth of stock, which was far short of break even, but that would have been an entirely unreasonable expectation after roughly a year of one way only cash flow! It did pay the expenses for the night at least and it put Siegfried Line on the dance map. So what went wrong?

Firstly Ken Livingstone's congestion charge. No sooner had we parked the van and unloaded than I took a quick scout around to find somewhere to pay it and get a receipt. Couldn't find anywhere, had he launched his venture without the infrastructure in place? As we had so much to do I asked one of our volunteer helpers to go have a look around, take his time, go a bit further than I had. Dave couldn't find anywhere either. Never mind, we'd just have to pay it by phone, I hate doing things that way, no receipt, but it was the only option. When we got through, "sorry, the system's down can you call back later?" We were very, very busy but we tried later, several times. As we were so busy and this was our big, big night we had friends try at regular intervals and we got on with what we had to do, meet, greet, explain, sell. Eventually, as it was getting late and the charge had to be paid by a certain time, or a fine would follow, our friend came to us and said I'm sorry, I still haven't been able to pay it.

Dave rang Ruth, his girlfriend and asked her to pay it via the internet. She tried, but apparently the system was down! Eventually, she called back. I got them to take my credit card over the phone she announced triumphantly, they said they'd put it through once the system's back up, so she had no name, no reference number, no proof. They never processed it and the fine duly arrived. Caron was still fighting it long after our business relationship had split up, on principle. It's immoral Mr Livingstone to fine people on a day when your system is malfunctioning. We went above and beyond the call of duty to try and pay that thing on a night when our time was quite simply extremely valuable, vital in fact, irreplaceable.

Were I not a pacifist, I think that if I saw Mr Livingston through a gun sight I could probably squeeze the trigger. And that's without going into the subject of whether it's a socialist policy, whether it hurts the poorer classes, or benefits fat cats in their chauffeur driven Mercedes. Or whether it's really a green policy or a cash cow that backfired, sorry about the mixed metaphors. The second problem was more serious in its implications. We had our stock displayed on the stage and people could come up and look, we used two back stage areas as changing rooms and I had my briefcase in the men's changing room. Behind was a staircase and a door to the street, locked however. So anyone wishing to remove my briefcase would have to cross the stage and anyway, we knew about ninety percent of the people there and we had friends, specifically looking out for anything crooked, particularly theft of watches or jewellery, but at least there was a level of security.

At the end of the evening, tired, but happy with the way things had gone and relieved to have paid the congestion charge, as we thought, we set about clearing everything away. My briefcase was missing. There was nothing in it of value to a thief, no cash, no credit cards, no Mont Blanc pen, nothing of value to anyone else. However, all the passwords for our website, all our addresses and contacts, all our stock records, cards and leaflets, all sorts of things we needed, for our business were in there. More fool me for taking it. I had used it during the evening to look things up for people so it was of value in that sense, it wasn't necessarily foolish to have it there, but I should have had everything backed up, and/or had the brief-case in a safer place. I couldn't believe that one of our guests had taken it and I still don't.

Instead of enjoying a feeling of triumph, the following days were a nightmare of rush, rush, rush. Get in contact with the website company, get all the passwords changed and take control again. Remake stock lists, get new address books and put everything down from memory or scraps of paper, or look people up again. Weeks later I was still coming up with problems, damn the answer to that is in my briefcase. However, one day out of the blue, we got a call from Conway Hall, The South Place Ethical Society. "We've found your briefcase in a cupboard upstairs, you must have left it when you had your event here."

After the launch event we'd spoken to every member of their staff that was present to say the brief case had been stolen. We'd searched the building from top to toe. We'd even scoured nearby streets and skips to see if the thief, having realised there was nothing of value inside, had simply tossed it away. I find it very hard to believe one of our guests snuck upstairs with my briefcase and the only motive would have been for our research, but everything was still in there. Who had keys to the back door and the upstairs cupboard? That's what I cannot help wondering.

Anyhow, we got it back, but too late, the damage was done. The trouble it caused was the final nail in the coffin of my relationship with Caron, the congestion charge the final nail but one. After the launch we were more stressed than ever, we didn't agree on anything. I told her we could no longer work together. I would leave and she could buy me out, for the price of half the stock. The website and the credit card reader, hardware and print I'd just give her. She didn't have much money, she felt let down, but the partnership was shot. Only one of us could continue and I chose to give that opportunity to Caron, which I was sure she would want.

Eventually I took some money and some of the stock for my share. I took all the menswear that fitted me, all the unsold men's watches, which meant I had the nucleus of a collection, so for a while I became a collector and developed an interest in mechanical watches. I also took some women's wear. I never got around to selling it. A few items I've given away.

Caron was very bitter towards me for a long while, but eventually we danced together once or twice, I guess the hatchet is buried. If you did an internet search for Malcolm Snook, whilst the Siegfried Line website was up and running that's where it would take you. Much later I repeated the exercise out of curiosity, I was amazed, that my sixth place finish in the vintage bike race at Deland came up. Who would have thought it?

CHAPTER 30

Wannabee Actor

EVERY NOW AND again a TV or film company, producing a period piece will need dancers for a ballroom scene and they'll approach clubs like Jitterbugs or the London Swing Dance Society. Diane and I had once danced in a film about a wartime all girl band, which starred Dame Judy Dench. Caron got to dance, before I really knew her, in an episode of Foyle's War. As a result of these experiences, Caron and I decided to enlist with an Extras agency called Casting Collective. We stressed our dance qualifications and hoped we'd get dance calls.

The people at the agency were lovely and they found us work, albeit mostly background work, without any dancing. It was enjoyable however, for the most part. It made a nice day out sometimes, but not always. I started to observe the film and television world at close quarters. I noticed that some of the actors struggled even to remember their lines; of course I don't know how long they'd been given to learn them, but watching the treatment they received, adequate I should think. Even actors in quite small soaps seem to get the star treatment. Of course some actors are very professional; Robert Lindsay, Zoe Wannamaker , Martin Shaw and Michael Kitchen amongst others, struck me as being very on the ball.

In other cases I remember thinking, hell I could do better than that, without three years at drama school, in fact I did do better at Thruxton Players, actually we all did, amateur or not! With a mortgage to pay and so much else going on in my life, child maintenance and trying to run my own business, I simply couldn't take three years off with no income to go to drama school and get myself a real agent, but I'd have loved to. I'd bluffed my way into an advertising career though, as a skydiving instructor, maybe I could become an actor through the back door too. I'd watch, learn and look for opportunities.

Generally, being an extra is, I'm told, an impediment rather than a help, but my ambition was encouraged by a radio interview with an established actor who had started his career as an extra.

The difference between jobs was quite remarkable, big calls, with hundreds of extras were often a real pain. Costume and make up could take hours, queues were interminable. Often starts would be very early and a long journey might be involved. No limousine for the extras, and last to get breakfast, lunch or dinner. Not that I'm complaining, these are the logistical realties when big crowd scenes are called for. Of course that's no reason to be treated like cattle and the attitudes one came across, were varied. On the set of Life And Death of Peter Sellers, I did actually find myself sitting in make up alongside one of the actresses. She was stunning too. Her role was to be one of the starlets Peter Sellers had dabbled with. We chatted and hit it off. Later, on set, during a break she came across and talked to me again. One of the crew firmly took her aside and said none too quietly that it wasn't done to be seen talking to extras. Scenery then, not real people eh!

On the other side of the coin, Gillian Taylforth on the set of Footballers Wives, was entirely natural, friendly and relaxed, and not at all, how shall we say, up herself! You find both sorts of people on film sets that's for sure. Some of the other extras were fascinating people too. I came across retired people, who'd been very senior police officers, and others who'd been directors of large companies, when I saw such people being talked down to, pushed around or otherwise being mildly insulted it made me wonder somewhat about the nature of life. I met very beautiful women, still hoping to be discovered although it was probably too late for some of them. I even met Zoe, the younger of my two bridesmaids at my first wedding, now a fully grown and exceptionally beautiful woman. She had her feet firmly on the ground though, odd really given her other job, she was just doing extra work for fun, when not on call as a flight attendant, purser these days, for the Virgin airline.

The best calls were the small ones. In those situations it was at least feasible for the company to treat you as part of the team and some of them did. Oddly one of the really small soaps I was involved with was one of the friendliest. The soap was a Sky TV drama called Dream Team, about a football team, at this point in the story the team was in financial difficulty and I played a banker. It wasn't even a speaking part, but I had to go back to the studios several times and hand out new contracts to the players and things like that. When I went back ,they all said hi and treated me as if I was a regular, it was so much more pleasant and human than some sets I've been on. One evening I got on the tube to go dancing after filming, one of the regular actresses got in the same carriage and we had a pleasant chat all the way into town. Jericho with Robert Lindsay was another very friendly outfit and so was Foyle's War and My Family. Why can't they all be like that?

Caron and I had once been involved with a TV programme called Celebrity Fit Club, we'd taught them to dance, at an up-market health spa, but the sequence was cut from the finished programme. It may have been because there was a bit of a drama when one of the 'celebrities' decided to quit, or it may have been simply that the director didn't like it. It didn't really matter to me, I got paid, that mattered to me. However, when I met one of the actresses again on the set of a soap, she was very much of the I don't talk to extras brigade!

When I started doing 'extras' work I was still living in my house in Tunbridge Wells. For the final year I was living on my boat in central London, whilst preparing it to travel the world. I decided I'd try and get as much work as I could and I'd try to get things with lines, or at least some action. If by some miracle I got a regular part, in even the meanest of soaps, I'd postpone my trip, for the sheer joy of being a professional actor for a while. If not, then once the boat was ready, I'd simply sail away. Fate could decide, but I'd make the effort!

I signed on with as many agents as I could find. I looked

them up in reference books, I spoke with other extras and asked who they were with. I met a chap on a Bollywood film set who'd once been in a commercial with Joan Collins and possibly had come close to making the big time. He recommended an agent who might get more than simple background work. I went to see her and she agreed to put me on her books. Even walk on parts and one liners were very hard to come by, but I still enjoyed nearly all of what I did.

One of the most enjoyable calls was for Foyle's War, I played a German prisoner of war. There was a small group of us and we had great fun kicking a football around our prison compound most of the time. However, in the plot one of the prisoners is killed by an assassin sent from Germany, because he knows too much. I was called on to recognise the assassin in a corridor and show fear as well as recognition. Not a great challenge, but it all added to the fun.

I got a line in Judge John Deed, well a few words anyway at an enquiry. In Family Affairs I had a line or two, as the Borough Ambassador, when one of the characters got involved in local politics. I had a couple of words in Mile High as well, where I was an airline first officer in the Sky TV soap about the goings on between airline staff. I danced in a movie called Piccadilly Jim, based on the PG Wodehose novel. It starred Sam Rockwell, who played the real baddie in The Green Mile. I think he's a great actor, but I've never seen the movie, it got slated and went straight to video, without a cinema release.

I also danced in the ballroom scene in Vera Drake, I've not seen that either to see if I can recognise myself, or even my feet! And I danced in a TV series called Blackpool, I can't see myself in that, well maybe for a moment, but I rather enjoyed watching it. I was in any number of crowd scenes, Love Actually, Layer Cake, Mrs Henderson Presents, Stage Beauty, Bridget Jones, a movie about Pocahontas and many others, like the ING commercial. However, it's rarely possible to pick oneself out. In one period drama, I think it was The Return of Sherlock Holmes, a Christmas special, there were two scenes, on two days, with early calls and long waits, so as always I took a book.

The book I was reading was on the life story of Captain James Cook. For one of the two days of shooting we were in a stately home. I sat in the basement reading; costume and make-up would take an age and there was itchy facial hair to be applied. In my book Captain Cook was, as yet, not a Captain at all, but a junior Royal Navy officer, in the squadron of Admiral John Byng. The book explained how Admiral Byng was subsequently tried for dereliction of duty, after failing to relieve the British Garrison at Fort St Phillip, Port Mahon, Menorca. He'd been executed by firing squad on the poop deck of one of his own ships back in Portsmouth. Menorca fell to the French. Admiral Byng had it seemed to me, not acted in the finest traditions of the Royal Navy, but was he in part a scapegoat? Opinions vary and I believe, as I write this that he's just recently been pardoned along with those soldiers executed in World War I. The surreal thing about it was that earlier that morning I'd never heard of him, when I went upstairs I found I'd been reading about his life and his death, in the basement of his house.

Since I was very against Britain becoming embroiled in the war in Iraq, I was very happy to play a small part in a documentary about the work of, and subsequent death of, Dr David Kelly, the Iraq weapons specialist. I felt the UN weapons inspectors were doing a good job, that Saddam was effectively neutered, that he could no longer kill thousands of his own people and so it was wrong for us to put them in danger. Had the existence of weapons of mass destruction been proven I might have felt differently, but of course there was no proof and we all know about 'that report' and the subsequent failure to find any such weapons, so the documentary fascinated me.

The most high profile movie I was in was Harry Potter and The Prisoner of Azkaban. They wanted dancers, but all the dancing I really had to do was take a few steps and sway a little, although there was another little piece of action. There were two costume fittings and we had to meet the Director before the day of filming too. All this, merely to be a living portrait in Hogwarts, a few seconds, inserted by computer in the background of a scene, covered from head to toe in a gown, head entirely covered, face hidden behind a mask. It's no wonder movies cost so much to make, although I can understand the need to get every detail right on such a big project. Why risk spoiling the ship for a hapeth of tar?

The actual filming took about half a day I think. Secrecy on those sets is paramount, if that's not a pun, until the film is released, and the extra who takes photos would be in breach of contract and in deep trouble if caught. I know some do. I never did, except for a little memento on my phone from Piccadilly Jim. The costume department take lots of polaroids on big productions in case you're needed back and have to be attired exactly the same. I asked one of the costume ladies on Harry Potter if, once the film was out, she'd send me a picture or two so I could prove to my daughter that the man behind the mask really was Daddy. She promised faithfully, but nothing ever came.

So the Borough Ambassador never reappeared in Family Affairs, nor did the banker in Dream Team, or the first officer in Mile High, no regular work came along and walk-ons and little features were rare treats, such as one line in Judge John Deed. So, finally, when the boat was ready I sailed off into the wild blue yonder, a wannabe actor no more, unless you have a part for me?

CHAPTER 31

The Road to Dromina

By which I mean the path that lead me to become the boat gypsy I am today, to find a yacht called Dromina and to prepare her, re-christen her Francesca, after the daughter I adore, and to sail thousands of miles in her, exploring this wonderful world. I think I started walking the path when I joined the sailing club as a child, I was on it when I resolved to try not to live as others do, to try and avoid commuting, lawnmowers and mortgages, and that I was purposefully striding along it when I attended John Ridgway's school and later became a skydiving instructor. A conventional life was already becoming something beyond my understanding.

And other forces were at work. In 1973, when I was on my schoolboy expedition to the arctic, an ex royal Marine Commando named Shane Acton was setting off to explore the world in an eighteen foot plywood yacht, of a type known as a Caprice. It wasn't that Shane Acton wanted to set records, he just wanted to explore the world by boat and an eighteen foot plywood boat was what he could afford. He'd thought about exploring the great rivers of Europe, but decided that was too tame for him. So off he went, sailing around the world, he was still at it whilst I was jumping out of aeroplanes from 1975 to 1981. It was in 1981 that Shane's book, 'Shrimpy', was published.

Due to my childhood interest in boats and sailing, I'd followed the exploits of Sir Francis Chichester, Sir Alec Rose, Claire Francis and Sir Robin Knox Johnston. The last of whom, I think, performed the greatest feat of seamanship the world ever has, or ever shall witness. To sail solo around the entire globe, without a single stop, or re-supply, with no GPS, in a boat neither designed for, nor entirely suitable to the purpose, a boat that leaked and had to be repaired single-handedly, from outside, at sea, a boat with contaminated water tanks. It defies belief. In his book Sir Robin talks of the spirits of Drake and Nelson watching him. They must truly have done so in awe.

However, it was Shane Acton who inspired me and in more recent times I've discovered the writings of Joshua Slocumb, the first man ever to circumnavigate the globe single-handedly, his departure year 1895. Neither of these men set out to do things in the hardest possible way, they took what was available to them and employed their considerable talents to explore, discover and to revel in the world. When I read Shane's book it wasn't just what he'd achieved with the sailing that inspired me, it was the love of life, the joy of discovery. You won't find that in Chichester's writings. Slocumb is suffused with joy also, and despite his old world look of Bostonian Puritanism you can sense the twinkle in the old man's eye, in almost every page. In Knox Johnston's book and in Shane Acton's there are seminal moments that bring home their achievement. In the former case, it is right at the end, when the customs officer at Falmouth asks, "where from sir?" The reply of course "Falmouth".

In Shane Acton's book there is a delightful moment in a Mediterranean marina, I'm in one myself as I write this in fact. He told other yachtsmen, that he'd come the long way round, by which they thought he meant across Biscay and around Spain, through the straits of Gibraltar like myself. "No" he said "I mean via the Atlantic, Panama, the Pacific, Australia, the Indian Ocean, Red Sea and the Suez Canal." I wonder who believed him.

I knew when I read Shrimpy that one day I would sail, travel and discover the world too. I also knew I had many other ambitions, but foremost motor racing, which had to come first or not at all. Chichester and Rose proved you don't have to be young to sail, professional racing drivers generally are. When I left on my trip I felt that this was what my life had been leading up to, and that my travels would inspire and inform a follow up book to this one. In fact the long periods alone have inspired another idea which may or may not change the course of events one last time. We'll come to that later.

For the moment lets go back two or three years. Tradewind Advertising is providing a very modest income, my office is now my living room. No Limits Publishing and Dealer-World.com have come to nothing for me, so have Savers, Liqui Moly and Siegfried Line, how hard do you have to try? I'm getting a little work as a film extra, often long hours and poorly paid. And now, my ex-wife Heidi announces that she and her third husband are emigrating, with their new daughter Hannah, and my precious daughter Francesca to Australia.

Can things get any worse? It is years since I've even thought about Shane Acton, or sailing and my mind is too full of other things now for them to intrude. I spoke to my first solicitor, the one who handled my first divorce. Heidi has asked for my permission to take Francesca to Australia. I'm advised to give it with a smile on my face. Do fathers have rights in this country? I can delay them I'm told, I can cost them and myself money, but ultimately, if they've got everything properly arranged the court will give its permission in my place!

I cannot stop them starting a new life, for all that it will deprive Francesca of her natural father, despite the fact that we are close and love one another, that I have kept up contact. " I only know of one case where a father has successfully prevented the ex-wife from emigrating with a child and that was in the case of a woman who wanted to go to Canada. However she had no job, no home to go to, she could not even tell the court what State she intended to settle in and so the court, naturally, said no, you cannot take the child on a wild goose chase. In cases like yours, where the wife has everything properly arranged all you can do is delay them, cost them money and so they will become your enemies, your child will end up on the other side of the planet anyway, and how will you know if your letters and e-mails will get through? They may even relocate, when they are out there, without telling you. Keep it friendly" I was advised. I didn't want Heidi to be my enemy whether in Australia or anywhere else anyway. So I gave my permission, much to Francesca's confusion and Heidi promised that she would not expect child maintenance in view of the distance, I could use the money to visit.

Heidi has kindly extended the agreement in the actual event, which saw me leave the country rather than her. It enables me, despite living on a shoestring these days, to maintain my relationship with Francesca and I'm very grateful. In the unlikely event that my writing makes a profit perhaps I can do more for Francesca's future too, although my travels have given me much time to think and in turn inspired a new idea, more of which at the end.

It turned out that Heidi and her new husband had all the points they needed under the Australian system for their visas, that Heidi's mother's brother lived there, and that her parents and even her best friend were going too. They were all going out there, to buy some land to build their dream home on and for Heidi to meet her uncle. It seemed unstoppable, inevitable.

Meantime I had a friend, Mandy, from dancing who wanted to buy a Dutch barge to live on. She was going away on holiday and she asked me to buy a copy of a magazine called Yachts and Boats for Sale while she was away, so she wouldn't miss it. I duly bought it and scanned through it. The prices of boats were a revelation, some were of course highly expensive, but not all. I'd long hankered after living in London, being closer to the dancing. I saw an old tug boat for sale, it had been converted into a home, was moored near Hammersmith and the price was not astronomical. Thoughts were whirling in my head, maybe there was a way I could afford to live in London after all, what if I sold the GT40 and the Harley-Davidson, cashed in my endowment policy, possibly sold the house, or rented it out.

I telephoned the family with the tug, "could I come and see it?" It was already under offer, they promised to call back if the deal fell through. I was acting on impulse, not thinking rationally, but I returned to the magazine. I saw a boat called Ned Kelly for sale. It was described as a 'Passage Maker'. What the heck does that mean? I asked myself. It was also described, which needed no explanation as a 'live aboard'. I looked up 'Passage Maker' on the internet. It seemed that the retired Captain of a World War Two US aircraft carrier had invented this new class of boat. He'd wanted to travel by sea after retiring, but had no interest in sails. So he'd come up with a formula for a 'Passage Maker', it had all sorts of requirements. It had to have two engines, both with their own transmission, prop shaft and prop, for safety. It had to carry a certain amount of fuel, have a minimum range, in order to cross oceans and there was something called the Trawler Truth Ratio. It was to do with stability and went straight over my head.

In short, a passage maker was a motor boat that could cross oceans with a reasonable chance of making it in safety at the right time of year, given the same sorts of considerations yachtsmen and women have to think about. Ned Kelly was a boat that could travel, she could be a home and she was only £28,000. I went to see her. Like most Passage Makers she was a converted fishing boat, in this case a shrimping trawler I was told. She certainly could serve as a home, her owner had already purchased a larger Passage Maker, being wedded to the concept, but Ned Kelly was big enough for me and already converted. She was made of steel, so she'd be tough. She had a big Gardiner diesel engine, and a Volvo Penta 'wing' engine as a back up, with its own gearbox and prop. The engine room was so big, the owner had installed a work bench and tools such as a grinder. She even had stabilisers that swung down, like the ones in the movie Perfect Storm.

Dave, the owner explained to me that she could carry 5,000 litres of fuel and that there was room for another tank if desired in the bulbous section at the base of the bow. I was told I could get a road tanker to call to fill her up with diesel, given the volume, and get it at a very cheap rate accordingly, plus of course it was red diesel, with a lower rate of tax. "Fill her up once and it'll last you a year or more" he said, I was hooked. "Will you accept an offer, subject to survey" I asked. "What do you want a survey for?" He asked with a very good impression of incredulity, "she's only eight years old." I stuck to my guns, I was on unfamiliar territory and I simply didn't know enough about the subject to spend that kind of money without professional advice.

"I can't accept an offer subject to survey" he said "because then I'll have to wait, there's another chap coming down on Friday to have a look and he seems very keen. I've already got my new boat and I'm anxious to be off." He's just putting the pressure on I thought, but I started to line up the friend of a friend, who did know a lot about boats to come down on Saturday, the first possible day, today being Wednesday and at least get an informed opinion. It came to naught though, the other chap came down on Friday and promptly bought Ned Kelly, without a survey.

I looked at another trawler, converted to be a live aboard in Greenland Dock, part of South Dock Marina in East London. She was nice, but there was no guarantee of keeping the mooring. She had just the one engine, an old BMC diesel, less fuel capacity, no stabilisers, unlike Ned Kelly she wasn't a boat to explore the world in and she was about the same money, slightly more I think. I almost regretted not charging in and just buying Ned Kelly on the spot. However, today I can't help thinking someone was looking after me. For now I slowed down, started to think things through properly. To plan out a course of action rather than act on a whim.

I remembered that I loved sailing, and that the wind is free! I realised that a sailing boat with an auxiliary motor also has two forms of propulsion for safety, that a sailing boat can make a home too, and that when you sail, there's just the wind in the rigging and peace and serenity. Barring storms, thunder and lightening of course! I remembered Shane Acton and Shrimpy. Yes, and I could sail to Australia, I could follow my beautiful, wonderful, marvellous daughter! I started to think about boats, their types, what they cost, what they're made from. I weighed and researched the pros and cons of wood, fibreglass, steel, aluminium, ferro-cement. I wanted to get the safest, most robust, most comfortable boat I could afford, speed was not an issue. I wanted a wheelhouse so I could control the boat whilst being sheltered, rather than in an open cockpit. And steel would be my first choice material.

I discounted wood entirely, as being too fragile, too expensive and too high maintenance. Aluminium I thought wouldn't be robust enough, but in fact I know more about it now. Friends I made while sailing back from the Baltic have an aluminium boat, and the hull is very heavily constructed. However, salt water is corrosive and when you have different metals employed (engines and prop shafts etc not being aluminium) then you've got a floating battery and you have to take very great care to avoid electrolytic corrosion. Besides aluminium is very expensive. Fibreglass was a possibility, there are many fibreglass boats to choose from and it's easy to keep clean, but what about osmosis? I couldn't afford a new boat, what was this thing osmosis?

The marine environment is harsh and whatever a boat is made from there are problems; wood rots, steel rusts, aluminium corrodes, fibreglass suffers from osmosis and ferro- cement boats, reinforced concrete if you prefer, have a basket of steel rods inside the concrete which can rust, and you can't even see it. I looked into osmosis. You'd think that a fibreglass, or 'plastic' boat as they're often thought of, would be as impervious to water as say a plastic washing up bowl. It's not the case apparently. In time sea water can work its way into the material, where it attacks the resin, as this breaks down it becomes acidic and the process of decay accelerates. Many owners of fibreglass boats take them out of the water every winter to dry out, but that's no good if it's your home! Attitudes towards osmosis vary, I'm told that in France many people regard it merely as a cosmetic problem!

I decided steel would be my first choice because it's very tough, an impact that would sink a wooden or fibreglass boat, might just dent a steel boat. Rust, the Achilles heel is very visible and easily treated with chemicals if it hasn't gone too far. And a steel boat can stay in the water for extended periods, no need to dry out. First choice steel then, wood and aluminium an absolute no-no on account of cost and maintenance worries. What about ferro-cement? They're less expensive, I could afford quite a large and luxurious yacht. I wrote this off too, on account of the fact that many of them were home builds by amateurs and that it's more or less impossible to survey what's going on within the structure of the hull, without destructive testing.

Again I've learned more since. In Seville I made friends with Terry and Liz, whose ferro-cement boat was made by a qualified engineer and the workmanship is self evidently superb. The hull is thick and clearly robust, second only to steel I would think. Terry told me about one that had fallen off a delivery truck on the motorway, it had bounced but not cracked. So a good one just might be a bargain. However, at the time, I was looking for my boat, I'd written off everything but steel, or just possibly fibreglass, early fibreglass boats were very heavily built as it was a new technology and no one really knew how good they'd be, they were arguably over engineered. New ones are possibly made from better materials, but they build them lighter today in most cases and I don't like vulnerable, exposed rudders and propellers, so I considered keel design too.

I wrote off catamarans as well, due to the strain on the rigging and the fact they don't roll to spill wind in a sudden squall, something else I've re-thought since meeting a few owners. Anyhow, I came up with an idea of my ideal boat. Steel, with a wheelhouse, a long keel that protects the prop and rudder as much as possible, low draught, so I can get over sand bars and up rivers. And comfortable to live on, with sails and a powerful engine to get me out of trouble in an emergency.

I found a boat to suit me perfectly and I really liked the elderly owner Geoffrey and his wife. He had been in the Royal Navy during Wold War Two and had been an officer on a frigate which accepted the surrender of the Nazi U Boats in the Irish Sea at the end of the war. By that time the life expectancy of a U Boat was very short indeed, probably around two weeks, since sonar and depth charges had become very good, their operators very experienced. There was a framed photo in Geoffrey's lovely ketch-rigged motor sailor, showing the crew of a U Boat at the surrender. The Captain was a scowling, grizzled old Nazi, the crew, all little more than kids, all grinning broadly with the joy of life, they'd survived! It was a moving picture.

Geoffrey's wife had done wonders with the interior, the boat was everything I wanted. Before I made an offer, subject to survey however, I thought I should look at another boat. I owed it to myself after all the research I'd done and my careful planning, not to just buy the first boat I saw. There was another steel motor-sailor advertised, it was in Waterford, Southern Ireland. This one had crossed the Atlantic. My friend David O'Brien and I flew to Waterford to have a look. Her owner Peter was a larger than life German man with a great sense of humour, who'd married an English lady and after travelling on his boat had settled in Ireland.

The layout was different, Geoffrey's boat had a tiny cockpit at the back and then a small wheelhouse, with all the accommodation in front of that, this layout gave her a roomy, airy feel. The boat in Ireland had a large central wheelhouse, part wooden, part canopy, its wooden floor was almost large enough to dance Lindy, and a table could be erected to make the wheelhouse a dining room when in port, the table could even be employed as an ironing board I thought, as this might become home. Behind the wheelhouse was a cabin with two single beds, or berths whilst in the bow was a double bed. My girlfriend and I could sleep in the bow, guests could have the privacy of the aft cabin and if they weren't a couple there were two beds. The layout was incredibly practical and made great use of every inch of space, but of course the main cabin and bathroom where much smaller, the space for the aft cabin and large wheelhouse had to come from somewhere. The décor was pretty DIY compared with Geoffrey's boat too. It was a tough decision, but I decided to go for the light and airy feel, the more luxurious and better presented boat. I told Peter that I'd been genuine and a serious prospect, that I'd not flown to Ireland to waste his time but that I'd chosen to make an offer on another boat. Peter and I parted on good terms.

Geoffrey accepted, my subject to survey offer, by telephone and I sent him a cheque for the deposit. I felt I was on my way and that I'd made a new friend in Geoffrey. I took Francesca to see the boat and meet Geoffrey. I told my daughter that in this boat I would sail to Australia to be reunited with her. She's pretty switched on and said "but what about storms Daddy?" I reassured her as honestly as I could.

Before I could actually complete the purchase on a boat I had to find somewhere to base it. I travelled around a bit, largely up and down the Thames as I wanted to be within striking distance of London and not too far from my daughter and friends until the time came to set sail. I settled on the sailing club at Gravesend as somewhere to base myself initially.

On the day of the survey on Geoffrey's boat I was on a modelling assignment in Manchester. Oh yes, I did a bit of that too! It was just an extension of the acting and extras thing really, one of my agents handled both. I had a phone call from the surveyor. He'd only done a few hours work, but he recommended I walk away from the deal. He said he'd finish the survey if I wanted, but if he stopped now the bill would be reduced. He told me there was rust in inaccessible places which would need the interior ripping out to treat, as well as rot in the wooden masts. I was virtually crushed, I'd set my heart on that boat and after all the research I'd done, all the care I'd taken after calming down from the initial whim, it had seemed so right. As soon as I could I went to see Geoffrey, with a letter from the surveyor and half a report. The offer was subject to survey and Geoffrey honourably returned my deposit. His house was on a river front and he said he hoped that one day I would sail up there in whatever boat I did eventually buy. He supposed it would be the boat in Ireland. I thought that to return in another boat would be to rub salt in the wound and I really, really liked the man, and his wife. I've not been back.

I telephoned the broker handling the sale of the boat in Ireland. "Sorry, it's sold, someone local has offered the full price without a survey". It was Ned Kelly all over again. As always I'd backed the wrong horse. I wasn't giving up though, it was back to the magazines and I found a Nicholson 38 at a price I could just about afford, but only just. The boat was at Eastbourne and it was stunning. The roomiest of all the boats I'd looked at, but with a layout like the boat in Ireland, wheelhouse and all, the aft cabin even had a porcelain wash bowl and the interior of the main cabin looked like it had been made by a proper cabinet maker, right down to the wine cabinet. This was a glamorous boat, way more so than either of the other two. Could I really afford a boat like this? Well yes, just, because of its age. Even so it was the 1,000th boat Nicholson's had built according to a plaque inside, so maybe they'd taken a bit of extra care on this one. It had been their Boat Show exhibit in the year it was made and all the boatyards were still building them very solidly in those days. OK it was fibreglass, but I thought it was exceptional. I made my offer, subject to survey, the owner was a friend of my friend Martin Sweet at Slipstream Motorcycles, and also knew one of my former colleagues at BBB, funny old world. Again I had that warm feeling that things would work out, possibly as a result of these coincidences.

The surveyor found osmosis, "no ones ever died of osmosis" said the vendor, "no" said the surveyor, "that we know of, but even so, one day someone will". That wasn't all though, there was a crack, a very small one, but from tiny acorns... We got a quote from a local firm with a good reputation to strip all the gel coat, fix the crack and apply a new outer coating or, however many layers are required and bake it all back on. The quote was £6,000 and with a new gel coat the boat could probably stay in the water for a few years without drying out. Problem was that I was at my financial limit, especially with the cost of this second, and this time full survey. To make it happen the vendor would have to reduce the price by the full £6,000. Sadly for me he was only prepared to go halves, and I simply couldn't find another £3,000 and so the deal fell through, my budget reduced by the price of that wasted survey. I was not happy to be back at square one again.

A day or so later I got a call from the yacht broker handling the sale of the boat in Ireland. The full price, no survey buyer was now messing them around. On two occasions the money was supposed to have been wired to their account they told me and it hadn't arrived. Peter would be interested in an offer from me, if I was still in the market. I was. I thought about my near miss with the Nicholson though and wondered how I'd feel now, buying the plain Jane, Dromina. I decided to go for it, she answered all the considerations I'd originally identified, steel, keel design, draught, big engine, wheelhouse, water and fuel capacity, everything, even the layout was the most practical really. OK she wasn't going to pull the babes in Monte Carlo, but what did I really want? Actually babes in Monte Carlo, but I made the offer anyway!

The offer was 1000 Euros below the asking price and I said she had to be off the market until my survey was done, I didn't want to pay for an expensive survey only to have the other chap come up with the money. I say expensive, because steel boats are more expensive to survey than fibreglass, this is due to ultra sound or ultra sonic testing that reveals the thickness of the steel, when you can't access both sides to measure it physically. Dromina was largely made from 6mm steel over thirty years ago, she still had well over 5mm left. At that rate she'd still be a tough old bird in another thirty years. Due to the wide geographical spread of the three boats I commissioned surveys on, they were all done by different surveyors, which is a shame, it may be that some surveyors are more critical than others and I may not have been comparing eggs with eggs in a sense. However, I'd paid for those surveys, so I might as well listen. Dromina wasn't glam, but the survey said she was sound and the deal was completed.

Shortly afterwards Heidi decided not to emigrate to Australia. Francesca assumed I would not go travelling as a result. After all plan A had been to sail down to Australia in order to keep up with her. However, having closed my business down, bought the boat and made the move, and given that Heidi's parents still intended to go to Australia, which might mean Heidi would revise her decision, I decided to carry on with my plans, but to modify them. If I stayed in the northern hemisphere for the next few years it would be possible to come back for holidays with Francesca and for her to visit me while she grew up. We might even end up with the same number of days together overall. Flights from Spain, France, Greece, the Canaries, even the Caribbean and Florida are quite reasonable these days. And of course if Heidi did decide to go to Australia after all, I could be on my way at the drop of a hat.

No sooner was the deal on Dromina finalised than the vendor of the glamorous Nicholson rang to say he'd reconsidered and would drop the price by the full cost of the remedial work. Too late. I may or may not have ended up with the best boat, but I'm still here. I've sailed from London, to Scotland, Norway, Sweden, around Sweden to the northern Baltic, down to Gotland, Denmark, Germany, Holland, briefly back to Dover to see Francesca, then along the French side of the Channel to Guernsey, across Biscay, around all of Portugal and up the Guadiana, then up the Guadilquivir to Seville, then Cadiz, Gibraltar, southern Spain and all of the Balearics, before back to southern Spain to see my daughter once more on holiday.

That's not to mention the journey back from Waterford to the Thames. Dromina is now christened Francesca and together we've sailed thousands of miles, seen a force eight and two force nines, one of them all but force ten and we've endured three lightening storms. So she's a pretty alright kind of a boat, although there have been some failures and some large repair bills. I also did a lot of work her on her, before leaving.

So, to finish the story. It was December 2003 when the deal was finalised and I made it a condition that Peter would sail back with a friend of mine and myself to show us how everything worked. He was familiar, we weren't. Further, with three on board we could have three hours on watch, six off during the night. We'd all get some sleep.

I booked a direct flight to Waterford, with a minor airline. The flight was delayed, then eventually we were called to the departure gate, there was no aircraft at the gate however. Eventually they announced the flight was cancelled, apparently due to a technical problem on an earlier flight, which supposedly had a knock on effect. We could have our money back or come back tomorrow, no hotel, no compensation, no nothing.

There were some very angry people! I decided we'd get to Waterford somehow, even if it meant getting to another airport, flying to Dublin and getting a bus. Which is what it did mean, and that is what we did. We were both extremely tired when we finally made it, met Peter, and got ourselves on board for a few hours sleep. Next morning we got supplies for the trip and Peter showed me how a few things worked. Then we got the sail covers off and made the boat ready to leave.

Peter said goodbye to his wife and that he'd see her soon in England. They had friends or family, actually quite near where I lived in Kent. My car was at Gravesend waiting and I'd run Peter back when we arrived, where his wife would also join him for Christmas, perfect. The sun was now shining after torrential rain, there was a gentle breeze and a good forecast we all felt pretty good as we motored out of the river.

My travelling home, from where I now write, at that moment, in the charming harbour at Eyemouth, Scotland.

It was one of those un-forecast storms that kind of sneaks up on you unawares. The wind gets up a bit, you put some sail out, the wind and waves get up a bit more, you bring some sail in and then you suddenly realise you're in the middle of the Irish Sea in a force eight with big waves breaking right over you. My friend was seasick, and I was thinking about it. Peter's smoking did not help, but what can you do, the man's addicted and it's still technically his boat, the money is being held by the broker until the boat is safely delivered and we're sailing on Peter's insurance.

One wave was so big it broke the helmsman's seat clean off. We had been on a course for Lands End, we diverted for Milford Haven, it was still a long way. We got into the marina about 3am the following morning after a lot of pounding and slamming. We tied up and went to sleep. The next day was no better, so I found a local firm to weld the support on the helmsman's seat, this time with solid bar, not tube. The next day we stuck our nose out, turned around and came straight back. It wasn't nice out there, but Christmas was a-coming, and we all wanted to get the job over. The following day we went for it.

Until we got around the corner into the English Channel it was still very rough, and so that day and during the night, there were really only two of us to take watches, due to the third member of the crew being sick and incapacitated. When we got to Gravesend the tide was out, we tied on to a hippo buoy in the stream until there was enough water to get up the cut to the lock gate and into the canal basin. Finally, I drove Peter to his friends' and said goodbye, before returning to my lonely house in Tunbridge Wells.

That Christmas I split from another girlfriend and so I spent Christmas Day with my sister and Boxing Day with my sister and daughter. Then I moved the things I needed, in order to live there, on to the boat. Things I didn't need, but couldn't leave for the tenants went into the garage and my watch collection, important papers and other things I distributed between Dave and Steve, my closest buddies. Then I moved from my lonely house to my lonely boat, in Gravesend, where I knew precisely no one except a couple of people at the sailing club I'd met once or twice.

Louise had taken over Yamaha, Ernie, at Boyer Bransden, decided to manage for himself and just keep things running as they were really, New Hampshire I resigned as I could no longer handle it. I'd get an income from the house, once the estate agents found someone to rent it and my only other income was from the film and TV work, pretty thin. In addition I had a boat to do up if I wanted to sail and travel extensively. I took the sails to be valeted as the surveyor had suggested. Three of the four need replacing said the sail maker. I took the life raft to be serviced, this isn't safe said the company, you need a new one. I gave the old one to my daughter for a paddling pool. Maybe there's a business opportunity there for a life raft company, but not for me. It was as well that I'd built in a budget for this sort of thing when I made my plans, I knew I'd be buying an old boat no matter what. If I'd gone the extra three thousand for the Nicholson and then had to spend even a fraction of what I spent on Dromina I'd have been bankrupt before I left.

Fortunately I found a companion for my labours and my nights. Jacquelyn had been a very successful fabric designer, but had made the mistake of a romantic involvement with someone she employed, or of employing someone she was romantically involved with. Either way disaster was on the horizon. They were splitting up in the most acrimonious of circumstances. However, Jacquelyn and I had a passionate relationship, she came to live on the boat at Gravesend. When friends of hers came over from the USA we moved the boat to South Dock Marina, so they could visit us in London. We loved it there and made many new friends, it was twice the price of Gravesend, but with two of us paying, we could just about manage, if they'd let us stay. They did and we lived there for eleven wonderful months doing the boat up. We also took sailing courses, radio and radar courses, diesel engine maintenance courses, first aid and sea survival, we learned to dive together. Jacquelyn helped me strip old paint and anti-fouling, mix up and apply copper coat to the bottom, she ran up new curtains and much more. And the whole time the sex was fantastic too. I'd found the girl who would travel the world with me. I thought.

Our new friends Steve and Anita on the other side of our pontoon were preparing to jack it all in and travel the world too. They had bought a brand new boat, but were more cautious about money than we were, they planned to wait another year or so and have more funds behind them. We hoped they'd catch us up in the Mediterranean, as we were going to the Baltic first. Our neighbours in South Dock were Dawn and Jay. They lived on a Humber keeled barge, which is virtually to say a flat bottomed barge, with lee boards like a Dutch or Thames barge. It's about seventy feet long and is wonderfully luxurious, with a proper bathroom and wonderful Victorian roll top bath. It wasn't always so however. When Dawn and Jay bought her, Gainsborough Trader was about to be broken up for scrap. They've done nearly all the work themselves. Not only have they saved a historic boat, one of the Dunkirk Small Ships, in fact the last to get off the mole with survivors, but they've transformed her inside. Jay is a financial advisor, Dawn a hairdresser, neither could weld, so they tossed a coin. The upshot was that Dawn went to college to learn to weld and it's she who fabricated the roof over the cargo hold, cut out the old floor and replaced it, she who made the huge new leeboards. Incredible people, who've also learned how to grow and produce their own bio diesel for when they realise their dream, a riverside home in France for Gainsborough Trader and a holiday business for themselves.

I found I liked Jacquelyn's parents and her favourite Aunt and Uncle. I helped her find legal help to fight her battles. We were lovers and we were a team. Then, about six weeks before departure Jacquelyn announced she was scared of the North Sea and scared of the cold. She left to return to Florida. I felt she would look for someone to marry, she wanted a green card. Once, her business had been based there and that's where her heart lay. She said she'd be back for me, I doubted it. Ultimately, her Aunt broke the news by telephone that she'd not be coming back.

I sailed without her. That, as they say is another story, it will be in book two, if I get that far, which is intended to be about my travels, my last big adventure. However, there may yet be another twist in the story. Whilst sitting alone on a mooring in a bay in Portugal I had an idea I called Dancer's for Peace. Over time, as I travelled it evolved into an idea I called the World Peace Foundation. Both ideas are attached here as appendices and I'll leave fate to decide. When this book is published, if it reaches enough people, then maybe a backer, or backers, with the resources to make my World Peace Foundation a reality will come forward. If they do, I'll give up my travels and devote the rest of my active life to that. It would be my preferred outcome and the best legacy I could leave. My mother and father went through one world war, my grandparents two. I know they hoped that my generation would do better. We haven't done very much better, but there's still time, if people are willing to help me. Please read the Appendices.

Dancers For Peace

I love to dance. For me dancing expresses the joy of life. Dancing brings people together. Dancing makes people happy. Many dances encourage people to hold one another, make contact, physically and emotionally. Share.

It's hard, if not impossible to think of war or violence when you dance. Dancing makes you think about joy and love.

I particularly like to dance to swing music, Lindy Hop, Balboa and Shag are the dances I love, but I enjoy Rock and Roll too and I've tried Salsa, and ballroom dances like Tango, Fox Trot and Cha Cha Cha.

At school we did Country dancing, Scottish dancing, Morris dancing and I've even tried that traditional London dance they call 'Doing The Lambeth Walk'.

They're all fun. Frankly if everybody danced nobody would go to war. The only logical argument against pacifism and disarmament is that it requires all countries in the world to do likewise. If you live in fear of your neighbour, you feel the need for some protection.

I dream of a mature, grown up world where no country is prepared to go to war. A world where every country cares about its neighbour's well being, its neighbour's economy, standard of living, health and safety as much as its own. And caring for our planet goes hand in hand with that.

For such a world to exist all people need to love their neighbour, despite religious or cultural differences.

Yesterday I had the idea for the concept 'Dancers For Peace'. Today I am compelled to do something about it, to take action instead of just dreaming, on hearing the news that three school girls, on the way to school in Indonesia were beheaded, by a group of young men, on account of religious differences. The poor kids hadn't even finished growing up and forming their beliefs about God, religion or nature.

Peace goes hand in hand with truth and reconciliation,

three cheers for South Africa in that regard at least. We need to accept that others have their own way to God. That many people don't believe in God and that is their right, debate the meaning of life, ways to find God, discuss whatever you wish with your neighbour, out of love, don't kill him because he doesn't agree. Whether life is a gift from God or an accident of nature, either way it is a tremendous gift. Dancing brings this truth home to people. If enough people danced, in every country in the world, if the majority in every nation danced and knew the joy and human contact, sharing and interaction it brings, if they openly declared and displayed their belief that war is wrong, then what politician or leader, religious or secular, would dare espouse war. Better still lets get the politicians dancing!

The idea behind Dancers For Peace is to take these thoughts out to the world and encourage millions more people to dance and to declare openly their opposition to conflict, their love for their neighbour. It doesn't matter what the dance is. I would like to promote dances that bring people together, make contact, but in some countries there may be cultural or religious reasons not to, that's fine, people can still dance and maybe we'll help to keep some traditional dances from dying out.

To start things off, my friends and I have designed a Dancers For Peace T shirt and enclosed with every T shirt is this little leaflet explaining what it's all about. Wear your T shirt until it's worn out, when it is buy a new one, better still buy two, so you can wear your Dancers For Peace T shirt even when it's in the wash!

Don't just wear it to go dancing, although that helps too. Wear it to work, to the cinema, to parties, walking the dog and whenever someone asks you what it's about you can tell them, or give them a leaflet, or keep a stock of T shirts and sell them one too. Then invite them to go dancing with you and don't take no for an answer. At the dance or lesson, help them, introduce them around, demonstrate the fun to be had.

All the money from T shirt sales will get ploughed back to

print more T shirts and leaflets, until we have enough money to launch Dance For Peace Day.

On Dance For Peace Day it's hoped that dancers of all kinds, millions and millions of them will hold events in cities, towns and villages all over the world, ideally, in every country in the world, yes every country. It's a high target. These events should be in public wherever possible, free lessons, free shows. Get on your local television channel if you can. Take the Dancers For Peace message out to more and more new people every year. When more than fifty percent of the population in every country, province, town and state in the world dance frequently, there just might be a world without war. A world of joy, friendship and love.

We may inspire others with other interests to form their own peace movements too, who knows, Athletes For Peace, Footballers for Peace, Skiers for Peace, Sailors for Peace, Motorcyclists for Peace, Chess Players For Peace, over generations we may help to change attitudes for ever.

In the words of veteran peace campaigner and musician Arlo Guthrie, they may call it a movement and friends that's what it is.

Since writing this somewhat emotional piece I had the idea for a World Peace Foundation. The germ of which idea appears in the last but one paragraph above. It's probably unrealistic to get the whole world to dance for peace, but it's not unrealistic to attach the peace message to other peaceful pursuits and hobbies so that everyone can join in. Dancers For Peace though, is still, to my mind, a wonderful idea and a great starting point. A Dance For Peace Day, with at least one dance in every country of the world from North Korea and Iran to Greenland and South Africa is a tough but achievable goal and a terribly powerful media opportunity.

Please read this in conjunction with the World Peace Foundation concept which follows.

World Peace Foundation

My idea for a World Peace Foundation grew out of my previous idea for Dancer's For Peace and from listening to a radio debate about the United Nations. On the radio some people supported the UN, some thought it a waste of time. Others said well it's the best we've got, which is true, but it needn't be.

The UN is a club of governments, which means political self interest, even if there are some very good people there. Furthermore, it's a club without equality, as the select governments in the 'Security Council' will never relinquish their advantageous position. What about CND then? Surely real power rests with the people? In the end I believe it does. However, in recent years, the Campaign for Nuclear Disarmament seems to have ground to a halt. One still sees the famous logo sometimes, most frequently in graffiti, but that's about all. However, nuclear arms proliferate in many countries around the globe. More than this, conventional weapons now have terrible power too.

What is needed is not just an end to nuclear weapons, but an end to war. When I was young it was still politically correct to hold beauty contests such as Miss UK and Miss World. It became part of the formula for the compere to interview the girls at the end and ask them what they wanted. World peace was a common answer and the grown ups chuckled to see such naiveté. Yet what more honourable goal is there? Given world peace, how much easier will it be to feed everyone, educate everyone and find ways to protect the planet. What if the billions of dollars, euros, pounds and other currencies spent on arms were used to clothe vast swathes of desert with solar panels, or on other radical projects to reduce global warming and provide clean energy?

When Tony Blair announced his intention to take the British nation to war in Iraq there was a huge demonstration against the proposed action, probably by over a million people, certainly the biggest demonstration London had ever seen. It was not enough. What would happen though if eighty or ninety percent of a nation's population openly expressed anti war feelings. What leader, be they democratically elected, religious or even a dictator could lead their country to war with those numbers ranged against. What if recruitment to the armed services simply dried up. Everywhere.

I can understand a young man's thirst for adventure and the armed forces offer that, I applied myself as a teenager and fortunately failed to get in. Since then I've discovered lots of ways to have adventure and excitement, without being a marine, without shooting anyone. I've also discovered what a wonderful world we share and how good the majority of people are, the variety of interests and activities we indulge in. Peaceful activities. Most of the World's businesses are also involved in peaceful pursuits. The arms manufacturers may be rich and powerful but compared with all the world's other manufacturers and all the world's peace loving people they're a small minority, we could and should compel them to turn swords into ploughshares.

Tomorrows' politicians haven't been born yet. How they are raised is crucial to the world's future. I know that world peace is not going to happen in my generation, or my daughter's, but might it be possible in her children's, children's generation. Maybe we can start the snowball rolling down the hill, getting bigger and faster until it's unstoppable. To create a world where children are taught in school about their ancestors, who started by throwing spears at one another, then stuck swords in each other and fired bows and arrows, they developed gunpowder, musket balls, cannon balls, artillery, rockets, fighter planes, nuclear bombs and inter continental delivery systems, they even took war into space and came so close to destroying the world that supports us all. How those children will laugh at their forebears' stupidity.

To make this vision a reality I want to employ the marketing techniques that have made the Coca Cola and McDonalds logos and others like them, recognisable around the globe. I want to harness the power of marketing and ally it to people's love of peaceful pursuits, to make the open proclamation of pacifism the norm rather than the exception in every country, to create the culture shift that will educate and inform future generations, prevent leaders from undertaking ego or greed driven acts of violence and make weapons a thing for the history books.

Let us accept the borders we were born with, but open the world up to freedom to travel, equal opportunities and free speech. Let people pursue their own religions or none as they see fit. There is no reason to kill.

The World Peace Foundation will have its own logo which will be seen on t-shirts, ties, lapel badges and all manner of clothing, casual and formal, it can be worn discreetly on the office suit, or tie, or proclaimed loudly on the most extrovert outfit. Yet The World Peace Foundation is an umbrella organisation. Its website will link to a thousand others, starting with Dancers For Peace and including, Motorcyclists For Peace, Skiers For Peace, Divers For Peace, Parachutists For Peace, Chess Players For Peace, Ten Pin Bowlers For Peace, Anglers For Peace, Athletes For Peace, Musicians For Peace, Book Clubs For Peace, Drama Clubs For Peace and so it goes on and on.

And if future demonstrations are called for, can you imagine the impact of a thousand banners, from a thousand 'For Peace' organisations representing a thousand peaceful pursuits, everyone's against it will be the unmistakable message, everyone!

The World Peace Foundation will aim to launch many such organisations itself, starting with the highly visual Dancers For Peace and Dance For Peace Day, but will happily embrace those organisations started by other people who understand the concept and also want to embrace it. To make it a reality. Before long, dance outfits, ski suits, motorcycle leathers, waterproofs for a whole variety of sports, even the sails of yachts and dinghies and a million different T-shirts will proclaim the love of peace, in every corner of the globe, to change the face of the globe forever.

That's the plan anyway. My sister told me I won't achieve world peace until women rule the world. However most of the women rulers we have seen were not pacifists and women still marry, soldiers, sailors and airmen. Mothers still let sons, even daughters these days, go to war, sometimes encourage them. I know they look great in their uniforms, but they look a lot less attractive in their coffins. We all know that small acts of re-cycling, made by millions of us have an impact on the health of the planet, making a stand against war in a small way, if it is embraced by sufficient of us can make a similar difference. Where's the point in warplanes, warships, guns and tanks if no one will operate them? Let's spend the money where it's really needed, industry will adapt and survive.

One can't have the effect of a Coca Cola or a McDonalds, without the kind of budgets employed by those kinds of corporations. Indeed the World Peace Foundation must become a multi national corporation itself. Just to start the snowball rolling we need staff, offices, design, advertising, computers, warehousing, clothing and other stock, distribution, legal, accounting and human resources. We need qualified, multi lingual representatives to go and recruit volunteers in every country of the world, we need information technology specialists and much more.

Currently I am travelling the world on a small boat and writing a book or two. As stated in the original Dancers For Peace, concept I thought about producing a few Dancers For Peace T shirts and selling them as I go along to try and start something happening, but that would be just to play at it and would in reality change nothing even if it made me feel good. If I can obtain the finance needed to create an effective organisation, be it from book sales or from backers inspired to help as a result of reading the book I will give up my travels and devote the rest of my active years to this cause. I will happily sit down and discuss, costs, staffing levels and all aspects with any serious backer. My hope is that this book will provide the first foundation or stepping stone.

Since writing this and searching the internet I discovered there is already a World Peace Foundation, I'd never heard of it. It was started in 1910. It appears to be a study organisation, looking at ways to create peace, or prevent conflict. I don't intend a criticism when I point out that since 1910 we have had the First and Second World Wars, war between Japan and China, the Chinese invasion of Tibet, the Russian invasion of Czechoslovakia (as it was then), the Korean War, the Vietnam War, the Suez crisis, Aden, the 'six day war' and on going conflict in Israel, Lebanon and Palestine , the Angolan war, the Falklands war, two Gulf wars (plus war between Iran and Iraq), genocide in Cambodia, Rwanda and Bosnia and other conflicts. I am not an academic, but clearly it's time to try new ways. Please help if you can. My World Peace Foundation will of course have be called by another name, I have several options in mind and if we can work with other organisations whose aims are the elimination of war then so much the better.

I chose to describe my book as a record of my escapades, it could as easily be described as a memoir, since it is composed of my memories. Not unnaturally it describes things the way I remember them. Others may remember things slightly differently, or may recall details I've forgotten, that's just a part of the human condition. When it came to some of the earlier memories I sent the book to people like John, Ken and Bob to read prior to publication. Sadly I'm not in regular contact with Paul. Although I asked my parachute buddies to read the whole thing, they all cut to the chase and read the bits that included them, ie the parachute club chapters. Ken criticised me for not being humorous enough, and also reminded me that Paul had left the Foreign Legion after being promised a transfer to Para, which was then reneged upon. The latter is a salient point which I had forgotten and in no way did I intend to portray Paul in a negative light. Day to day Paul was my mentor at the parachute club, he taught me a great deal, I owe him much and respect him immensely.

Ken's other point about humour is more complex. Paul's teaching was always very matter of fact, my courses included a lot of humour, the majority of the jokes I've forgotten now, but mostly they involved the ridiculous mistakes people can make under stress and so acted as a warning as well as making people laugh, often hysterically. I'm sure some students preferred Paul's style and I hope some preferred mine. It became easy to have classes in stitches, pretty much whenever I wanted since I could refine the act week in week out. It's also easy to make people laugh when they're full of nervous energy anyway. I felt that the long class room lectures benefited from a few good laughs to keep people awake. I also managed to make audiences laugh when I was a compere on Yamaha's stage show, it's a skill that sadly seems to be waning these days and I wish I knew why. Although, I'm told by other friends that my regular e-mails are also more amusing than the book. However, I didn't set out to write a humorous book as such, maybe I'll try to inject more humour into the next one. My writing style is still evolving and I'm not a natural comedian like Bob and Ken, although I can ad lib quite well when relaxed.

On the occasion when John phoned and pointed out to me that he'd never chromed the hose clips on his Norton Commando, he then went on to tell me about the new bits he'd bought for his current Ducati, I'm glad he hasn't changed. John was also very upset that I accused him of dropping the grapefruit and assured me we'd called it Max, I don't remember that I'm sorry, he also said that if I didn't admit that I'd thrown the grapefruit too low for him to catch then he'd spread a story on the internet about how he'd caught me in the packing shed, indulging in a sexual act with a six foot squaddie. I told him he exaggerated both his stature and his military credentials. So that's a little example of the sort of banter that was a daily occurrence at the parachute club, nothing changes. Very kindly, John suggested the sub-heading 'The Autobiography Of a Modern Day Adventurer'. It had been 'The Autobiography Of An Unknown Man', which I considered more modest and hoped was intriguing. One confidant felt that should be the sole title, nothing about land, sea or sky! Where two opinions are possible you'll get three, but the final version a mixture of John's improvement and my last thought on the matter does give a better indication of what the book is about, even if some of the adventures are to do with business, drama or dancing rather than activities one normally thinks of as adventurous!

So there it is warts and all. I hope you enjoyed it and I hope you'll help spread the word about the World Peace Federation idea, or whatever it's finally called. Each book sold will help to make it more likely that I can raise the funds or find a backer. So buy some more and give them out as birthday and Christmas presents! Book two was planned to be about my sailing around the world, it may still be, however, if in fact

I don't complete that exercise but go on to launch a World Peace Campaign (the outcome I hope for) then book two may be rather different. I also have ideas for a novel or two! What next? We'll see is all I can really say at this point.

Another of my Grandfather's sketches, from the dark days of World War One.

Lightning Source UK Ltd.
Milton Keynes UK
UKOW051141161012

200655UK00005B/1/P

9 781425 157593